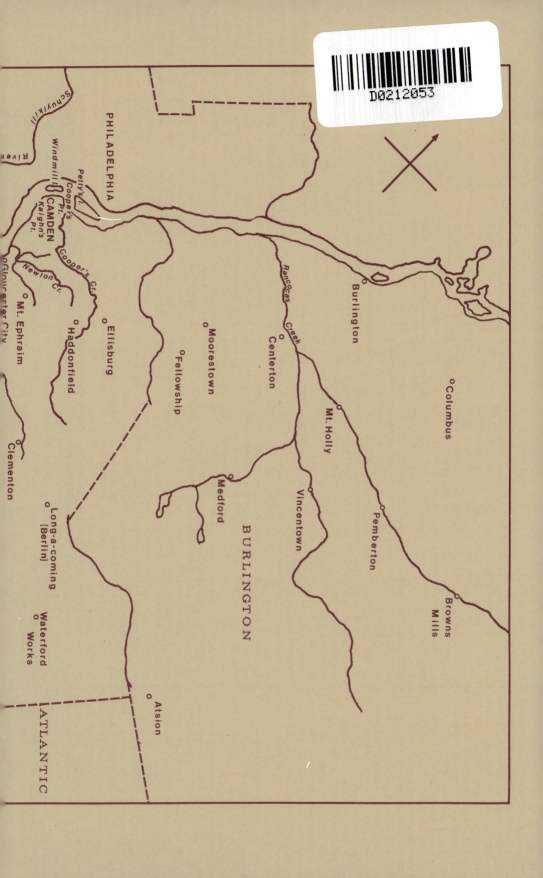

PHILADELPHIA

Schuylkill River

Windmill I.

Petty's I.

Cooper's Pt.

CAMDEN

Kaighn's Pt.

Cooper's Cr.

Newton Cr.

Mt. Ephraim

Gloucester City

Clementon

Haddonfield

Ellisburg

Fellowship

Moorestown

Centerton

Rancocas Creek

Burlington

Mt. Holly

Vincentown

Pemberton

Columbus

Browns Mills

Medford

Long-a-coming
(Berlin)

BURLINGTON

Waterford
Works

Atsion

ATLANTIC

A Gentleman
of Much Promise

Isaac Mickle, 1840

A Gentleman
of Much Promise

The Diary of
Isaac Mickle
1837-1845

VOLUME ONE

Edited, with an Introduction, by

PHILIP ENGLISH MACKEY

University of Pennsylvania Press

1977

Endpaper maps prepared by Muriel Ketcham

Library of Congress Cataloging in Publication Data

Mickle, Isaac.
    A gentleman of much promise.

    Includes bibliographical references and index.
    1. Mickle, Isaac. 2. Camden, N. J.--Biography.
I. Mackey, Philip English. II. Title.
F144.C2M52   974.9'8'030924 [B]   76-53190
ISBN 0-8122-7722-8

ACKNOWLEDGMENTS

The editor wishes to thank the many colleagues, students, and friends who helped in the long and laborious task of preparing the diary for publication. Special gratitude is due Camden County Historical Society President, David C. Munn, Rutgers University Professors Gerald Verbrugghe, James Muldoon, and Rodney P. Carlisle, photographer Jan Guidotti, and the library staffs at Rutgers University-Camden, the University of Pennsylvania, the Free Library of Philadelphia, the Historical Society of Pennsylvania, and the Camden County Historical Society. Thanks are also due to my wife Ann Mahoney and to the following Rutgers-Camden students: Margaret Amos, Paul Brandimarto, Clair Brumbach, Jerry Buckley, Eric Burleigh, Dennis Campbell, Cheryl Chatburn, Steve Cirillo, John Cliver, Joe DeAngelis, Frank Domico, Wayne Evans, Mark Frizell, Len Gigliobianco, Mark Hendricks, Sue Hoffa, Anita Johnson, Mark Kaizen, Robert Kangian, Linda Kirkpatrick, Craig Knaup, Coleen McCarthy, Jack Marquess, Janet Matlack, Bruce Mayer, Frank Memmo, Dave Morgan, Stan Mroz, Walt Novoshielski, Jeff Richardson, Barry Root, Wanda Sammartino, Grace Sciamanna, and Robin Zeff.

Much credit for the diary's publication is due Robert W. Wythes and Richard H. Hineline of the Camden County Historical Society who conducted early negotiations with Mickle's descendants. The New Jersey Historical Commission, the Rutgers University Research Council, and especially the Camden County Historical Society provided essential financial assistance.

Of course, the whole undertaking would have been impossible without the interest and determination of Marjorie H. Williamson, Mickle's nonagenarian granddaughter. Her wit and energy served as an inspiration to those but a fraction of her age. This book is dedicated to her.

FOREWORD

The Camden County Historical Society is pleased to be associated with the University of Pennsylvania Press in the publication of the diary of Isaac Mickle. It has been over forty-five years since the last such joint effort resulted in Charles S. Boyer's *Early Forges & Furnaces in New Jersey*. The Board of Trustees has encouraged this work because it believes that the observations, wit, and wisdom of Isaac Mickle should be made available to a wide audience. The diary provides a rich addition to New Jersey history and the trustees hope that it will become a much-used historical source.

The Society is grateful to the University of Pennsylvania Press for the interest and cooperation they have shown in this project. We also acknowledge the support of the Camden County Board of Chosen Freeholders and the Camden County Cultural & Heritage Commission.

David C. Munn, President
Camden County Historical Society

CONTENTS

ILLUSTRATIONS

VOLUME ONE

VOLUME TWO

INTRODUCTION

PHILIP ENGLISH MACKEY

The Man

Died. In this city on Saturday last, Isaac Mickle, Esq. Editor of the "Camden Democrat" after a tedious illness; a gentleman of much promise cut off in the prime of life.

(Camden *Mail,* 5 December 1855)

Such was the humble obituary which announced the demise of Isaac Mickle (1822–55), lawyer, editor, historian, politician, musician, translator, inventor, and diarist. Not many of his contemporaries recognized his merits. His name is virtually unknown today. The diary which follows, written between 1837 and 1845, may help to rescue him from oblivion. For in it, Isaac Mickle not only reveals his own precocious gifts but also illuminates the years in which he wrote.

The Mickle family arrived in America as part of the Quaker migration of the late seventeenth century. Isaac's great-great-great grandfather, Archibald Mickle (d. 1706), a native of County Antrim in Ireland, settled in Newton Township, Gloucester County (now Camden County) in the early 1690s. Initially, Mickle's farmlands, covering over five hundred acres, stretched from his home on the Delaware River west to Joseph Cooper's property on Cooper's Creek. In subsequent years, the Mickles acquired more land to the south and, by Isaac's lifetime, owned virtually all the land between the Delaware and Cooper's Creek, from Little Newton Creek (about where Camden City's Jackson Street is today) on the north to Newton Creek on the south.

Isaac Mickle was born at Walnut Grove, one of the farms in this large and valuable tract, on 18 October 1822. His father, Isaac (1791–1823), died of tuberculosis less than a year later. His mother, Rebecca Morgan Mickle (1791–1875), soon moved in with her brother-in-law, Captain John W. Mickle (1793–1861), who, family tradition relates, gave up his beloved nautical life to help raise his brother's son.

Isaac was a bright and precocious child, perhaps partly because he was given early encouragement and the advantages which only a wealthy family could afford in early nineteenth century America. Books were plentiful in the household and Isaac took great interest in them. His mother made a sort of game of book-collecting, founding what she called "The Washington Library" on Isaac's third birthday and installing Isaac as "president" of the institution when he was twelve. Rebecca Mickle's clever strategy was amply rewarded. Isaac proudly listed over one hundred volumes in this library at age twelve, was an avid book collector at fourteen, and retained a love of books and reading throughout his life.

More formal education began in late 1828 when the first of a succession of tutors began to instruct the boy. Such lessons continued until at least 1831 and perhaps went on until Isaac's departure for boarding school at Franklin Park, New Jersey, sometime before October 1833. There, he and some twenty-five to fifty other boys studied reading, writing, "cyphering," grammar, orthography, and geography. Isaac seems to have enjoyed the company of his classmates and the competition they offered him. His letters to his mother and his Uncle John reveal an eleven-year-old scholar, proud of his academic success and already scattering his fine English prose with phrases in Latin and French. He was obviously already fascinated by politics as well. In describing his fellow-students at the school, he was pleased to note that a large percentage of them were "Jackson men."

Little is known of the other schools Mickle attended. In 1835, he commuted across the Delaware to Joseph P. Engle's Academy on George Street in Philadelphia. From 1836 to early 1838, he attended a school run by Oliver Cox in Camden. In March 1839, he again left home for a boarding school, operated by Baptist minister Samuel Aaron in Burlington, New Jersey. His studies at the Burlington Academy included Latin, French, Greek, algebra, and English.

It was at Burlington Academy that Isaac reviewed his options for a career and chose to study law. Uncle John and his mother wished him to become a gentleman farmer, but that promised to be too "monotonous." He rejected study of divinity because "I will not attempt to interpret that which I cannot understand myself." Medicine? "No—

while a pittance can be earned by honest toil, I never will kill one person to learn how to cure another." It was the legal profession that attracted Isaac most, a career which he saw as "almost the only way to offices of government and jurisprudence." John and Rebecca Mickle were not pleased with the boy's choice, but they did not discourage him. Uncle John, in fact, was instrumental in arranging for Isaac to study law with prominent Philadelphia attorney James Page. Though the diary sometimes seems to paint the author as a delinquent legal scholar, it is clear that, for all his protestations of difficulty, Mickle flourished in the study of law. Indeed, the seasoned president of his bar examination board, in May 1844, felt that the student had made one of the best presentations he had ever heard.

Mickle's success as a law student is the more remarkable given his devotion to other interests in the same period. Above all, the young man was consumed by a fascination with politics, which seems to have been the motivation for choosing a legal career in the first place. Mickle grew up in a political family and in highly partisan times. Uncle John was a leading South Jersey Democrat and spent much time attending meetings, organizing support, and running, often successfully, for political office. John Mickle does not seem to have possessed the sort of personality which would have endeared him to the electorate. But he was bright, businesslike, and had strong connections with the most powerful corporation in the state, the Camden and Amboy Railroad Company.

There can have been few more exciting decades in American politics than the 1830s and 1840s. Andrew Jackson dominated the scene while president (1829–37) and after, defining issues in such a way as to guarantee extreme partisanship. The new Whig party formed in opposition to Jackson's Democrats and, with the help of a severe financial depression in the late 1830s, built a movement strong enough to threaten Jackson's successor, Martin Van Buren (president, 1837–41), with retirement after a single term. To the Mickles' astonishment and disgust, clever Whig campaign techniques—including the use of placards, floats, parades, and slogans—helped sweep William Henry Harrison and John Tyler to victory. Isaac, a confirmed "Jackson man" since age eleven, now dedicated himself to a life of politics.

As Democrats and Whigs sparred for position in future elections, the Mickles and other Americans watched a curious scenario unfold in Washington. President Harrison died after only one month in office and Tyler, a former states' rights Democrat from Virginia, proved an impossible ally for congressional Whigs, pledged to support a national program. An inevitable split developed in Whig ranks, causing consternation in Washington and making the president essentially a man without a party. At the same time, Democrats wrangled over the question of how far and fast to push national expansion and whether to give the American people a "sober second chance" to reelect Van Buren in 1844.

Isaac followed events in Washington with the keenest interest, seeing some awful fate at work in Harrison's demise and gloating at Whig factionalism. Among Democrats, he shied away from radical Jacksonian economic positions and allied himself with the expansionist "Young Democracy." This wing of the party, with very strong support in the slave states, fought the nomination of Van Buren because he opposed the immediate annexation of the Republic of Texas. They sought a man with more aggressive instincts and, in the Baltimore convention which Isaac describes, found him in dark horse James K. Polk of Tennessee.

If the exciting election campaign of 1844 was not enough to disrupt the final months of Isaac's legal studies and the beginning of his career as an attorney, two other political contests demanded almost the entire remainder of his attention that year. John Mickle and other Democrats saw 1844 as the opportunity to create a new county in South Jersey, with Camden as its seat of government. The northern half of old Gloucester County would regularly vote Democratic, the Mickles and their allies believed, and local affairs would henceforth be controlled by Camden's leading citizens, without the interference of interests from the old county seat of Woodbury. It was during the same year, too, that agitation for a revision of the New Jersey constitution culminated in a constitutional convention and a new fundamental law for the state. Mickle had been advocating such a move since early 1843 and became a leading campaigner for the reform in 1844.

Isaac's ability to become a modest force in New Jersey politics by age twenty-one was partly due to his editorship of an important South Jersey newspaper, the Camden *Eagle*. Mickle had exhibited a fine writing style by age eleven and by fourteen was publishing polished letters in local newspapers. His writing skills and intelligence commended his talents to Whig editor Philip J. Gray of the Camden *Mail*, who began publishing Isaac's articles and letters in 1838, when the boy was only fifteen. His political convictions had him working for the *Mail*'s rival, Charles D. Hineline's *Eagle*, anonymously in 1843 and as official editor after January 1844. The *Eagle*, a weekly, was not a large paper. Like most newspapers of the 1840s, it offered only four pages and at least two of those were given to advertisements, notices, and features. Still, it is difficult to fathom how Mickle found time to acquire knowledge of the law, campaign for political causes, and edit the *Eagle*.

Astoundingly, it was during the same years that Isaac conducted the research for and wrote his *Reminiscences of Old Gloucester*, a one-hundred-page history of the area comprising today's Gloucester, Camden, and Atlantic Counties. Although the book contains errors and exaggerations, it is, on the whole, an invaluable source of information about the area. Its text and notes make clear that Isaac read many books, sorted through original documents, and conducted interviews in trying to trace over two hundred years of the area's history. The *Reminiscences* received highly favorable reviews at the time of its publication and has become a standard source for the history of South Jersey.

It is not surprising that a diary which chronicles the author's fourteenth to twenty-second years should reveal great changes in his life. In that period, Isaac moved steadily away from his family's influence, supplanting his mother's and uncle's values with his own. At first he erected a rather rigid code for himself, attending several church services every Sunday and avoiding alcohol. His romances, too, were marked—and perhaps marred—by Isaac's sense of duty, pride, and propriety. But increased contact with life outside his home and his town made the young man far more independent of his prim Quaker heritage. By the end of the diary, Isaac shows little or no guilt as he drinks, dances, and consorts with women of questionable character. At age twenty-two, Isaac has shed his innocence and seems comfortable in the world of politics and journalism, in the world of adulthood.

Mickle's life after 30 March 1845, the date of the last diary entry, is far more difficult to trace. A profound and happy change occurred in late 1845 or early 1846 when Isaac met and fell in love with a beautiful young Philadelphian named Clara Tyndale (1827–1910). Daughter of china importer Robinson Tyndale and his wife Sarah Thorn Tyndale, Clara had attended several boarding schools and was back in Philadelphia when Isaac first saw her at the opera. The young attorney contrived to meet her by scheduling sittings with portrait painter Thomas Buchanan Read immediately following hers. Soon Isaac and Clara were courting and, in June 1846, were engaged. Their marriage took place before Rev. William J. Furness of Philadelphia's First Congregational (Unitarian) Church on 26 January 1847. After a wedding trip to New York and New England, they returned to Isaac's home in Camden. The couple had hoped to rent a home on Front Street in that city, but that plan fell through at the last moment and they were forced to stay with John and Rebecca Mickle until other quarters could be found.

To this end, Isaac bought from his mother the 108-acre Bloomfield Farm, a few miles east of Camden near the junction of today's Routes 70 and 38. There he began building the house he called "Bloomfield

Cottage" which the couple occupied in June 1847. The next few months were probably the happiest of Isaac's life. A poem he wrote shortly after moving to the farm celebrates the "secluded, rural, ornamented spot" with its handsome white mansion overlooking a wide lawn and a reflecting lake. This physical setting for the couple's "wedded bliss," Isaac wrote, would provide an ideal environment for the child Clara would soon bear. There too, Mickle continued,

> . . . she the partner of his active life,
> Shall join, to aid and urge his high career
> Along the paths of fame, amidst the strife,
> Of warring mind, with mind and thus to cheer,
> Will be to gain for *genius,* triumph's greenest wreath.

Mickle's immodesty is blatant, but perhaps excusable. By mid-1847, at age twenty-four, he had proved his abilities as a lawyer and editor, had become influential in local and state politics, and was friendly with the vice-president of the United States and many other powerful politicians. He had recently published several pieces of music, a history, a speech, and a play, and had invented a means by which gunpowder could be used to drive a piston engine. Surely a man of such accomplishments, a man possessed of great wealth, intelligence, industry, and social standing, might expect a "high career along the paths of fame."

In fact, the last eight years of Mickle's life were a lamentable tale of illness, tragedy, lack of accomplishment, and intimation of scandal. The idyllic stay at Bloomfield Cottage was very brief. Isaac, Clara, and their newborn son, Isaac, Jr., abandoned their country home sometime before October 1848 and returned to a house on Bridge Street, Camden. The reasons for this sudden reversal are unclear. That Bloomfield Cottage soon became known as "Mickle's Folly" suggests that Isaac had insufficient funds to make the house habitable. The Mickle family, though possessed of valuable property, did not always have an ample supply of liquid capital. Another possibility is that Isaac's poor health required his return to Camden where physicians' services were more readily available. While the diary gives few indications of serious health problems, Isaac had written a friend as early as 1844 that he was forced to travel to upstate New York for his health and that a European trip would be necessary if there were no improvement.

> Sam! [he wrote] with what avidity could I not study, if I had a reasonable assurance that my acquirements would ever be of much service. You know my constitution—and you know therefore that it matters but little whether I study or play.

Isaac's condition must have been much improved at the time of his Bloomfield Cottage euphoria. Perhaps he even believed himself cured. The disease, tuberculosis, was a recurrent one, however, and may have necessitated Isaac's removal to the city.

Clara and Isaac's life in the house on Bridge Street mixed pleasure with intense sorrow. Three more children were born there or in another house just across the street to which the family moved in 1849: Rebecca in 1848, John in 1850, and Clara in 1851. As a lawyer, Isaac never acquired an extensive clientele, but he secured additional income by selling part of the Mickle lands and the family never suffered privation. A crushing blow came in December 1850, though, when scarlet fever claimed the life of both Mickle boys in one numbing week. Isaac's own illness came and went. Fragmentary family correspondence indicates that he was relatively healthy in November 1851, seriously ill in mid-1853, improved in August 1853, but a wasted invalid in 1855.

Isaac's financial worries, parental bereavement, and illness were compounded by some sort of personal tragedy at which family records only hint. A letter of condolence to Clara from her sister Elizabeth in December 1850 took a remarkable twist when it expressed the wish that Isaac might profit from the death of his two sons. Then, in a passionate outburst, Elizabeth addressed the father himself:

> Oh! Isaac, my dear brother arouse yourself. You *know*—you *feel* that you are capable of good; then why debase the gifts of your almighty father. Determine to honor his gifts, for Oh! a terrible day of reckoning must come to those who abuse his favors.

Other clues to the existence of the same problem exist in three mutilated letters, from which remarks of John W. Mickle and Sarah Tyndale have been excised. The context of the missing material suggests that Uncle John had cause to chastise Isaac about the secret problem in 1850 and again in 1853. Two possibilities are that Isaac was spending money recklessly, perhaps on something his relatives deemed improper, or that, despairing of his health, he had begun to drink immoderately.

But Isaac's many misfortunes did not completely quell his talents or cripple his ambition. He had long wanted to own, as well as edit, a newspaper and, after much haggling, he secured possession of the Camden *Democrat* in 1853. That he remained influential in South Jersey politics is indicated by the fact that President Pierce appointed him collector of the port of Camden in April of the same year. Mickle, apparently, remained a man to reckon with in Camden right up to the time of his death.

The Setting

Camden, New Jersey, was a small town when Isaac Mickle was born in 1822. Spurred by the growth of Philadelphia, directly across the Delaware River, and by the arrival of the Camden and Amboy Railroad in 1834, the population began to increase. While the village contained less than 1000 citizens in the early 1820s, it held almost 2000 in 1830, 3400 in 1840, and 9500 in 1850. Many of the new inhabitants came from the smaller towns or farms of Camden, Gloucester, or other South Jersey counties. Others, encouraged by new and improved ferry service in the 1830s, moved across the Delaware from their former homes in Philadelphia.

With the influx of thousands of new townsmen, the character of the area changed abruptly. The five distinct hamlets which occupied the site of modern Camden in 1840 lost their identities as the fields, woods, and ponds which once separated them gave way to streets and small housing developments. Industry, too, began to dot the area, especially along the Delaware River and Cooper's Creek. Camden products included iron, lumber, shingles, carriages, wagons, candles, and pork sausage.

The rest of Camden County, part of Gloucester County until 1844, changed far more slowly. The only other towns of any significance were newly industrialized Gloucester on the Delaware, just south of Camden, and Haddonfield, a quiet community six miles southeast of the burgeoning city. Elsewhere, a score of villages provided the only interruption of the low, fertile farmland or woods. The county, especially the northern half, possessed a reasonably good network of roads, almost all leading to Camden and the ferries to Philadelphia.

Philadelphia had been the commercial and intellectual focal point for Camden County and most of South Jersey since its founding in 1682. In the 1840s, Penn's "greene country towne" was a sprawling metropolis of a quarter of a million people. Here Jerseymen came to sell their produce, to attend private schools, to shop, to attend plays, concerts, and speeches, or like Mickle, to learn and practice a profession.

The Diary

Isaac Mickle's diary has remained in his family's possession since his death, most recently in the hands of his granddaughter, Marjorie H. Williamson, of West Chester, Pennsylvania. She has presented it to the Camden County Historical Society where it is available to qualified visitors.

Mickle wrote his first diary entry on 7 April 1837, but he was far from a consistent diarist during the next three years. Instead, periods of faithful daily entries were followed by long stretches (of up to a year and a half, assuming all of his volumes are extant) of silence. Almost all the entries of these years were written at home in Camden. Presumably Isaac was too busy writing letters and exercises while at school at Burlington. Beginning with 4 July 1840, however, Mickle kept his diary for over four years without missing a day. A few of these entries may have been back-dated, but it appears that most were written in the evening of the day described. Isaac sometimes thought of the diary as a record for his descendants, sometimes as a purely private journal. Nowhere does he seem to be writing with publication in mind. While some of his friends and relatives knew of the diary— indeed, a few even read parts of it—most of the people Mickle quotes or describes were probably unaware that their words and actions were being recorded.

The gap in the diary from 14 September 1844 to 1 January 1845 probably represents the author's temporary abandonment of the time-consuming effort during the last hectic weeks of the political campaign of that year. Once New Year's Day reflections brought him back to his notebooks, he again wrote daily entries for three months before abruptly abandoning them altogether. The pages preceding the last entry, that of 30 March 1845, give no clue as to why Mickle stopped writing. He may have felt himself too busy or may have suffered a severe attack of his recurrent illness.

The contents of Mickle's unedited diary are considerably more extensive than what is presented here. Omitted from the present edition are hundreds of letters Mickle copied into his notebooks, some of his fledgling literary efforts, and those entries or parts of entries which would strike most readers as dull or repetitious. No material has been removed or altered out of deference to maligned ethnic groups or families. The editor hopes that readers offended by some of Mickle's intolerant remarks will remember that they are retained here in order to enrich our knowledge about beliefs and prejudices of the ante-bellum years. In no case does their retention imply that anyone associated with the production of the book shares or approves of Mickle's sentiments.

Mickle's writing style is faithfully reproduced in the pages which follow. Misspelled words, incomplete sentences, and inappropriate punctuation have been zealously retained. Abbreviations have been left in short form and foreign words and phrases in the original language. At the same time, a desire for readability has necessitated some minor changes in the text. Foreign words and names of books, plays, songs, ships, and law cases have been italicized. Obvious slips of the pen, like the repeat of a word, have been removed. Where Mickle places both a dash and some other form of punctuation at the same point in a sentence, the less appropriate mark, usually the dash, has been stricken. Mickle's mixture of styles for the headings of his daily entries has been standardized. For the period 29 January to 28 February 1845, when Mickle kept two diaries (one labeled "secret," though it contained much the same sort of material as the other), entries from both have been joined. Transitions from the regular to the secret diary are marked [SD], those from the secret to the regular diary, [RD]. Finally, the editor has clarified a very few sentences by adding a word or two, but in each case the addition is enclosed in brackets and italicized (to differentiate it from Mickle's own bracketed material).

The notes are designed to elucidate names and terms which readers of the diary might find puzzling. Words and phrases in standard English dictionaries are not explicated, nor are names of well known people or places. Frequently mentioned place names in Camden or in the Philadelphia-South Jersey area may be found on the maps in the end papers and are not identified in the notes. People are identified only at their first mention in the diary, but readers may use the index to find relevant information about any name they encounter. Of course, correct spellings, so far as they could be established, have been employed in the notes and index, regardless of Mickle's occasional misspellings in the text.

The illustrations scattered through the text are of two kinds. Those at the beginning of each year have been reproduced from John W. Barber and Henry Howe, *Historical Collections of the State of New Jersey* (New York, 1847). The remainder are Mickle's own drawings, mostly from the volumes for 1837–40. Those referring directly to a diary entry are placed in juxtaposition thereto. Those with no specific reference have been distributed throughout the text.

CHRONOLOGY OF THE LIFE
OF ISAAC MICKLE

18 Oct. 1822	Born at "Walnut Grove," Newton Township, Gloucester, N.J.
22 Aug. 1823	Father dies of Tuberculosis
Dec. 1828–Nov. 1831	Tutee of Andrew Mein and A. Danny
Oct. 1833–May 1834	Attending boarding school in Franklin Park, N.J.
7 Apr. 1837	Begins first diary
1836–38	Attending Oliver Cox's school in Camden
Mar.–July 1839	Attending Aaron's High School, Burlington, N.J.
Nov.–Dec. 1839	Again attending Aaron's school
4 July 1840	Begins consistent daily entries in diary
3 May 1841	Begins law study with James Page, Philadelphia
19–26 July 1841	Trip to Bethlehem, Mauch Chunk, Pottsville, Reading, Pa.
5 Jan. 1842	Founds Camden Debating Society
11 Feb. 1842	Elected to board of Camden Temperance Society
13 Oct. 1842	Helps form Amateurs Music Association of Camden

Oct. 1842	Working as an editor
10 June 1843	Sees President Tyler in Camden
4–17 Aug. 1843	Trip to New York City, New Haven, Boston
11 Sept. 1843	Pamphlet calling for New Jersey constitutional reform published
22 Dec. 1843	Becomes editor of Camden *Eagle*
Feb. 1844	Begins publishing historical sketches of Old Gloucester County
21 May 1844	Passes bar examination in Pennsylvania
22 May 1844	Takes oath as attorney
6–10 May 1844	Witnesses nativist riots in Philadelphia
25–29 May 1844	Attends Democratic National Convention in Baltimore
10 Aug. 1844	Helps form Camden antinativist organization
11–23 Aug. 1844	Trip to New York City and upstate New York
9 Jan. 1845	Court debut as lawyer
1 Mar. 1845	*Reminiscences of Old Gloucester* published
1–6 Mar. 1845	Trip to Washington for Polk inauguration
30 Mar. 1845	Last diary entry
6 Nov. 1845	Elected member, New Jersey Historical Society
10 June 1846	Engagement to Clara Tyndale
Oct. 1846	Publishes *Old North Tower* (adaptation of a French play)
Late 1846	Invents engine powered by gunpowder
1847	Member of Camden Common Council
26 Jan. 1847	Marriage to Clara Tyndale in Philadelphia
27 Jan. 1847	Appointed first lieutenant in state militia by Governor Charles C. Stratton
June 1847	Moves to "Bloomfield Cottage" (returns to Camden before Oct. 1848)
July 1847	Three pieces of music published

2 Nov. 1847   Isaac, Jr., born

8 Feb. 1848   Appointed lieutenant colonel in state militia by Governor Daniel Haines

10 Oct. 1848   Rebecca born

29 Apr. 1850   John born

15–22 Dec. 1850   Isaac, Jr., and John die of scarlet fever

4 Nov. 1851   Clara born

Apr. 1852   Assumes editorship of Camden *Democrat*

1853   Becomes owner of *Democrat*

Apr. 1853   Appointed collector of port of Camden by President Pierce

1 Dec. 1855   Dies in Camden

CHRONOLOGY OF NATIONAL AND STATE EVENTS

Nov. 1836	Martin Van Buren and Richard M. Johnson elected president and vice-president of the United States
Mar. 1837	Van Buren and Johnson inaugurated
Early 1837	Panic of 1837, followed by depression until 1843
Dec. 1837	Canadian raiding party captures U.S. steamboat *Caroline* in an attempt to end rebel attacks on Canada
1838–39	Disputes over boundary of Maine and New Brunswick lead to the Aroostook "War"
Aug. 1838	Wilkes marine exploration expedition leaves for the South Pacific
Late 1840	Presidential election campaign. William H. Harrison and John Tyler elected
Mar. 1841	Harrison and Tyler inaugurated
4 Apr. 1841	Death of President Harrison
11 Sept. 1841	President Tyler's cabinet (except Secretary of State Daniel Webster) resigns in protest of Tyler's policies
9 Aug. 1842	Webster-Ashburton Treaty settles Maine-New Brunswick boundary

Apr.–May 1842   Thomas W. Dorr of Rhode Island leads effort to replace the constitutional government of that state in the so-called Dorr Rebellion

Feb. 1844   New Jersey legislature passes act creating Camden County

1 May 1844   Whig National Convention nominates Henry Clay for president

6–8 May 1844   Nativist riots in Philadelphia

14 May 1844   New Jersey State Constitutional Convention meets at Trenton

27–29 May 1844   Democratic National Convention nominates James K. Polk for president

5–8 July 1844   Nativist riots in Philadelphia

13 Aug. 1844   Voters of New Jersey approve new constitution

4 Dec. 1844   Polk defeats Clay for the presidency

1 Mar. 1845   Congress votes to annex Texas to the United States

4 Mar. 1845   Polk and Dallas inaugurated

MY JOURNAL

When the toils and cares of the day are o'er
And the hum of the city's heard no more—
When night wraps the earth in her sable sheet,
And the nightingales sing—and lovers meet,
To pledge and to swear their loves eternal—. . .
With what joy I haste home to **my Journal;**
There to record the events of the day,
To register in it my work—my play
My actions, my thoughts—my observations,
To note *en passant* the state of nations:
Revolutions, wars, machines infernal,
Are touched upon, in thee, my Journal! . . .
Though small the book and mean the external
I hope you will not condemn **my Journal** . . .

Isaac Mickle, 1838

The Diary

1837-1841

Friends Meeting-house, Haddonfield

1837

The improvement arising from the recording of occurrences which daily take place, or in other words, keeping a Diary, is admitted by all to more than compensate for the short time consumed each day, in making such record; more over—it may happen that the record be referred to at some future day, to settle a disputed point, provided the keeper thereof is known to pay a strict regard to Truth, which I shall endeavour to do. An instance of this occurred at the March term of the court of Oyer and Terminer, Gloucester, 1837, before Presiding Judge Ryerson.[1] The suit involved the question of the validity of the last will and testament of Andrew F. E. Mickle, M.D.[2] One of the witnesses of the will, named Frees,[3] at the time he signed the paper,

1. Thomas C. Ryerson (1788–1838) was Associate Justice of the New Jersey Supreme Court from 1834 to 1838. The trial hung on whether Dr. Mickle, Isaac's uncle, had executed a legal will granting property in Gloucester County to James Matlack. The jury determined that the will was a legal one and that Matlack, rather than Dr. Mickle's brother, Benjamin W. Mickle, should receive the property. This decision survived several appeals and John W. Mickle eventually bought the property from the Matlack family. See entry of 17 August 1841.

2. Andrew F. E. Mickle was Isaac's half-uncle, the son of Isaac's paternal grandfather and his second wife, Mary Matlack.

3. The witness is called Henry Freas in the New Jersey Supreme Court's later decision in the case.

wrote down the particulars—not omitting to notice the posture, words, actions and looks of the testator and the others present. The consequence was, at the trial, he was able to give in a clear and uncontradicted testimony, concerning the most trifling points on which he was questioned; the paper seemed to dispel the mist which three or four years cast over one's remembrance, and to bring him back to the time and place of the execution of the will. Another witness, named Lord,[4] having no memorandum, became so completely tangled, during his cross-examination, that he fainted in court, and was obliged to leave the stand.

These, and many other reasons which I could name, have induced me to commence this "Record of Every-day Occurrences."

7 April, Friday.

The weather is dull and oppressive; the wind S.E. and S, light but squally. At 1 o'clock P.M., I took a sail (as the expression is,) in the "Custom House Boat" of which I have the care; but finding the squalls to be too heavy, I was obliged to take in a reef, after which I enjoyed a very pleasant sail to "Windmill Island," notwithstanding some ten or fifteen gallons of water, which, to the great inconvenience of my feet, found its way over the lee gunnel of the boat.[5] At 4, P.M., I landed and walked to Kaighn's Point; and returning, I resumed *Don Quixote de la Mancha*, who was on his march to Micomicon, to sever the head of the gigantic usurper from his "head pedestal" (as some writers are pleased to term the shoulders,) and restore the lawful sovereign to her throne. . . . And I close the volume to pen the first page in this diary. . . .

8 April, Saturday.

In the morning the weather was cloudy; wind S.W.; in the afternoon the rain fell in torrents, the thunder pealed and the lightning flashed terrifically; a thunderstorm is sufficient to strike awe in the breast of man, and convince him of the power of God. S. S. E. Cowperthwaite[6] borrowed *Don Quixote* vol 1; and John W. Barrett borrowed *The Histories of Celebrated Pirates*.

9 April, Sunday.

Cloudy; the wind blowing a gale from the westward. I went in the

4. The witness is identified as James A. Lord in New Jersey Supreme Court records.

5. The boat belonged to the United States Customs Office in Camden. Mickle sometimes refers to the craft as the "Custy." Windmill Island, in the Delaware River between Camden and Philadelphia, was dredged out of existence in 1898.

6. Samuel S. E. Cowperthwait (often called "Sam" or "Master Sam" in the diary) was one of Mickle's closest friends in these years. He made his living as an engraver in 1840, but later became a Camden dry goods merchant.

afternoon, to the Methodist Episcopal Church, where "Brother Taylor"[7] delivered a laboured discourse from Matthew 5:8, "Blessed are the pure in heart, for they shall see God." Nothing remarkable occurred to day.

10 April, Monday.

The weather is clear, cool, and bracing; wind N.W.; To-day I commence school, after a week vacation, with Oliver Cox, A.B.[8]

Samuel S. E. Cowperthwaite returned *Don Quixote* vol 1, and borrowed Vol 2 of the same. Mr. Cox borrowed *Rights of Women*. Isaac Mulford, M.D.[9] borrowed 3 nos. of Atkinsons *Evening Post*.

In the evening I went to Miss Sarah Haine's[10] Birth-day party—where there were twelve or fourteen "young ladies" (!) of my own age, in whose company I enjoyed myself a great deal.

11 April, Tuesday.

The weather very pleasant; wind N.W. The directors of the Camden and Amboy Rail Road and Transportation Companies holding a meeting to day at New-Brunswick, I accompanied my uncle, starting at 7 o'clock, A.M., per steamer *Trenton* from Philadelphia to Bordentown—from Bordentown to Spottswood, per Rail Road—and from Spottswood to New Brunswick, per stage, arriving at 6 P.M.[11] Immediately on arriving, I made a survey of the town, which is very thriving, and which, from the romantic scenery, which a walk along the banks of the Raritan presents, is rendered very interesting to the naturalist. . . .

Being very much fatigued "I laid me down to sleep" on a bed, which reminded me of the one occupied by the valiant *Don Quixote* on the night his jaws were broken by the "enchanted Moor" (as he supposed;) however I slept very well; and on the morning of

7. The speaker may have been Edward Thompson Taylor (1793–1871), a noted Methodist missionary preacher from Boston.

8. Cox, a graduate of Cambridge, operated the Camden Classical School in the basement of the Methodist Church, beginning in March 1836. Mickle attended the school from then until 1838.

9. Mulford (1799–1873), one of the most prominent physicians in the Camden area, and later an historian of New Jersey, was Mickle's uncle. He had married Mickle's paternal aunt Rachel and had fathered three children, Mary, Emma, and Anna.

10. Sarah or Sally Haines was Mickle's cousin, the daughter of his paternal aunt Mary and Samuel Haines of Woodbury. Sally's sister Rebecca appears later in the diary.

11. The Camden and Amboy Railroad, incorporated in 1830, soon became a great economic and political force in New Jersey by virtue of its monopoly of New York to Philadelphia traffic. In the diary it is sometimes called simply "The Company" or "The Monopoly." John W. Mickle (1793–1861), one of the leading citizens of Gloucester County and of Camden City, was an officer of the Camden and Amboy Railroad. A former sea captain, "Uncle John" had returned to Camden upon Isaac's father's death and now lived with Isaac and his mother. The phrase "my uncle" in the diary almost always refers to him.

12 April, Wednesday.

The weather being very pleasant—I set out on my return, per steamer *Napoleon* from Brunswick, to South Amboy, from whence, per Rail Road, to Bordentown, and from Bordentown per steamer *Trenton*, to Philadelphia, where we arrived at 4, P.M.

This being the first time I was ever in New Brunswick, I was very much delighted with my visit.

13 April, Thursday.

Pleasant weather; wind W. Went to the city (of brotherly love) A.M. and P.M.; saw the corner stone of the Old Second Street Market[12] taken up, but did not see the contents of the leaden chest examined; in the evening I attended the meeting of the "Youths Debating Society" where the question "Which of the two is the worse, open or sly robbery?" was debated upon. . . .

16 April, Sunday.

Clear weather; gales from the westward; could not go to church on account of the toothache; slept none last night.

17 April, Monday.

Clear weather; wind N.W; confined to the house by the toothache; slept none last night.

19 April, Wednesday.

The weather being very pleasant, my friend, E. Drayton, D. Harvey and myself, walked to the Philadelphia Navy Yard to see the ship-of-the-line *Pennsylvania*—or as it is more commonly termed "the big ship."[13] I there procured a piece of red cedar, which is much used in building the aforesaid ship—and set about making a Baltimore schooner, or at least the copy of one, which I intend to present, when finished, to Edward Drayton, as a token of the friendship I bear him. . . .

Took the Custom House Boat to receive some repairs, (which she needed very much) agreeably to Messrs Croxall's and Bullock's[14] orders.

---

12. The old Second Street market building, built at the site of today's Head House Square in the mid-eighteenth century, had been torn down and replaced in the first decade of the nineteenth.

13. Mickle's good friend Edward (Ned) Drayton was absent from Camden for much of the period of the diary, attending Lawrenceville School and Princeton College. Harvey is not mentioned in Camden City directories.

The *Pennsylvania*, 210 feet in length, was the longest man-of-war yet constructed.

14. Morris Croxall, a Camden attorney since 1821, was collector of customs for the port of Camden. Isaac Bullock was the city's postmaster.

U.S.S. *Pennsylvania*

20 April, Thursday.
Recommenced school, there having been none since Tuesday 11th instant on account of sickness in Mr. Cox's family. . . .

21 April, Friday.
Clear and calm; I went to school in the morning, but in the afternoon I crossed over to "the city of brotherly love" to purchase the book in which this is written, and for which I paid fifty cents.

The sloop *Ohio*, belonging to Jacob Ellis[15] and Brother, was sunk during a "South-easter," in the autumn of 1836, in the river Delaware, between Market and Arch Streets—having on her deck some four or five tons of rail road iron. The owners attempted to raise her, but were not successful; she after that, drifted with the ebb, to somewhere in the vicinity of the Point House; then up with the flood—and lodged in the middle of the Mickles fishing ground.[16] To-day, having obtained a bill of sale for her, my uncle, John W. Mickle, departed with the sloops *Alexander* and *Eliza and Ruth*—"to try his luck." We will see if the sailor's proverb "'Tis bad luck to begin an enterprise on Friday" comes true or not.

22 April, Saturday.
Clear weather; light breeze from N.W; launched my batteau *Napoleon*; my uncle was sweeping for the wreck but had got no purchase; I went to a party at my uncle Mulfords, this evening, where there were some half dozen **young ladies** (!)

23 April, Sunday.
The snow is two inches deep on an average, while I am writing this

15. Ellis may have been the Philadelphia merchant of that name at 7 North Second Street.
16. The "Point House" was probably the Kaighn's Point Tavern on Kaighn's Point. The Mickles owned the fishing rights on the east side of the Delaware, from Kaighn's Point south to Newton Creek.

(7½ o'clock, P.M.) it having snowed incessantly, since 5 o'clock P.M.; the flakes are as large as hickory nuts; wind N.E. I did not go to church to day, though I made two essays.

24 April, Monday.

Clear weather; wind blowing a gale from N.W. The snow which fell yesterday, still remains in spots on the ground. I walked down to "Poplar Hill"[17] this morning, and went off in a fishing boat, to the wreck, . . . and remained on board until 1 o'clock P.M, when I returned. They had got a purchase fore and aft, and were in a likely way to raise her.

25 April, Tuesday.

Clear weather; wind N.W. Went to the wreck in the morning, and in the afternoon to the city,[18] where I bought some books.

26 April, Wednesday.

Clear weather; wind N.W. Went to school; toward evening I went to the city where I bought the following books: *Glory of America*, for which I paid $1.00; *History of the United States*, 1.10; *Souvenir*, 15; *Book of Pleasures*, 37 1/2; *Romantic Tales*, 50; *Devil on Two Sticks*, 25; *Napoleon-Poem*, 8; *Roman and Grecian Geography*, 18 3/4; *Columbian Plutarch*, 22; *Coronal*, 20; Grimshaws *Napoleon*, 22; Parley's *Ornithology*, 50; *Vicar of Wakefield*, 31 1/4; *Life of Lafayette*, 25.[19]

27 April, Thursday.

Clear and calm; went to the wreck in the morning, and to the school in the afternoon. Went to the Debating Society Meeting in the evening; no quorum.

30 April, Sunday.

Clear and sultry; wind S W. I went to the wreck; the largest cable had broken "in twain." Dull times; nothing worthy [*of*] remark, only a complete muddying, received by falling into a ditch. . . .

1 May, Monday.

Clear; wind blowing a gale from North West; I went "a maying" with Mrs. Mary Haines, and some others.

3 May, Wednesday.

Clear in the morning, wind S.W. In the afternoon, rain, with thunder and lightning. In the meeting of youth, to adopt proper measures for

17. Poplar Hill was one of the Mickle family farms, in today's South Camden.
18. Diary references to "the city" always refer to Philadelphia.
19. United States mints issued half-cent coins up to 1856. There never was a quarter-cent coin produced in this country, but Mickle may be using foreign coins of such a value.

the institution of a society for the attainment and promotion of useful knowledge, there were twenty one attended. Mr. Cox, A.B. was appointed President; more concerning this anon. To day I received the first no. of *The Youth's Literary Messenger*.

8 May, Monday.
Cloudy; wind S.E. The wreck was raised this morning and drifted as far up as Kaighn's Point. In the afternoon I went down to her. Dr. Mulford borrowed Grimshaw's *Napoleon*.

15 May, Monday.
Cold and hazy; wind N.E, N. and N.N.E; went to the city with my uncle; when in the neighbourhood of Front and Willow Streets, the **larboard** wheel of the gig **unshipped**, and my uncle was "cast overboard" but did not receive any injury; for my own part I clung to windward like a good fellow; and weathered the gale; In the evening the Lyceum meeting was slimly attended, on account of a heavy shower.

17 May, Wednesday.
Clear; wind SW; went to school in the afternoon only; in the evening an adjourned meeting of the "Youths Lyceum"[20] was held; the Constitution was adopted; owing to a misunderstanding, there were only nine present; Samuel S. Foster[21] borrowed the *Coronal*.

19 May, Friday.
Cloudy; wind N.E. It is one month to day since my uncle set about raising the sloop *Ohio*. Nothing occurred to day worthy of remark.

21 May, Sunday.
The weather is clear; wind S.W; I went down to Kaighn's Point, to see the *Ohio of Wilmington*, who had been drawn in during the night, with a **crab**; after working two or three hours, and rowing a batteau a mile, I returned home at 3 o'clock, in expectation of getting some dinner; but "alas for human prescience"—I was accosted by a dandy of the first water, who, when he meets me in the city, where he dwells, would run over me and trample me to the ground.
"Will you walk in, sir?" said I as we arrived at the door.
"Yes, I believe I will."
"Have you dined?"
"Yes."

20. This is the society, the organizational meeting of which was held on 3 May. It was defunct by April 1839.
21. Foster was an apprentice harness-maker who lived in the house next to Mickle's in "Garrett's Row."

I then invited him to see my library; and he, after examining some three hundred volumes said "Will you lend—" "Did you ever hear this tune?" said I—hastily interrupting him, and putting a musical box in motion which played *Napoleon's March.* He laid *Don Quixote* and "The Bard of Avon" upon the shelf, and went to the table on which the instrument set. "No!" said he, in reply to my interrogation. He examined the box over and over, and having succeeded in misplacing some of the machinery by which it is propelled, he invited me to take a walk, having forgotten all about his books; I agreed, and we trudged along through sand somewhat less than knee deep, the hot sun beaming down on our heads with an almost tropical heat.

I had risen early in the morning, had been at work overhauling cables two or three hours—had had no dinner, and notwithstanding these inconveniences, had to walk a mile or two; the journey was rendered more tiresome by his trifling questions, such as these,

"Is this red quartz?" picking up a small piece of brick, and

"Is this a nettle?" pulling up a bunch of clover.

He wanted to loan some books, but whether he could read or not is what I cannot fully ascertain.

We at last got back to the place of departure; he desired me to bring him some water; I did so; the shoe brushes came next in demand, but I was surprised to find he did not "politely request" me to black his boots; then came the clothes brush, then the hair brush—then the hat brush—in order from the feet up. After a half an hour spent in brushing and other indispensable requisites to enter the city of brotherly love, he said he would like me to row him across the river in a boat; I, being greatly rejoiced to get rid of him in any way, said I would **with pleasure**. On stepping on board the boat, he asked me if I would be so kind as to lend him my handkerchief; I did so, and the handkerchief, which was clean, was soon engaged in rubbing the mud off the seat on which he was to sit. I rowed a good half hour against a current which runs at the rate of four knots per hour, and landed at the foot of Market Street—the sweat standing in drops on my forehead.

"I spose you're goin to treat, aint you?" said my visiter, as I handed him up on the wharf; and he went to a booth & purchased 1s. 6d[22] worth of cakes, candies etc., and telling the woman that I would pay, which I did, he thrust a half of a gingerbread into my pocket, darted up the hill without even saying "Good day."

I rowed back and made amends in my supper for what I lost in my dinner.

22. British and certain other foreign coins were legal tender in the United States until 1857.

22 May, Monday.

Clear; wind S W, W & N W. I met my visiter of yesterday in the city, who passed with a slight nod of the head. "O! Gratitude, thou art a virtue!"

26 May, Friday.

Cloudy in the morning; wind N.W & N.E. To day "Mingo" the champion of the north was beaten, on the Camden Race Course,[23] by Lady Clifton. . . .

29 May, Monday.

Clear and calm; nothing worthy of remark. I do not feel very well, having a cold on my breast.

30 May, Tuesday.

Clear and exceedingly hot; light breezes from SW; Mr. Cox returned Shakspeare Vol 7. To day I finished *Don Quixote,* and I think it exceeds any book I ever read, for ingenuity of the plan, wit and amusement and instruction which it contains. It is said to have nearly done away the chivalrous spirit of the Spaniards. Perhaps, on a second perusal, I may be enabled to pass some of my criticism upon it.

31 May, Wednesday.

Clear; wind W. Went on a sailing excursion; nothing remarkable.

1 June, Thursday.

The summer comes in with pleasant weather, and wind S.W. I was sailing again to day; the *Custy* beat everything that came before her, notwithstanding she was close reefed. . . .

4 June, Sunday.

Clear in the morning; in the afternoon thunder and showers which the farmers needed very much. Made an addition to my Library of 64 volumes.

5 June, Monday.

Went to school; after which was dismissed I went a-riding on my (as I call her) little mare.

6 June, Tuesday.

Clear; wind N W. Went on a sailing excursion at noon and riding after school.

23. The Philadelphia and Camden Race Course was built in 1835–36 on farm-land formerly belonging to Samuel C. Champion in old Newton Township, about three miles from Camden, now West Collingswood. It included a one-mile track, a hotel, a grandstand, and stables, and attracted some of the finest racehorses in the East, before its demise in 1847.

8 June, Thursday.

Went to school; wind N.E. with rain; went a sailing after school, notwithstanding the shower; "**wet** fun!" . . . Went to the Debating Society meeting in the evening; "Ought or ought not the Ferry Boats to ply between the cities of Camden & Philadelphia on the Sabbath?" was discussed; I in the chair, decided "ought not!" "Was General Jackson the cause of the present pressure was next discussed; decided by Jas: Ballantine, pres. pro tem "he was not."[24]

10 June, Saturday.

Clear, calm and cold; Did not go to school. Went to the Philadelphia Museum.[25] E. Cole[26] borrowed Turners *Chemistry*.

11 June, Sunday.

Clear; light breeze from N.E. So cold that we are obliged to keep a good fire on the hearth. Last night, about 12 o'clock, the house of Josiah Sawn, in second street, about two hundred yards from our own dwelling, was discovered to be wrapped in a sheet of flames. The work of destruction was so quick that Sawn, his wife, two children, and old lady and her daughter, the inmates of the house, were obliged to effect their escape by leaping from the second story window, by which the old lady was considerably injured. The alarm was not given in time to save the building or any of its contents, and it was with the utmost difficulty that the store of Joab Scull, adjoining, was saved.

The steam boat *William Wray*[27] was dispatched for assistance from the city; and it is a notorious fact, that the Philadelphians pilfered everything that came in their way; the fire was extinguished before they arrived.

12 June, Monday.

Cloudy and cool; wind E. Went to school, but did not translate any Caesar, or say any Mair;[28] engaged in writing "A Tale for Youth."

---

24. The second quarter of 1837 had been marked by a sharp drop in stock and commodity prices and a severe banking crisis, early signs of the depression of 1837–43. James Ballantine, mentioned many times in the following pages, was a close friend of Mickle.

25. The Philadelphia Museum, or Peale's Museum, founded by artist Charles Willson Peale (1741–1827) and once located in Independence Hall, was now in the Philadelphia Arcade on Chestnut Street, between Sixth and Seventh.

26. Mickle's good friend Edward Cole would become a druggist in Philadelphia in the early 1840s.

27. The *William Wray* was one of the Camden to Philadelphia ferries, named for the owner of the hotel and ferry house at the foot of Market Street, Philadelphia.

28. Mickle refers to John Mair's, *An Introduction to Latin Syntax* (Edinburgh, 1797).

Sent the **article on the Bath house** on Smith's Island[29] to the office of the *Mail* for publication. Attended a meeting of the Lyceum; and [*after*] a good deal of electioneering & a LITTLE bribery, and some pleading I got my **suspension bill**[30] through, which enacts that the next meeting of the society shall be held on, or after the first day of September 1837—or in other words, it is the funeral dirge of "poor young Lyceum." I am like the hippopotamus—I destroy my own begotten!

16 June, Friday.
Wind N; very cool; went to school; said 7 sections in Caesar. Nothing occurred worthy of remark.

17 June, Saturday.
Clear and cool; wind N.N.E: Went to Peales Museum with a friend.

18 June, Sunday.
Clear; light breezes, A.M. from N.E; P.M. blowing a gale from N.N.E; it is so cold that we are actually obliged to keep a "rousing" fire on the hearth, if not to keep our toes from freezing, to prevent the chills from running up and down our backs.

21 June, Wednesday.
Cloudy in the morning, but in the afternoon clear; took a sail in the Custom house boat.

25 June, Sunday.
Clear. Fell into the river; nothing remarkable.

1 July, Saturday.
Clear, but rather cool; went to Philadelphia in the morning; and sailing in the afternoon.

4 July, Tuesday.
This great day is extremely pleasant; neither too cool nor too warm; a good breeze stirring from N.W.

8 July, Saturday.
Cool and pleasant; in the morning I was engaged in making some improvements in my study, and consequently did not go to school. In the afternoon I went to the navy yard in Philadelphia, and saw "the big ship" and all the clubs on parade. In the evening I attended the meeting of "The Union Debating Society" but was very much disappointed in my expectations of hearing "good speaking."

29. The bathhouse and beach on Smith's or Windmill Island in the Delaware, attracted bathers whose dress or behavior Mickle found objectionable. Mickle's letter, signed "Decency," appeared in the *Mail* of 14 June 1837.
30. Suspension bills were those authorizing banks to suspend specie payments in view of the current financial crisis.

View in Woodbury

1838

1 January, Monday.

The new year comes in with remarkably pleasant weather; Farenheit is 16° above the freezing point—to the great detriment of our "fun" on the ice. Concluding that it would not do to sit in the house all day, poring over *C. Julii Caesaris Commentariorum*, I went, with a friend to the "city of right angles"—to see, but not to **be** seen—as I had not shipped my "go ashores" if I may speak *a la matelot*. The streets were all crowded, but Chesnut Street, the fashionable **promenade**, was literally a black mass, as far as the eye could reach. My friend and I, seeing several persons on the State House, resolved "to rise above the vulgar crowd" also—which we did, notwithstanding a scowl from the bellman, who as Shakspeare has it, "being clothed in brief authority" feels very consequential; he certainly is an **elevated** man. After having inscribed my name and anothers (a la mode) we proceeded to enjoy the fine view, which the State House[1] commands, of the city and environs.

1. Mickle's "State House" is Independence Hall.

14

On the east, the majestic Delaware, with its numerous shipping, the town of Camden, and the blue highlands in the background, all strike the eye at once, and produce a sublime effect. On the North the Delaware is still seen pursuing its serpentine way; steamboats and vessels of all classes speckle its bosom; Petty's Island, Dyott's Glass Works,[2] continually sending forth a dense volume of smoke, which reminds one of Aetna and Vesuvius—country seats and forests, render the scene extremely pleasing. On the West, the Schuylkill river, Fairmount water works, Moyamensing Prison, Girard College, and the romantic scenery beyond the Schuylkill, excite the admiration of every beholder. Nor is the South prospect less attractive; you see the Navy Yard, which is rendered "classic ground" since the launch of the *Pennsylvania* man-of-war—the largest ship afloat; "John Bull" has one larger on the stocks, but if she should ever grapple with "Uncle Sam's skiff" I "guiss" (as the Yankees say) she'll be "Fletchered"[3] (*id est*—she will get into a scrape that she will not get out of as well as she might wish.) But I digress. You can see Kaighn's, Gloucester, and Greenwich Points, "from the latter of which, General Washington crossed with his army, during the Revolutionary struggle. . . ."[4] With a telescope you can distinctly see Red Bank—where Greene bled and Donop fell.[5] I have been in the house where Count Donop exclaimed, a few minutes before his dissolution—"See in me the vanity of all human pride! I have shone in all the courts of Europe, and now am dying here, on the banks of the Delaware, in the house of an obscure Quaker!" This Friend's name was Whitall. The city below you, much resembles a chess board—the streets crossing each other at right angles. Close to your feet is the United States Bank—(alias Monster—) the bone of political strife; adjoining which is the Philadelphia Bank, a new and

2. Thomas W. Dyott (1771–1861) operated a huge and renowned glassworks in Philadelphia's Kensington section.

3. Mickle seems to have coined this term, possibly in reference to U.S. Navy Capt. Patrick Fletcher. Fletcher and his ship, U.S.S. *Insurgent*, ran into a mysterious "scrape" in 1800, disappearing without a trace while on patrol off the Atlantic coast.

4. Mickle comments elsewhere that an old revolutionary soldier had spoken the words quoted here, but that he was apparently incorrect. Washington had never crossed the Delaware at Greenwich Point, just south of Red Bank, though perhaps Col. Christopher Greene had on his way to garrison Fort Mercer; see next note.

5. The Battle of Red Bank or Fort Mercer was fought on 22 October 1777, when Col. Carl Emil Kurt von Donop led twelve hundred Hessian troops in an attack on the strategically situated fort. The Americans, commanded by Col. Christopher Greene, repulsed the attack, administering grave casualties in the process. Donop was mortally wounded and died several days later in the nearby home of James Whitall. Greene was not wounded, but about forty of his men "bled."

splendid edifice.[6] The Merchant's Exchange, the Girard and Pennsylvania Banks—the Arcade and Chestnut Street Theatre—Independence and Washington Squares, can all be seen at a glance![7] Indeed, what can you not see?

Independence was declared in the East Hall of the State House; a statue of *"Patriae Pater"* stands where President Hancock sat, on the pedestal of which is inscribed "Washington—the first in war—the first in peace—and the first in the hearts of his countrymen." Two or three Presidents of the United States have been inaugurated here.

Having enjoyed the prospect around and below us "to our hearts content," we descended and returned to Camden.

As I attended the funeral of '37, I felt somewhat of a desire to "turn in;" a game of chess, however, with my friend E. Drayton dispelled this. I took up Peyrouse's Journal[8] and read 40 pages, after which I surrendered myself to Somnus, at the seasonable hour of 12 o'clock!

2 January, Tuesday.

Summer weather in winter! I went to Philadelphia, walked up Market Street in great haste, as if on important business—down sixth to Chesnut—and down Chesnut very slowly, as if promenading for my health or amusement! ! ! Upon my return I took up Peyrouse, and—laid it down again! I have not been in a disposition to study since the Christmas holidays; four parties in one week is rather too much for my nerves! I then played a game or two at cricket, after which I resumed Peyrouse and read twenty pages; I find this book to be very interesting; but if the French Government had been as dilatory as ours is, in reference to Exploring Expeditions, perhaps I should not have had the pleasure of its perusal.

3 January, Wednesday.

The duties of Mr. Cox's school were resumed to day, but having business on hand which could not be delayed, I did not go. "Madame Rumor with her thousand tongues" says that Mr. Cox is about to take

6. Andrew Jackson had "destroyed" the Second Bank of the United States in 1832–33 when he vetoed a bill rechartering it and transferred federal deposits to state banks. The bank remained a political issue until its failure in 1841. The Bank of Philadelphia, incorporated in 1804, had moved to a new building at Fourth and Chestnut Streets in 1836.

7. The Merchants' Exchange at Third and Walnut Streets, the Girard Bank on Third below Chestnut, the Bank of Pennsylvania on Second below Chestnut, the new Arcade on Chestnut above Sixth, and the Chestnut Street Theatre at 201 Chestnut were among the most imposing landmarks of early nineteenth century Philadelphia.

8. Mickle apparently refers to the writings of French navigator and explorer Jean François de Galaup, comte de La Pérouse (1741–1788).

both rooms of the Camden Academy,[9] and that he is to be assisted by ——— ———! who is a first rate Latin scholar, inasmuch as he—cannot decline *penna*, or conjugate *sum*! as a mathematician he is unequalled by—few! But he has been declared to be the "Newton of Camden!"—and not many years ago he was "Number 1" at an impartial (?) examination! These are qualifications sufficient! !

In the evening I went to the Baptist Church with the expectation of hearing the Rev. Mr. Tyng,[10] of Philadelphia, deliver an oration on Temperance; circumstances preventing him from coming, the meeting was addressed by Isaac Mulford, M.D. President of the Camden Temperance Society, and Rev. Mr. Dandy,[11] of the Methodist Church, to the great satisfaction of all present. I was not a little amused to see a certain gentleman's eagerness to let the audience know and admire his powers of oratory; whenever opportunity offered, he would rise—"tell us that which we ourselves did know"—and take his seat again with Ciceronic dignity! I was informed that he is an engraver.

My uncle, Jno: W. Mickle, went to Bordentown this morning, to meet the Directors of the Camden and Amboy Rail Road.

4 January, Thursday.

The weather is remarkably fine; I have known colder days in June. I commenced school this morning; Caesar and Euclid are like rolling a stone up a hill.

5 January, Friday.

This day is more like winter than yesterday. I went to school in the afternoon; in the morning I went to Philadelphia to buy some books; on my return I found the new ferry-boat (which I proposed to call the *No Monopoly*—as her mate is the *State Rights*) lying at the Rail Road Wharf; she is a splendid vessel, and there is quite a rivalry existing for the Captainship of her.[12]

6 January, Saturday.

Clear and somewhat cool. I went to Philadelphia twice; saw nothing but people and houses. I met James Cassady, a certain impertinent

9. The Camden Academy was built as a schoolhouse, in 1803, at the corner of what became Sixth and Market Streets.

10. Stephen H. Tyng (1800–85) of St. Paul's Church in Philadelphia, was reputed to be one of the great orators of his times.

11. James H. Dandy had been pastor of Camden's Third Street Methodist Episcopal Church since 1837.

12. Mickle proposes a name for the ferry, which like *State Rights*, was a motto of Jacksonian Democrats. Though Mickle persists in applying this name to the boat, it was actually called the *John Fitch*, after the inventor of the steamboat. The "Rail Road Wharf" stood at the Delaware River terminus of the Camden and Amboy Railroad, at the foot of Bridge Avenue.

up-start, well known and much despised about town, and felt a great desire to break his head, for slandering me; but not wishing to make a black-guard of myself by fighting in the street, I let him pass unmolested. I can bear a good deal—as much as most persons of my age; but "there is a point, beyond which forbearance ceases to be a virtue. . . ."

7 January, Sunday.

In the morning I walked with a friend to Cooper's Creek Bridge. POST MERIDIAN, three o'clock I went with the same person, to the Methodist church, and took my seat as usual, in the gallery. The sacrament was to be administered and the house below was nearly full. I had not been seated long, ere Mr. Dougherty[13] made his appearance at the top of the stairs, and seemed, by an authoritive beckon, to want those in the gallery to come down. No one obeyed, and he came and whispered in each one's ear "There's plenty of room below, you disturb the congregation up here"—which was not so. My companion hurried down stairs and out of the door; but I went into the lower part of the church. A certain would-be orator now commenced a prayer, snuffling and snorting like a wild horse. Some of his audience were sitting, some standing, and some kneeling—many of whom embraced that opportunity to reconnoitre those behind them; the men to see if there were any pretty girls, and the women to see if there were any handsome men—what kind of a bonnet this one had on—or if that one wore her new cloak—in short any thing that would add to their budget of slander for the ensuing week. But some of the congregation showed "the workings of the spirit" by long and loud "Amens!"—"Glory Hallelujah!"—"Lord, have mercy on us!!" "O, my savior!"—"Glory, glory!"—and many other similar expressions, formed such a jargon as nearly drowned the voice of the reverend orator, altho' it was raised to the highest pitch.

After the prayer was ended, I made a "straight wake" for the door, and meeting an acquaintance, I walked with him to Coopers Point, and—back again of course.

If any one should ever chance to look over this my "Diary" let him not call me a scoffer at religion, because I have hinted at a few of the scenes witnessed in a Methodist church.

Reader! If you are a disciple of Wesley, you are prejudiced; if not— if you do not agree with me in censuring this clamorous way of wor-

13. Edward Daugherty, who sold "provisions" at a store on Third Street in Camden was an active Methodist layman, and later president of the Camden temperance organization.

shipping God, as incompatible with his own scriptures—then am I surprised.

8 January, Monday.

This is the twenty third anniversary of the glorious achievement of the American troops at New Orleans, under the command of our late venerable chief magistrate, Andrew Jackson. A few flakes of snow fell this morning. . . . I spent the evening with Edward Drayton, with whom I played a game or two of chess.

9 January, Tuesday.

Very damp and disagreeable. I went to Philadelphia on business; a report is afloat of the capture of the ship *John Sergeant,* but the "Much ado about nothing" affair of the *Susquehanna* is too fresh in their memories for the report to gain credit.[14] (I suppose three or four sloops of war and a steamboat or two will be sent in pursuit of the pirate! The merchants have not yet held a meeting in the Exchange!)

My uncle, Jno. W. Mickle, departed this evening for Harrisburg, to advocate the passage of a Bill now pending before the Pennsylvania Legislature, to authorize the Camden and Philadelphia Steam Boat Ferry Company to cut a Canal through Windmill Island.[15] He promised to take me with him, but—

"Promises are easily made and easily broken." James Ballantine spent the evening *chez moi.*

10 January, Wednesday.

In the morning I went to the "shin plaster city."[16] In the evening I attended a Meeting of the Camden Temperance Society at the Baptist Church, and heard an able address delivered by Mr. Marsh[17] of Philadelphia. As the **pledge** was being handed around for signers, a son of Erin who sat near the pulpit, took the floor and made an **eloquent harangue.** O'Connor[18] himself would have quailed before the orator's withering glance; and his herculian arm would have "smashed any negroe's head in Africa" as it moved swiftly up and down, like the

14. Rumors abounded in late 1837 that the Liverpool packet ship *Susquehanna* had been captured by pirates. The *Susquehanna,* however, arrived unharmed in Philadelphia in early January 1838 on her return voyage from England.

15. Mickle's Uncle John was a member of the board of directors of the company. Windmill Island lay athwart the most direct route between Philadelphia and Camden. The canal was completed in 1838.

16. Mickle derides Philadelphia as the source of many "shinplasters," privately printed paper money issued in the wake of the financial panic of 1837.

17. John Marsh (1788–1868) was a renowned Congregational clergyman and editor of the *Journal of the American Temperance Union.*

18. Daniel O'Connell (1775–1847), was a great Irish orator and political agitator.

walking beam of a steamboat, I suppose to "drive his words to his hearer's hearts" as I once heard a D.D. say.

After having bound his audience in admiration for about three minutes, he was called to order by a knight of the mortar,[19] who seemed to think that as the meeting was called to **promote** the cause of Temperance, no one had a right to **oppose** it. Paddy did not much like to resume his seat, and a faint hiss was heard in the gallery; some one who sat behind me, in a Stentorian voice, cried "Turn him out!" The assembly was now somewhat confused, by those who took the side of Patrick. Order was soon restored however, and after the Society was adjourned, they commenced distributing "The Temperance Almanac." A rush towards the pulpit now ensued; and the aisles being full, many climbed over the pews. I had nearly arrived at the **place of destination**, when ——— ——— tapped me on the shoulder and exclaimed "Good evening Mr. Mickle, Philopoena!"[20] (how d'ye spell it?) After returning the salutation, I proceeded to the desk, but alas! all the Almanacs were gone! I spent the remaining part of the evening in reading (for about the twentieth time) the *Life of Washington.*

11 January, Thursday.
The thermometer stands at 16°. . . .

In the morning I went to "the city of brotherly love" to purchase a book. At half past three in the afternoon I got aboard of the Moorestown stage at Toy's Ferry and was soon under weigh; there's no opposition on this line and **consequently** we went on a snail's pace the whole journey.[21]

The roads were very rough on account of the recent freezing weather, and such a jolting I never had, since I used to "go to town" on my mothers knee. The stage pitched and plunged like a yawl in a heavy sea, tossing the passengers about in all directions, and causing many *tête-a-têtes* much against the inclination of the parties.

The moon rose just as we entered the town, "lighting up" the spire of the new church in an elegant manner.

The stage stopped at West's tavern,[22] and I was glad to exchange

19. By "knight of the mortar" Mickle either means a bricklayer or an apothecary.

20. A custom in the Northern states at this time held that under certain circumstances, when two people met, the first to cry "Fillipeen" or "Philopena" was owed a present by the other. Hereafter, Mickle sometimes mentions paying a "philopoena" to someone; that is, he already owes something to that individual, probably as a result of losing some sort of parlor game.

21. Toy's Ferry was one of the ferry terminals at the foot of Federal Street in Camden, operated by Isaiah Toy. By "no opposition" Mickle means that there was no competition on the route.

22. John West had been the proprietor of the William Penn Hotel in Moorestown until 1837.

my unpleasant situation for a seat by a good **Hickory** fire. I proceeded the rest of the way in a thing 'clept a dearborn, ten times worse than the stage itself; I was obliged to hold fast with all my might to prevent myself from being thrown out of the **phaeton**.[23] I arrived at my uncle Hugg's about 7 o'clock, and found the list of my cousins **plus** one![24]

Reader, the situation of Falstaff in *The Merry Wives of Windsor* is more enviable than that of a passenger in a stage coach, driving over frozen ground—isnt' it?[25]

12 January, Friday.
After breakfast I started off in the same stage for Camden, where I arrived about 10 o'clock, *engourdi de froid*.

13 January, Saturday.
I went to the city across the water with my friend E. Drayton, and walked out to Broad Street, via Arch, returning via Chesnut. We saw the New Mint and many other things "too numerous to mention." At the **horse market** there were plenty of Jockeys trying to palm upon unsuspecting Jonathans, their old broken down nags, **warranted** "without a blemish," and plenty of Shylocks jockeying the jockeys, and beating down, "a quarter" at a time, the price asked. O, gold—o, silver!—o, shinplasters! !

14 January, Sunday.
I spent the morning in reading; in the afternoon, I went to the Episcopal Church and heard Reverend Mr. Whitesides[26] preach a good sermon, but from what text I cannot say, for it is fashionable "in the present enlightened age" to begin an oration in a whisper.

16 January, Tuesday.
In the morning I went to school and after a hard struggle, *vici Pons assinorum*, or the 5th problem of Book 1 of Euclid.

In the afternoon I assisted Mr Cox to move his desks etc. to the Camden Academy.

In the evening I enjoyed myself very much in the company of a few "lassies" of my own age, at my uncle Dr. Mulford's.

17 January, Wednesday.
I went to school. Some of the boys who "could not get the hang of

23. A dearborn, similar to a phaeton, was a light four-wheeled carriage.

24. Richard Hugg, who lived near Moorestown, had married Mickle's maternal Aunt Hannah. Their children were Mary and the newborn Joe.

25. Falstaff is successively soaked, pummeled, and pinched in Shakespeare's play.

26. Henry F. M. Whitesides (d. 1861), ordained in 1835 and recently a missionary in Michigan, lived in Pottstown, Pa., in 1838–39.

the new school house," like the boy in the anecdote, "got the **bang** of it" under the law which enacts that "no young gentleman shall play during the hours allotted for study." A large **rod of correction**, alias hickory, alias **gad**, made its appearance this morning under Domine's desk, indicating that the "rules were to be exacted to the uttermost farthing" as he says in his advertisement, by foul, if fair means fail.

18 January, Thursday.

Although in the very middle of winter, yet every window in the school house was thrown up, and even then the boys were complaining of heat! There was not a spark of fire in the room.

Such a winter was scarcely ever experienced before in this climate.

19 January, Friday.

Blowing a gale from N.W. Farenheit now (10 o'clock P.M.) stands at 27°. I wrote a portion of my speech for the twenty-second, and learned 20 sections of *Epitome Historiae Sacrae*.[27]

20 January, Saturday.

Farenheit is at about 34°. I went to the city this morning and bought Grimshaws *England* Grimshaws *South America* and Falconer's *Shipwreck.*

The Woodbury Rail Road[28] went into operation this afternoon, by taking sixty or seventy gentlemen from Camden to the above mentioned town, "to drink toast" in **celebration of the event!**

The trip to Woodbury was performed in 24 minutes, and coming back, in 18. We gave her nine cheers when she (the locomotive) returned. . . .

21 January, Sunday.

Is not very sunny. Sol has not cheered us with "one genial ray" since last evening when he made his exit in the western horizon. I saw, or thought I saw a flake or two of snow. The Colonel is off for Harrisburg this afternoon where business with the Sons of Solon requires his presence.[29]

The evening was passed in a very pleasant manner with some friends. One would narrate his adventures "by flood and field,"—another his "hair breadth 'scapes," and a third some *affaire d' amour* (don't frown, ye stoics—ye bachelors!).

---

27. Mickle was working on a Washington's Birthday address and studying Charles François Thomond's *Epitome historiae sacrae,* a popular Latin reader.
28. Chartered in 1836, the eight-mile Camden and Woodbury Railroad was never much of a success and ceased operations after only a few years.
29. John W. Mickle, infrequently called Colonel, was off again to lobby among the members of the Pennsylvania legislature for a Windmill Island canal.

After the party was broken up, I opened Goodriche's *History of the United States,* and drawing near the fire, commenced reading the battle of Trenton. . . .

After having fought the battle of Trenton over, I concluded I had "glory enough for one day," and retired instanter.

22 January, Monday.
The thermometer varies from 22° to 24°. The Delaware begins to assume the appearance of winter; it is not likely however that anyone will walk across it—yet a-while. . . .

23 January, Tuesday.
May weather! light breeze from S.S.W. In the morning I learned 40 sections of *Historiae Sacrae Epitome,* and a portion of *Commentariorum Caesaris.* The school in the afternoon went into committee of the whole, on the subject of **fighting.**

The circumstances were these; James Lane, a school boy was punished by Mr. Cox, for some misdemeanour. After the school was dismissed, Thomas Neall was laughing at the beauty of Lane's phiz while undergoing the aforesaid castigation, whereupon Lane waxed wroth and a battle ensued. The furious combattants were parted, and Wm. Burrough said Neall flogged Lane, who called Burrough a liar; hereat another fight took place, in which Jim got the worst.

He passed on a little further, and Henry English called Lane a coward. To settle this, they went into a narrow alley, that they might not be seen.

Now came the tug of war! One would strike a tremendous blow at his antagonist, who would dodge, and as a matter of course, the others fist would come in contact with the bricks. This was repeated several times; at length they **closed in,** and each attempted to gain the victory by knocking the others head against the wall. Thus they kept swinging backward and forward, like a pendulum, until the thumping caused thereby brought Mrs. ⸺ to the door, who put a stop to this well contested but novel battle.

Both appeared in school this afternoon with a large "bump of combattiveness" as a Phrenologist would say.

After an impartial hearing, Presiding judge Cox sentenced each of the **bullies** to have a good flogging which he himself executed in a manner that would not have disgraced any boatswains mate in Uncle Sam's service. . . .

24 January, Wednesday.
Pleasant weather. After learning a portion of *Historiai Sacrai* and Euclid, I drew [a] . . . map of Camden, which I believe is pretty correct.

Camden was first settled in 1681–2 by Messrs. Runyon, Cooper and Morris.[30]

At the period of incorporation, 1828, the population of the district
was 1143
In 1830, it was 1987
And in 1833 2341
The Increase in three years being 1354

Now . . . [3 *years is to 8, as a population increase of 1354 is to 3610⅔ and*] 3610⅔ + 1987 = 5597⅔ = Pop. in 1838.[31]

There are five separate divisions, all included in the act of Incorporation; Cooper's Point, Carmanville, Camden, Fetterville and Kaighn's Point.

At **Cooper's Point** there are a ferry,[32] from which the steam-boats *Citizen* and *Kensington* ply, a tannery, a cake shop and twelve or fourteen dwelling houses.

Gordon, in his *History and Gazetteer of New Jersey*, says: "The land at Coopers Point was taken up in 1687, by Wm. Cooper, one of the first and distinguished emigrants to the province, after the sale by Lord Berkeley to Byllinge; the whole of which is, at this time, not only possessed by his decendants, but actually, by decendants bearing the name of Cooper; no portion of it, [*having*,] in the space of 146 years, been aliened by the family."[33]

Cooper's Point is supposed by some to have been the place where Blackbeard, the celebrated pirate, deposited his ill gotten treasures. . . .[34]

Carmanville is about midway between Coopers Point and Camden, and contains a steam sawmill and lumber yard, a steam grist mill, an extensive cap-factory and eight or ten dwellings. It derives its name from William Carman.[35]

30. Mickle refers to William Roydon, William Cooper, and Samuel Norris. He fails to mention Richard Arnold, generally thought to be the first white settler on the site of Camden.

31. Camden was growing rapidly in these years, but not to the degree indicated here. The city had a population of 3371 in 1840.

32. Proprietor of the ferry at Cooper's Point was William Cooper (1770–1849).

33. Mickle quotes Thomas F. Gordon's *Gazetteer of the State of New Jersey* (Trenton, 1834). In 1664, King Charles II of England had granted New Jersey and other lands to his brother James, Duke of York. James granted New Jersey to Sir George Carteret and John, Lord Berkeley, the latter of whom, in 1673, sold his half to Quakers John Fenwick and Edward Byllynge.

34. New Jersey folklore has long included tales of treasure buried by such pirates as Blackbeard and Captain Kidd.

35. Carman had married Mary Ann Cooper, daughter of Daniel Cooper, and had begun a lumber business at the foot of Linden Street in Camden.

Camden, the third and principal part, is immediately opposite Philadelphia. There are in it an Episcopal Church, Baptist, Methodist and Friends Meeting Houses. A town house which formerly answered the quadruple purpose of jail, church, poll and lodge. The second story of this building is dignified with the name of City Hall; the quarter sessions are held here. An Academy and two or three school houses; two fire engines—the "Niagara" and "Perseverance"—neither of them very effective.

There are four ferries; Englishe's from which the *Delaware* plies, Paul's from which the *Camden*, Toy's from which the *William Wray* and *Philadelphia*, Elwell's from which the *State Rights* and *No Monopoly*, ply.[36] At each of these ferries there is a bar to **accommodate** passengers! There are three public gardens, Johnson's "Vauxhall"— Edmund's "Columbia"—and Weatherby's "Rail Road."[37] At the Vauxhall there is a reservoir or cistern, surrounded by a railing, in which is a great number of the **golden fish of Tagus**. In the centre of this reservoir, standing on a rock, is a female, holding in her arms a swan, from whose mouth comes a *jet d'eau*, which after rising about 15 feet, falls into the basin. This stream is supplied from another vessel on the top of a building, at a distance from, and apparently unconnected with, the fountain. "Water seeks to preserve its level" in an axiom in philosophy which needs no demonstration.

Statues of Hercules, Diana and other heathen divinities, decorate the Columbia garden.

In the Rail Road Garden is a platform, around which a miniature horse carriage is driven, by machinery underneath; a little engine plies a stream on a painted house. The whole is just calculated to please children. The council refused to grant the proprietor of this garden, a license to sell rum, so he "whips the devil around the stump" in this way. He has a box, on which is painted "**Charity Box**;" he **gives** his customers the rum and they put the money in said Charity Box! As there is no law forbidding a person's **giving** rum to another, nor giving **money** to another, he is not fineable.

There are seven taverns in Camden and a Temperance Society; to the honor of the town, let it be said that the latter is gaining ground on the former.

There are two public libraries—Harrisons and "The Washington."

36. Joseph and Israel English managed the ferry at Cooper Street, William S. Paul the ferry at Market Street and Isaiah Toy that at Federal Street. The Camden and Philadelphia Steamboat Ferry Company operated from Elwell's Hotel, also at Federal Street.

37. The proprietors were John Johnson, Nathaniel Edmonds, and Joseph Weatherby.

Two Debating Societies—the "Union" and the "Franklin." The Washington Library and Franklin Debating Society are conducted by boys. One Benevolent and one Beneficial Society, (the latter composed of youth.)[38]

Four physicians, six lawyers and one druggist. One Bank too many; two printing offices, from which two newspapers are issued—the *Mail* and the *Republican*—one neutral in politics, the other a whig; both would be insufficient to wrap a Lilliputan in.[39]

Nine groceries, seven extensive coach factories, one hair cloth manufactory, and four or five dry goods stores. Many other trades are carried on, but it is not necessary to enter into minutiae.

Fettertown, alias **Hard Scrabble**, is built on a bog between Camden and Kaighn's Point.[40] There is a **tavern**, a homony (*vide* Walker) mill,[41] a grocery, a garden for "the people of color" and thirty or forty houses, tenanted principally by that unfortunate race, "On whom Afric's sun has set his seal."

Kaighn's Point is situated opposite the Philada. Navy Yard, and has one ferry,[42] from which the steamboats *Kaighn's Point* and *Southwark* run to South Street, one tavern, a school house, a smithery and grist mill, a coach manufactory, a tannery, and several dwelling houses.

Rail Roads. The Camden and Amboy Rail Road, and the Camden and Woodbury Rail Road, terminate at Elwell's Ferry. . . .

Morals *vel* immoralities. I am sorry that I cannot say much in favour of the moral character of Camden. Being so near the **vortex of vice**, of which every great city is the centre, too few of its youth, I fear, are able to withstand its force. Thus I account for the depraved state in which Camden ever has been, since I can remember, and is now.

If you walk out in the evening, at every corner you will meet a group of lads from 12 to 20, swearing, cursing each other, lying,

---

38. The societies are probably the Howard Beneficial Society and the Youths' Lyceum.

39. A staunch Jacksonian Democrat, Mickle opposes banks in general. The local enterprise was the State Bank of Camden, incorporated in 1812. The Camden *Mail*, founded as the *American Star* in 1821, was owned and edited at this time by Philip J. Gray, a Whig. The Camden *Republican* had been founded in 1831, later changing its name to the *National Republican*. Josiah Harrison, a Democrat, was the current publisher of the paper.

40. Camden businessman and public servant Richard Fetters (1791–1863) had purchased land from the Kaighn family in 1833 and again in 1835 and sold lots at low prices and reasonable terms. Among the buyers were a number of Philadelphia and South Jersey blacks. Fettertown, more often called Fettersville, was originally bounded by the Delaware and modern Line, Cherry, and Third Streets.

41. Thomas Walker (1715–94), frontier physician, is credited with being the first writer to use the spelling "homony."

42. Ebenezer Toole owned and operated the ferry and tavern at Kaighn's Point.

insulting females, and using indecent and offensive expressions. At 14 or 15, they commence tippling and "loafing" at taverns; at 21 you find them habitual drunkards and **worse**; at 25 they are worn down by debauchery and disease.

The Race Course, situated near Camden, aids greatly in their downward course.

During the summer season, particularly on the Sabbath, our streets are filled with the **dregs** of Philadelphia. As I once observed on the floor of the **much puffed** Youth's Debating Society—"The Philadelphians seem to think that the Delaware bounds all order. The instant they set their feet on the shores of "Spain,"[43] they give way to all kinds of rioting; the profligate's oath and prostitutes billingsgate accompany the sounds of the organ, and the obscene song and sacred hymn are heard at the same moment."

May they reform. Thus ends this short History of Camden.

27 January, Saturday.

I was in Philadelphia this forenoon an hour or two. The afternoon I employed in reading.

At 6 ½ o'clock. P.M. I started off through mud and mire, for the Academy, where I arrived after a fatiguing and disagreeable walk, about 7. My pains were rewarded, however, by hearing an **able** discussion by the "Union Debating Society," on the question—"Was Washington a more praiseworthy character than Lafayette?" Decided in the affirmative.

28 January, Sunday.

I went to the Methodist church in the morning and to the Episcopal in the afternoon.

30 January, Tuesday.

Pleasant weather. At Algebra and Caesar all day, and at my address for the "22nd" all night.

The urchins are skating along the shore.

31 January, Wednesday.

. . .The present month has been very changable; sometimes like a southern spring, sometimes like a northern winter. The Delaware at one time would be full of ice, and at another not a particle was to be seen. There have been three snows, but I have not heard "The merry tingle of the gay sleigh bell." One day the boys would be **skating**, the next thinking of **swimming!**

---

43. New Jersey was jokingly referred to as Spain because Joseph Bonaparte, Napoleon's brother and former King of Spain, lived at Bordentown from 1816 to 1841.

1 February, Thursday.

This month comes in with remarkably clear and cold weather. The Delaware again assumes the appearance of winter.

I had some fine sport on the ice at Mount Meadows, and my aching bones are a convincing proof, that "pleasure is ever bought with pain."

3 February, Saturday.

. . . I attended in the evening a meeting of the "Washington Library" of which I was elected Vice President—an office of honor and profit.

4 February, Sunday.

Did not go out of the house, although the day was extremely pleasant.

I finished Goldsmith's *History of Greece,* with which I was very much interested.

5 February, Monday.

I went to Philadelphia in the morning, in the afternoon to school. I received a letter from my uncle at Harrisburg, and wrote in reply. . . .

6 February, Tuesday.

In Philadelphia from 9 'till 11 this morning. After dinner I went to Mount Meadows, to skate, with some friends.

7 February, Wednesday.

Wind S.E. with rain. At 7 o'clock I went to a meeting on the subject of Education. Dr. I. S. Mulford, A. Browning, and P. J. Gray, addressed the audience.[44]

44. Abraham Browning (1808–89), a prominent Camden lawyer, served as Attorney General of New Jersey, 1845–50. Philip J. Gray (1798–1875), newspaper editor of the Camden *Mail* and *West Jerseyman* from 1833 to 1860, was a leading figure in South Jersey politics.

8 February, Thursday.

After school I went to Philadelphia—on business of course. Finished reading Goldsmiths *History of Rome,* but do not think it as interesting as his *Greece.*

9 February, Friday.

Received a letter from my uncle—walked to Benjamin Mickle's,[45] a distance of two miles and a half—dispatched my business—returned—wrote a letter—and mailed it, in two hours after the reception of the letter which I answered.

Commenced reading Gillies *Greece.* . . .

10 February, Saturday.

In the evening I went to hear the "Union" discuss the question—"Which is the greater incentive to action—honor or wealth?" They talked me to sleep before long; there were no **invincible** arguments advanced on either side.

11 February, Sunday.

Reading Gillies *Greece* all day. I have become quite an antiquarian, and like Caius Marius, I should like to pass my life amid the ruins of Carthage or Athens or Sparta, and like Volney to meditate on "The glorious, by-gone days" of Roman and Grecian splendor, and on the Revolutions and downfall of Empires. . . .[46]

12 February, Monday.

My uncle, Jno. W. Mickle, returned from Harrisburg after an absence of three weeks—**all told.** The Bill passed Senate on Saturday, the 10th inst. . . .[47]

15 February, Thursday.

"It rains, it hails, it snows, it blows" as the Hunter's Chorus says, "And I could not go to school to day!"[48]

One week more, and the dreaded day comes in which I am to expose my ignorance and folly to a room full of critics!

Some acquaintances spent the evening *chez moi.*

---

45. Benjamin W. Mickle was Isaac's half uncle, the son of Isaac's grandfather and his second wife, Mary Matlack.

46. There is no evidence of Marius (155–86 B.C.), a Roman general, having had such wishes. Constantin François de Chasseboeuf, comte de Volney (1757–1820), was a French scholar and author of *Les Ruines, ou Méditations sur les révolutions des empires* (1791).

47. John Mickle's lobbying had helped secure passage of a bill authorizing construction of a Windmill Island canal.

48. Mickle may be quoting lines from some musical review. He is not referring to the most famous Hunters' Choruses in opera, those from *Der Freischütz, Lucia di Lammermoor,* and *William Tell.*

17 February, Saturday.

Did not go to school. The weather is extremely clear, and very cold. The mercury in Farenheit standing at 15°, at 8 A.M.

This evening at supper, by one of those mishaps "which flesh is heir to," the plate of my uncle was transferred from the table to his lap—and the contents with it. This would not have been worth mentioning, were it not that it led to the narration of an anecdote which I think deserves recording.

"On my return from sea" said he "I was invited to a tea party at neighbour S*****'s; and as there were several beauties from Philadelphia expected to be there, I equipped myself *cap á pie* in my best "go ashores."

"At supper, wishing to show my refinement, I took hold of the saucer with my thumb and one finger. When in the act of raising it to my lips, to take the first sip, it slipped from my grasp; quick as thought, with my right hand I tried to prevent the catastrophe; but, as the saucer was decending and my hand ascending, the concussion was more powerful than I expected. Up flies the mischievous saucer to the ceiling, and breaks into a thousand *morceaux*, and down comes the boiling beverage, into the eyes and on the clothes of the company, who were watching this extraordinary feat of legerdemain! I wished myself ten thousand times, on the fore top of my "bonny bark." It is superfluous to say that as soon as I could make an honorable retreat, I did so." We see the old adage realized here—"There's many a slip, 'tween the cup and the lip."

I have been in several dilemmas or quandaries (as Colonel [*Davy*] Crocket would say) like that of my uncle's.

Once in particular at a party, I was requested to "lade out" the ham. Accordingly I commenced operations with a knife on which I could have ridden a mile or two without any serious consequences. I gave two or three saws, when to my great mortification, and the merriment of all present, I capsized the dish, ham, gravy and all, on the superfine damask. I have no doubt but that the cook could almost have broiled a steak by my face; it certainly **burned** with shame, to think of making such an awkward **splash**, after having read Chesterfields *Principles of Politeness*! . . .

18 February, Sunday.

I remarked a few days ago that I had not heard the bonny sleigh bell this winter. The hail and snow which fell day before yesterday have frozen, and sleighs are running in every direction. The Delaware is fast (as the common saying is) at Coopers Point, and hundreds of people have walked across.

Did not go *a l'egise* to day for a **wonder!**—but was engaged in the house with my confounded address. I have seen from the window, a dozen persons get **hoisted**, or lowered, on the slippery walks. . . .

19 February, Monday.
Clear, cold, and good sleighing. At 8 o'clock this morning I got aboard of a sleigh with my uncle, and got a-weigh at the rate of 8 knots an hour, steering due South.

After a delightful ride of an hour, seasoned with several snow balls from the horses feet, which never missed to hit in the face, we came to an anchor off Smith's Hotel[49] in **Woodbury.** This, the shire-town of Gloucester County, is situated on a Creek of the same name, about [*three*] miles from its entrance into the Delaware, and eight from Camden.

Like Moorestown, it **consists** of one street only, about a half a mile in length; and contains a Court House, with a prison connected with it, three churches (Friend's, Presbyterian, and Methodist) three taverns, and three Academies or school-houses.

Lawrence and Decatur, whose naval exploits have astonished the world, and erected for them, on the page of history, a monument, more lasting than marble, received the rudiments of an English education, in the **log** academy, which "rears its venerable self" on the east side of the street, just above Denny's tavern.[50] The noble deeds of these heroes, have shed a halo of glory around this plain structure, in which they were once mischevious pupils, and in which they, who could brave the cannon's mouth without trembling, have smarted under, and supplicated against, the castigations of a man who would go into hysterics on hearing the bellow of an iron **Bull** [*cannon*]!

There are several respectable, and some handsome dwelling houses in Woodbury; but take it "all in all," it is a dead, dull place, fit for Timon or any other man-hater.[51] I would not live in it for **money**, and I think not for **love.**

The gloomy monotony, it is true, is broken once or twice a year, when the Courts are held; but this only serves to render the relapse more unsupportable. . . .

After walking about the town an hour or two, I returned to Smith's and took a seat in the bar room for want of a better place. Here as

49. Jesse Smith was proprietor of Smith's Tavern, or the Upper Tavern.
50. Mickle refers to James Lawrence (1781–1813), American naval hero in the War of 1812, and Stephen Decatur (1779–1820), famous for his engagement against the pirates of Tripoli and Algiers. There is no evidence that Decatur ever attended Woodbury Academy, though Lawrence certainly did. The Academy, built in 1791, stood near Joseph W. Denny's Eagle Tavern.
51. Mickle's reference is to Shakespeare's *Timon of Athens.*

usual there were a dozen loafers sitting around the hot stove, squirting their tobacco juice, and spinning yarns.

At 4 o'clock I started per Rail Road for "home, sweet home" and arrived in 27 minutes.

At 7 o'clock, I attended a meeting of the Franklin Debating Society. . . .

After the Society adjourned, I went "agreeably to an invitation," to my uncle Dr. Mulford's to a *soiree*. There were several handsome and accomplished young ladies there, and of course I enjoyed myself very much.

21 February, Wednesday.

At 8 o'clock, A.M. the mercury in Farenheit stood at 12° above Zero. Now, 8 PM, it is at about 10°.

I was in Philadelphia again, to day, on business for the "Washington Library." I crossed in the *State Rights*, and find it much more comfortable to be carried, than to carry one's self, across a river, with a piercing northwester blowing in one's face.

In the evening I heard an address on Temperance delivered by Mr. Acon or Achon, (to whom I was introduced at my uncle Mulford's.) He strung anecdotes like Sancho of Quixottic memory, did proverbs; and I verily believe that, had it not been in a church, he would have been cheered with hearty "Bravoes!" and "Encores."[52]

There was a brilliant Aurora Borealis or Northern light visible this evening from 7 until 10 o'clock. For a description of it see the gazettes of the day.

22 February, Thursday.

This immortal day is as pleasant as it is great; like the character of the illustrious **Washington**, not a cloud darkens it.

In the morning I skated across the river and saw the parade of the military companies of Philadelphia. The remembrance of Trenton, Brandywine and Yorktown flashed upon me as I stood gazing on the gayly attired columns, moving slowly onward. . . .

In the afternoon I was engaged in fixing the room for the evenings Celebration, and doing other little "notions." Item. My heart begins to go pit-a-pat.

Evening. Description of the Celebration. **The Room.** The upper apartment of the Camden Academy was brilliantly illuminated, and comfortably heated. The only ornament was a large flag on which was inscribed "COLUMBIA;" this was suspended over the officers, and had a great effect.

52. "Sancho" is Sancho Panza of Cervantes' *Don Quixote*.

The Members. All the members, eighteen in number, were present at an early hour, and presented a sight which every citizen of Camden should be proud to behold. They are composed of highly respectable youth between the ages of 14 and 20. Each one wore a badge on the left breast, with the inscription—"**He still lives in the hearts of his countrymen**"—under the portrait of *Pater Patriae*; over this was printed—"**A Nation's Gratitude.**" The badges were **red**—those of the "Union Debating Society" **white**. Should these institutions ever come to a rupture, it could properly be called "The war of the badges". . . .

The audience—was not as large as might have been expected, but it was respectable. Several bright eyes graced the room and by their encouraging looks, animated the speakers. Several members of the Union Debating Society have been very busy for several days past in circulating a report that we were to deliver our addresses with those of their Society, in the Methodist church; a great number were thus misled, and I have it from good authority that one half of the concourse at the church went there for the express purpose of **hearing the Juniors.** "Honesty is the best policy"—and they will gain nothing by this foul play.

The Orations. The "Legacy" or Valedictory Address of Washington was read in an admirable manner by Mr. E. J. Cole, although he was somewhat hoarse. Samuel S. E. Cowperthwaite was to have read it, but he **bolted!**—consequently Mr. Cole had no time to prepare himself.

Your humble servant next followed with an address on the life and character of "the Romulus of America."

Mr. John W. Barrett then took the floor; his subject was Education, and his address throughout bore the stamp of originality, and was delivered without the slightest degree of confusion. "May his course be onward!"

The audience expressed their satisfaction with the performances, and withdrew about half past eight o'clock. The Society having received an invitation to attend the Celebration by the "Union," marched two and two down to the church, where the front seats were reserved for them.

They had finished with the exception of Mr. Cox, (whose speech is declared by the critics to have been the best) whose subject was a comparison between Washington and Moses. If this oration was the best, the others were neither "**sublime**" nor "**unsurpassable.**"

The house was full, pit and lobbies—but half of them **belonged to us.** The performances were concluded about 20 minutes past nine, and I returned home, heartily glad that my dreaded task was accomplished, and **Resolved,** That I wo'nt volunteer my services in such a scrape as this, again, soon. . . .

23 February, Friday.

Went to school, although my head ached pretty severely. Public speaking does not agree with me.

24 February, Saturday.

Worse and worse! I am downright sick.

25 February, Sunday.

I am really ill! and under the doctor's hands.

Wm. Shaw called on me, and I was obliged to entertain him; he is an old associate of mine. . . .[53]

Shaw and I have had many adventures with the Philadelphia wharf rats, who cross the river in swarms, to pilfer fruit from "the Spaniards" as they contemptuously call the Jerseymen. I may record some of them hereafter.

This is the coldest day we have had yet, this winter. Mercury at 8 o'clock this morning stood at 6° above Zero.

26 February, Monday.

Clear and cold. I feel hearty as ever—(thanks to the doctor's little white powders) and for amusement, skated across the river six times. Horses were "introduced" on the ice to-day for the first time this winter. . . .

27 February, Tuesday.

Mercury, through his oracle, Thermometer, tells us that icy winter has relaxed his grasp a little—32° exactly, all day; it neither melts nor freezes.

28 February, Wednesday.

The last of winter. Icy season, with all thy "nor westers" I love thee still! and

>"Let others hail the coming season,
>I bow to him who's touch is 'freezin'."

I must exclaim with the good emperor of Rome, "I've lost a day!" for I have done nothing but skate.[54] On a moderate calculation, I think I have travelled 20 miles. . . .

1 March, Thursday.

The first day of spring is very pleasant. There are a great many sleighs and people on the river, which still affords a safe and easy passage.

---

53. Mickle's friend Shaw, who had recently returned to Camden after several years' absence, is not mentioned in Camden city directories.

54. The Roman emperor Titus (*c.* 40–81) is reputed to have expressed this lament upon reflection that he had passed a day without accomplishment.

2 March, Friday.

Clear and cold: Thermometer at 14°. In the morning I went to Philadelphia on business for my uncle; in the afternoon to school.

3 March, Saturday.

My uncle arrived at home from Trenton, whither he went last Wednesday, on urgent business—a suit pending before the Supreme court of New Jersey. I was engaged in drawing and writing.

4 March, Sunday.

This great day (with politicians) is rainy, foggy and oppressive.[55] I kept close house all day, and instead of going to some place of worship ("sinner that I am!") was busy writing. . . . Among other notions I wrote *vel* scribbled a "puff" for the *Mail* and signed it "WASHINGTON."

5 March, Monday.

The Gubernatorial Convention is held to day in Pennsylvania; they have a wet day for the choice of a Candidate. . . .

6 March, Tuesday.

Clear and pleasant; very spring like. The ice in the Delaware was very much weakened by the rain yesterday, and will probably drive to morrow.

I was busy all the evening in writing and collecting matter for another address, to be delivered before long—**provided** my electioneering powers and influence are sufficient to get a Resolve to that effect, passed by the "Franklin Debating Society."

7 March, Wednesday.

Comes in with a snow storm and goes out with muddy walking. The flakes of snow that fell this morning, were fully as large as a dollar! . . .

The *Mail* of to day does not contain my communication. The Editor says:

We have not room to-day for the communication of "Washington," which shall have a place next week. In the interim, we would have a word with him.

Well! I suppose I must go and hear what his "word" is. Perhaps he does not like my indirect charge of foul play against the "Union Debating Society;" or perhaps he wants to request of me, the names of those accused. But I will see.

I went, in the evening, to the Court House, pursuant to a notice signed "Many," to a meeting called for the purpose of expressing **public opinion** on the subject of **duelling**. The house was jammed with

55. 4 March was the usual date of presidential inaugurations.

tagrag, and bobtail-loafers, bloats and scavengers. I took some pains to ascertain, and found that there were seven respectable **men** present. . . .

8 March, Thursday.

Brings with it rain, snow, hail, a blow, cold, mud, and a flood **minor**. What a day! I made out to wade up to the Academy and to wade through two problems of Euclid. . . .

9 March, Friday.

My uncle returned from Trenton, whither he went on Monday last. The case—*Mickle* versus *Matlack*—came before the Supreme Court on Tuesday. Counsel for the plaintiff, Jeffers and Williamson—for the defendant, Halstead and Frelinghuysen.[56] More of this anon.

10 March, Saturday.

The navigation in the Delaware is open, and vessels of every description, from the noble Indiaman down to the mean shallop, spread the canvass to the breeze, and cleave the "dark blue wave" for their destined port.

11 March, Sunday.

Our good citizens, like black snakes, turn out en masse to sun themselves; the day being named right. For my part, I staid in the house to write and read the papers, from which I collected the following Section of Salmagundi, or Matters and Things in **General**. The duel or affair of **dis**honour, if I may be allowed to add three letters to a fashionable phrase, between the **Honourable** Jonathan Cilley and the **Honourable** Mr. Graves,[57] which "came off" before several other **Honourables**, on Saturday, February 24th, near Washington City, continues to occupy a thrilling interest in the minds of the public.

The **honour** of Mr. Cilley was vindicated by closing his eyes in the sleep of death, after aiming three several times at the heart of his unhated adversary, and the **Grave** was revenged and satisfied when its

56. The Mickle family was now appealing the outcome of the trial mentioned in the opening paragraph of this diary. This and a later attempt to set aside Andrew F. E. Mickle's will were unsuccessful. The four lawyers involved were a stellar group. William N. Jeffers (*c.* 1788–1853), uncle of Mickle's friend of the same name, was one of South Jersey's most prominent attorneys, first in Salem, later in Camden. Isaac H. Williamson (1767–1844), governor of New Jersey from 1817 to 1829, was currently practicing law in Elizabeth. Oliver S. Halsted (1792–1877), another Elizabeth attorney, would become Chancellor of the state of New Jersey in 1845. Theodore Frelinghuysen (1787–1862) was a Newark lawyer who had served in the United States Senate from 1829 to 1835 and who would become the Whig candidate for vice-president of the United States in 1844.

57. William J. Graves (1805–48), a member of the House of Representatives from Kentucky, 1835-41, shot and killed Jonathan Cilley (1802–38), representative from Maine, with a rifle during a duel at Bladensburg, Maryland.

silly victim uttered his expiring groan. I would sooner be the deceased than the survivor. . . .

The arms of the Patriots in Canada have not yet been very successful.[58] But, as I said in my address on the "22nd"—a community contending for LIBERTY will eventually triump although numbers and advantages be never so much against them. And I hope in a few years to see the **Republic of Canada** added to the list of independent powers. England is at this time so critically situated that she cannot spare a single troop, to extinguish the spark of Freedom, which is fast fanning into a flame, and which at no distant day will rock the now tottering throne of Albion, to its centre, if not level it, with its petticoat incumbent, to the dust.

England, Wales, Scotland and Ireland are kept in subjection at the point of the bayonet; and the East India Colonies are but a means to drain the Kingdom of its finest troops; for those who escape death by the natives, meet it by pestilence. These **conquests** are something like Alexander's—**all glory and no profit**. The West India possessions are of the same description.

"Under these considerations"—if Canada does not succeed in throwing off the yoke—if Victoria, the adulated queen, dies on the throne— if the Parliament is not **Cromwelled** before many years, why then you may say that I am no prophet!

The Florida war is about as near a close, to all appearances, as when the first scalp was taken in it, three years ago. They want the hero of the Hermitage among them a day or two; the way he'd use the poor red faces up, would be a caution to Crockett![59]

The affairs in Texas are at just about the stage of the wrathy urchins, one on each side of a wall; "**jawing**" each other in a fine style. The Mexicans are afraid and the Texans dare not to **go round the wall** to get at their enemies.[60]

I do not think that Houston is as vigilant or persevering as McKensie, the Canadian Washington.[61]

58. There had been an unsuccessful insurrection against British authority in Upper Canada in the autumn of 1837.

59. Ex-President Andrew Jackson (1767–1845), who called his Tennessee home "The Hermitage," had long ago earned a reputation as a fierce Indian fighter, a distinction also claimed by Davy Crockett. Mickle feels that such a leader is necessary to end the long Seminole War in Florida which had begun in 1835 and would end in 1842.

60. Texas had declared its independence from Mexico in early 1836 and, after the loss of the Alamo, had routed a Mexican Army at San Jacinto. Texas remained an independent republic until 1845, when it became the twenty-eighth state.

61. Sam Houston (1793–1863), commander-in-chief of the Texas army in its war for independence from Mexico, was currently the president of the Republic of Texas. William Lyon Mackenzie (1795–1861) led the brief and hopeless Canadian bid for independence in 1837.

The fifth of March Convention in Pennsylvania resulted in the choice of General David R. Porter, for the Democratic candidateship for Governor. The tories of '76, alias whigs of '36 nominated Jos: Ritner his present Excellency.

At the last election, in 1834, the democratic ranks were divided between Geo: Wolf and Henry Muhlenburg. Hence Ritner's election.[62]

Muhlenburg has been appointed by the Executive to a mission to Austria, and Wolf collector of the Customs for the district of Philadelphia. ["Tis strange but true."] Porter will have a clear coast. The above as the newspapers say, needs no comment. . . .

12 March, Monday.

Is very mild and pleasant. Nothing remarkable occurred except a fight between a **Gray** and a **black** personage.[63]

14 March, Wednesday.

The *Mail* of this morning says not a word about "Washington" or his communication; this is strange. In the evening I was preparing, at my *toilette*, (if so I can call the kitchen fireplace) to go to my cousin's birth day party, when the cry of "Fire!" told me that the **good servant** was playing the **bad master**. I hastened, half undressed as I was, to the scene of the conflagration, losing my slippers, and running afoul of divers fellow-mortals, repeatedly. The building on fire proved to be John Rue's Coach Manufactory, in Mulford's alley, below Second Street. The fatal spark was communicated to some moss in the loft, from the chimney, but fortunately it was discovered in time to prevent the entire destruction of the shop, which however is minus its roof.

Great praise is due the "Perseverance" and "Niagara" engines for the prompt attendance, and vigilant efforts to extinguish the flames.

A report is current which reflects no credit on Mr. Rue. But I leave the fire for a more pleasant—or perhaps I should say, **more pleasurable** —place, which is a room full of young Venuses (!) in whose company I enjoyed myself very much, (notwithstanding my—what shall I call it?—modesty or awkwardness?—*je ne sais pas quoi.*)

In my embarassment my foot (none the smallest by-the-by,) happened to become entangled in the lower rigging of a chair, upon which a gentleman was about to be seated, and in my efforts to disengage it, it, the chair, was "transported" a pace or two back, and, wonderful to tell! Master Frank suddenly found himself stretched on

62. It was in 1835 that Pennsylvania Democrats split and ran both Wolf, the incumbent, and Muhlenberg for governor. Joseph Ritner, the Anti-Masonic and Whig candidate, won the election with ease, and served as governor from 1835 to 1839.

63. Mickle refers to a fight between Philip J. Gray and a black man.

the **tapis**, when he expected he should have been sitting by the pretty Miss ———. I made the best apology in my power for the misfortune, which was—a hearty laugh!

An obvious inference: when we attempt to sit on "airy nothing" it's ten to one that we'll come to the floor.

15 March, Thursday.

The Delaware is entirely free from ice. I saw Mr. Gray and was astonished to find that he knew me to be Mr. "Washington;" he insisted on my coming to his office on the morrow.

16 March, Friday.

Wind N.E. with haze and rain. I had an interview with Mr. Editor, who seemed to think that the hits of "Washington," although just, were a little too hard and the satire too keen, for publication. He told me he would gladly insert any communication I may be pleased to send him, and many more things which it would not do for **me** to tell of **myself**.

17 March, Saturday.

Saint Patrick's Day is snowy, windy, cold and very disagreeable. Many a **Patrick** will this night **carry out** effectually, the words of the old ballad—"Come let us be merry, In drinking old cherry"—and many a son of the Emerald Isle will be, this night, **carried out** of the grog shanties, dead—dead drunk!

I wrote an article for the *Mail* over the signature "Junius.". . .[64]

18 March, Sunday.

I perceive by the papers, that the white washed whigs are endeavouring to turn the odium of the recent bloody murder at Washington, from the grave and wise gang, upon the friends of the late lamented Mr. Cilley. This, it will be seen in a moment, is done to decieve the "dear people" and to cause a reaction in favor of the Federalists, or Blue lights.[65]

Yes! although Mr. Cilley was the challenged party—although he acted in self defence—although he acknowledged his respect and friendship for Mr. Graves—although his eyes are closed forever in death, the detestable party of "The Swaggerer Webb," like curious

---

64. Mickle's letter proposed that the *Mail* begin a "Juvenile Department" which would publish essays by young people.

65. Here Mickle condemns Whig party leaders Henry Alexander Wise (1806–76) and William J. Graves (see entry of 11 March) and links Whigs in general to the long dead Federalist party and especially its so-called Blue Light members, that is, those so unpatriotic as to oppose the War of 1812.

dogs, growl and scowl over his bones and upbraid him with thirsting for his assassin's blood. . . .[66]

This day has been snowy and cold. I did not go out of doors, because [I staid within.] I was intently engaged in scribbling some "trifles light as air" for the "Juvenile Department" of the *Mail*, over the name of "Junius."

19 March, Monday.

There being no school, I employed the day in writing, reading, and such "notions." I composed two articles for the *Mail*—"Junius No 3 & 4;" one is on "**Boys and Books**," the other on "Diaries". . . .

The weather is warm, and the snow (which was a foot or 10 inches deep this morning) is fast yielding to the genial influence of the sun— or in two words, is melting.

20 March, Tuesday.

The weather is very pleasant; wind S.W. In the evening the Franklin Debating Society held a meeting. . . .

21 March, Wednesday.

Very pleasant weather; wind N. and N.E.—I went to Philadelphia in the morning.

The *Mail* contains both my communications. . . .

Mr. Gray as usual, murdered *"Pater"* into *"Pro."*—Confound the leather headed proof-reader, I say!

P.S. My uncle promised to take me to see the farce of *Plot and Counterplot*[67] to night at the American Theater, but it was "all talk and no cider."

22 March, Thursday.

The squib of "Washington" makes a great stir in town to day; the Opposition have put the shoe on—a sure sign that it fits. I heard something about tar and feathers and prepared myself for emergencies. Wo be unto the person who attempts *vi et armis* to crush my freedom of speech!

The frogs announce the approach of spring in earnest.

23 March, Friday.

I went to Philadelphia and bought the busts of LaFayette and Franklin.

---

66. James Watson Webb (1802–84), Whig leader and editor of the New York *Courier and Enquirer*, had challenged Cilley (see entry of 11 March) to a duel shortly before Cilley's death at the hand of Graves.

67. Charles Kemble's (1775-1854) *Plot and Counterplot* had played the American Theatre (a name then given to the famous Walnut Street Theatre) on 19 March, but was no longer being performed on 21 March.

In the evening there were several flashes of lightning to the South-
ward—the first this season.

24 March, Saturday.
I went to an evening party and dealt pretty extensively in the commodity called kisses.

25 March, Sunday.
I went to Philadelphia this morning to witness the embarkation of
a friend—a warm hearted, noble fellow—for New Orleans. He sailed
in the barque *Josephine* (strange coincidence)[68] and parted from the
place of his birth and the smiles of **dear ones** and dear friends to brave
the storms and dangers of the ocean, with a bright face and buoyant
heart.

26 March, Monday.
"Washington" continues to be slandered by the Union Debating
Society. I have made some noise in the world if I should never make
any more.

18 October, Thursday.
Well! To day I enter upon my seventeenth year. *"Tempus fugit!"* It
seems but yesterday since I used to mount a broomstick and romp
o'er the green o' the "Grove" in all the "pomp and circumstance" of
an infantile equestrian! Yet those blithesome days are gone, never,
never to return. Melancholy reflection—stubborn fact! But away with
al'lasses! Now I commence this volume, with the intention of sticking
to it (until I cease **to am**?—no, that's too poetical entirely,) until I
find some better employment for my leisure hours. . . .

This morning I got up (as all good citizens should) and, after
breakfast, went to Philadelphia on business which it is not expedient
for the reader to know. Upon my return Mr. Joseph B. Cooper,[69] a
lover of antiquities, called to show me his Cabinet of Curious Coins,
which, by the by, is large and interesting. He undertook to translate
some of the inscriptions, but between his stammering and his ignorance,
I was reminded of the fable of the blind leading the halt. . . .

In the afternoon I went over the river with the New York passengers
in the *John Fitch* but tarried not long.[70] And now, when Terra has

68. Mickle remarks upon the ship's name because he has long been interested
in a girl named Josephine Sheppard.
69. Cooper was a gentleman farmer from Newton Township, near Camden.
70. New York to Philadelphia passengers normally took a train to Trenton and
a boat from there to Philadelphia, but when the Delaware was rough or ice-
bound, they continued by train to Camden and ferried across the river.

assumed her black night gown (excuse me, ladies.) here I am in my studio, scribbling the nonsence you are reading.

The day has been about as long as usual, (is'nt that information?) and very pleasant. Farenheit indicates 69°. . . .

19 October, Friday.

. . . . I spent the morning in writing and the afternoon in doing nothing. In the evening I went to a Temperance Meeting in the Methodist church; but as the benches were likely to be inflexible hearers, the speaker saved his breath for a more favourable occasion. Tee-Totalism is a bitter pill to the Camdenics!

By to day's *Emporium* the triumph of Democracy in New Jersey is confirmed.[71] Farewell, Federalism!—your doom is sealed. Last year you carried the State by 1200 majority, but now **it** carries **you** by 83 minority! . . .

20 October, Saturday.

A strong wind from the North West and an unclouded sky. I was deeply engaged in what half the world consider as useless—namely, thought. . . .

21 October, Sunday.

This afternoon, I went with B. Wilkins, to St. Stephen's Church in Tenth Street, Philadelphia, but as we heard nothing by which we were likely to profit, we came out ere the service was half over.[72] There was too much mummery and too little sincerity for me. **Give me the Friends for true piety!** . . .

22 October, Monday.

This morning I went to Philadelphia and "took a station" (as some of our erudite Camden loafers would say, up Chesnut Street, to see the followers of *haut ton,* and the engravings at Nolens', which resembled the animated fops in two particulars—both were painted and both were brainless.[73]

"POST MERIDIAN, half past four" I was walking with my friend Drayton when we espied over our heads a balloon, which we found, upon reference to the *Ledger* to be Mr. Wise, "the celebrated Aero-

71. The Trenton *Emporium* had misinformed its readers about the outcome of the New Jersey legislative elections of 16 October. In fact, the Whigs won the close contest.

72. St. Stephen's Episcopal Church stood near Tenth and Market Streets. Henry Ducachet was the current rector. Mickle's companion was probably Benjamin Wilkins (1788–1873) of Woodbury.

73. Mickle presumably stationed himself at various points along Chestnut Street, including Spencer Nolen's mirror shop.

naut."[74] He was "battling with airy nothing" in fine style, and making for the South East. He ascended from Seventh and Callowhill Streets, Philadelphia.

I was to have gone to the theatre to-night, to see Forrest play, but as "there is many a slip 'tween the cup and the lip" here I am, in a better place. . . .[75]

7 November, Wednesday.

Well! Here I am again, with thee, "thou source of 'improvement' my journal!" Two long days have separated us; and whilst I was flying o'er the country thou wast neglected, and stowed away among thy inferior kinsmen, printed books.

In company with my friend Edward Drayton, I started from Camden in the 10 o'clock cars, last Monday morning and at 2, P.M. found myself safely "set down" at Snowden's "Trenton House."[76] We dined in company with Senator Wall,[77] who condescended to be sociable to me, altho' he would not notice my friend. At 3 we took a coach for Lawrence, and after a tedious ride of an hour found the High School bearing full on our quarter. I felt, as we were entering the sombre mansion, a little as if I were about taking lodgings in Newgate or Bridewell.[78] After waiting three hours I obtained an interview with Mr. Hammil, the principal of the school, who informed me that it was doubtful whether he could admit me to a seat as he had applications for more than his complement.[79] He promised to write me, as soon as he ascertained, and leaving Ned, I made a straight wake for the tavern, not that I was dry, but because I was hungry. There I supped (on almost bare dishes) with John Ross, a son of the celebrated Cherokee Chief of the same name: he is about going to old "Nasau Hall," having been in training for two years, at the Lawrenceville High School, of which he gave a very favourable account.[80] After tea Ned and I took a muddy promenade towards the Girl's Seminary, but, as he assured me that it was dangerous for one to be caught looking at it, we "tacked ship" before we reached it. I lodged at the

74. John Wise (1808–79) was a scientific pioneer of ballooning.

75. Edwin Forrest (1806–72) was one of the great tragedians of his times.

76. Col. William Snowden operated the Trenton House from 1834 to his death in 1846.

77. Garret Wall (1783–1850), a Democrat, was United States senator from New Jersey from 1835 to 1841. He was defeated for reelection in 1840 and lived in Burlington until his death.

78. Mickle names two London prisons.

79. Mickle's interview was with Samuel Hamill (1812–89), who directed the affairs of the Lawrenceville school from 1837 to 1883.

80. The elder John Ross (1790–1866) led the Cherokee migration from Georgia to Oklahoma in 1838–39. He was chief of the United Cherokee nation from 1839 to 1866. Young Ross was planning to attend Princeton University.

tavern, "on a pallet of"—(straw?—no, worse) stones, and on the bright, but blowy morning of Tuesday, Nov. 6th, I proceeded to Trenton, and went to the State House. The Legislature were in session, but were doing nothing. Dined at Snowden's and at 2 o'clock, to use a curious phrase "took the Railroad home." Arrived in Philadelphia about 7, and went to "old Drury"[81] but the play being miserable, I crossed the river in a small boat, and by nine o'clock was snoozing it bravely on my own bed. This jaunt is an era in the monotonous life which I have led for four or five months past.

The steamboat *State Rights*, to-day (Wednesday) entered the Windmill Island Canal from the eastward. . . .[82]

8 November, Thursday.
Wind N.E, with rain. I was in the house, engaged in drawing etc., all day. In the evening I went to a Meeting of the Library.

9 November, Friday.
I went to the Fair of the Franklin Institute[83] this morning—where there are a great many pretty things and pretty faces to be seen. The miniature Steam Engines in particular attracted my "attentention" as the stammering schoolmaster said, while the miniature flirts "took my eye." Returning, saw a man named Van Aurburgher killed by a stab from a fiend called Boman.[84] The fracas happened on board of the steam boat *John Fitch*.

10 November, Saturday.
I saw a young man this afternoon who had blown his brains out in the woods in the vicinity of Camden.[85] "A horrid sight forsooth!"

In the evening I went—where? to escort my cousins home. I saw—whom? and many other nice, blooming girls.

11 November, Sunday.
I went to the episcopalean Church this afternoon, and heard just exactly what I have heard often before, from the same mouth. Thinking that "variety was the spice of" religion as well as "life" in the evening I went to all three chapels—not at the same time, because that is a philosophical impossibility, but in succession. . . .

81. The Chestnut Street Theatre, near Sixth and Chestnut Streets, was sometimes called the "old Drury."

82. See entry of 9 January 1838.

83. Founded as an enterprise for the promotion of "Mechanical Arts" in 1824, the Institute occupied a building on Seventh Street, between Market and Chestnut.

84. Newspapers report the name of the victim variously as Daniel Vanbrugen, Vanburger, or Van Bergen.

85. The Camden *Mail* of 14 November 1838 reported that the man, named Wilcox, had committed suicide while on a hunting excursion near the Woodbury Road, one half mile from Camden.

1 December, Saturday.

Winter comes with a smiling face—a sign that he will go with a frown. I went to a Meeting of the "Washington Library" this evening, but there was no quorum. . . .

14 December, Friday.

Pleasant weather: wind N.N.E. I went to the Baptist meeting this evening, where Mr. Tyndale feelingly announced the death of Mr. Sheppard—"May he rest in peace."[86]

15 December, Saturday.

I was in Philadelphia all the morning, and this afternoon have been busied in—doing nothing.

16 December, Sunday.

I don't feel well, "no how you can fix it." I've got a pain in my head—an ache in my ear—a sore in my throat—a splinter in my finger and a peg in my boot; delightful variety—eh?

17 December, Monday.

The snow this morning when I got up, was at least "Three inches deep on an average, in spots" as the thing in the Almanac.

In the evening I went to a special meeting of the "Library," and had a bit of a bat with "Number One" about a certain Resolution.

18 December, Tuesday.

It is just two months since I commenced this volume, and I have not had the least cause to complain of my undertaking, or regret the pains I have taken. . . .

19 December, Wednesday.

The same old tale—no good done this day to myself or the country. When will my mother give up for me to leave this cursed town?

20 December, Thursday.

This day seventeen years ago, Rebecca Morgan became Rebecca Mickle.[87]

23 December, Sunday.

"Cold as blazes." The river is full of ice—

24 December, Monday.

—and fast to the Island from this side.[88]

---

86. Napoleon Bonaparte Tyndall or Tyndale was pastor of Camden's First Baptist Church from 1838 to 1841. Joseph Sheppard, father of four daughters of whom Mickle speaks often in the diary, had been pastor there from 1836 to May 1838.
87. Mickle speaks of his parents' marriage.
88. Mickle again refers to Windmill or Smith's Island.

25 December, Tuesday.
Pleasant weather.

26 December, Wednesday.
The river is "chock full" of ice, which is jumbled to the depth of 3 or four feet. The *State Rights* is fast at Kaighn's Point and the *Jno: Fitch* in the Canal.

27 December, Thursday.
The boats are still fast: So much for not repairing the "*Statesy*" as she ought to have been.

28 December, Friday.
The past night has been colder than any we have experienced this winter, and the river this morning presents quite a carnival scene. The *Fitch* was got out by loading her bow down, and the *State Rights* by persevering.

29 December, Saturday.
I was surprized when I arose this morning to find that the ground was covered with snow a foot deep, as last night I left an unclouded sky.

This afternoon I went to the office of the *Mail* to see the news, and when Gray got a chance, he inquired—"Is the ink in 'Junius' pen dried up?" I sat down and wrote a squib on "Latin, Lectures and the Like. . . ."

30 December, Sunday.
The New-ferry boats with great difficulty succeeded in opening a passage through ice eighteen inches thick—but—

31 December, Monday.
—to day, it is almost as bad as none at all. Farewell, old year!

Southern View in Bridgeton

1839

1 January, Tuesday.
The *Mail* came out this afternoon and contains my communication. The new year comes in with pleasant weather.

2 January, Wednesday.
Went to the American Theater to night, and saw *Oliver Twist* by Boz—good for nothing: *Swiss Cottage—le même*: but o! Miss Lee! Miss Lee![1]

3 January, Thursday.
Scribbled a peice for the paper.

4 January, Friday.
Did nothing, and—

5 January, Saturday.
—completed it!

1. *Oliver Twist* was one of the many adaptations of Charles Dickens' novel. Miss Lee, a dancer, appeared often in Philadelphia theatres and was most renowned for her performance as Lizette in A. H. Bayley's *The Swiss Cottage, or Why Doesn't She Marry?* The Walnut Street Theatre was then known as the "American."

6 January, Sunday.
Went to church and to sleep.

7 January, Monday.
The river is still firm as a rock—Weather mild.

8 January, Tuesday.
The *demos cratia* of New Jersey hold a Convention to-day at Trenton, to take into consideration the alarming fraud and outrage upon the elective franchise, recently committed by Governor Pennington and the Privy Council, in giving the "whig" would-be-Congressmen the Certificates of election when the "Republicans" were chosen by a clear majority. The Governor sho'd be hanged—but the Conventionists should let Congress, the rightful tribunal, investigate the matter.[2] My uncle is a delegate in attendance.

9 January, Wednesday.
Communication—newspaper—devil—murder. I'snt brevity a beauty?

10 January, Thursday.
Wrote a batch of trash for the *Mail.*

11 January, Friday.
The ice in the river is much weakened by the recent warm spell, but a few venturous persons still trust their lives upon its yielding surface. Below the Company's track the ice is drifting, making the crossing in their boats very tedious during the latter part of the flood tide.

Evening—Temperance Meeting—anodyne—vacuum—sleep.

12 January, Saturday.
The river (or the ice in the river) is all afloat, above and below.

13 January, Sunday.
Church—nonsense—night—Shakspeare.

14 January, Monday.
Adjourned Temperance Meeting—spouting—cold water—snow.

15 January, Tuesday.
I have had the winter (not the spring) fever—all day, and consequently—

16 January, Wednesday.
—did nothing.

---

2. New Jersey's congressional elections of October 1838 were so close that five out of the six seats were claimed by both Democratic and Whig candidates. Gov. William Pennington (1796–1862), a Whig, certified all five to the Whigs, but the House of Representatives later awarded them to the Democratic candidates.

17 January, Thursday.
The same—

18 January, Friday.
—as usual.

19 January, Saturday.
I went to Philadelphia this morning. *Pour-quoi?* None of your business.

20 January, Sunday.
As Gray did not publish my Criticism of "Melinda's" Reflections in his last paper, by way of spite (!) I to day scribbled some Sunday verses for the *Herald*.[3] They are my first attempt in the religious line.

22 January, Tuesday.
In the house, hammering at Horace, but could not make him any flatter than he was.

23 January, Wednesday.
It snew, or snowed, this morning till about 9 o'clock; the flakes were as large as saucers (excuse this *lapsus pinnae*)—sixpences, and fell as thick as a beggar's blessings.

When the squall ceased the thermometer stood at 30°, and it has been falling ever since; now (11 o clock P.M.) it is at 6°. I fear that the mercury will all be gone to nothing before to morrow morning.

The *Mail* of to day has got no "Tironiana" in; "cause vy" I dont know.[4]

25 January, Friday.
The weather seems "kind o' mysterious"—what's a' comin' now?

26 January, Saturday.
Will long be remembered on account of the almost unparalleled storm, which began about 11 o'clock last night and continued until two this afternoon. Detailed accounts of the destruction which it caused will be found among the files of newspapers in my Library.

27 January, Sunday.
Did'nt go to church, because—the walking is so sloppy that there will be no pretty girls there.

28 January, Monday.
"Melinda" told my aunt that she would like to see my library—and accordingly got an invitation from her.

3. "Melinda's" reflections had not appeared in recent issues of the *Mail*. Presumably they appeared in some other local newspaper. *The Village Herald and Gloucester Advertiser* had been published under various names in nearby Woodbury since 1817.
4. That is, there was nothing by "Tiro," one of Mickle's pseudonyms.

29 January, Tuesday.
I went this evening to the shop of my friend Samuel Foster, to initiate him into the "preliminaries" of English grammar.

30 January, Wednesday.
Went to Philadelphia. Gray's paper had arrived when I got home and contains my *"Iterum de Gubernatricem."*[5]

31 January, Thursday.
Having got a stove for my studio, I was engaged all day in moving up stairs.

1 February, Friday.
"Busy as a bee in a tar barrel" helping myself do nothing.

2 February, Saturday.
This afternoon, according to notice, "Melinda" came. I was "gone to the city"—(under the bed in my chamber!) with my diary and every other paper that could afford her any clue to the identity of "Tiro" in my lap.

Charles Garrett, a little boy who lives next door, got run over by a burthen car, under our window, and, (*credite posteri*) escaped minus a years growth—he was so "skeirt". . . .[6]

20 February, Wednesday.
I was informed to day of my unanimous election to membership in "The Youth's Debating Society."

21 February, Thursday.
Went to the Theatre to night and got asleep as usual. The narcotics were *Paul Pry* and the *Spitfire*—dancing and other obscenities.[7]

22 February, Friday.
The sun rose and set to-day, and, the wicked thing! did not stand still for a moment.

In the evening I went to a Commemoration meeting of the Society of which I have the new born honor (!) of being a member. As I saw the poor fellows look down their nose I thought how I was feeling about that time one year ago! . . .

---

5. Mickle had written a letter to the *Mail* declaring that an earlier correspondent, who used the feminine pseudonym "Gubernatrix," was actually a man.

6. The lucky child was the son of Charles S. Garrett, a saddler, of 6 Lanning's Row.

7. John Brougham's (1810–80) popular comedy *Paul Pry* and John M. Morton's (1811–91) *The Spitfire* were both playing at the Chestnut Street Theatre on this evening.

View of The County Buildings, Salem

1840

Ad Lectorem: OR
A FEW WORDS BY WAY OF INTRODUCING THE WORK.

I need not enter into any defence of myself before the bar of posterity for BEGINNING THIS DIARY; inasmuch as the manifold advantages of the step are so obvious that the reader, on reflection, cannot but acquit me of wasting the time necessary to its composition. **An hour spent at the close of the day in reflecting upon and recording what has passed, cannot be more profitably occupied:** I might say, indeed, that the mind, wearied by its previous duties, cannot be otherwise directed with any pleasure or profit to its owner, at all; for, in the words of the proverb, **the morning is the season for work, and the evening the brain's playtime.**

My life being for the most part one of monotony, passed in a little room measuring but ten feet square, the reader whose eye may scan the following pages will doubtless have reason to deem my little book **a very leaden production.** But no person ever led a life **totally devoid of incidents worthy to be preserved**; and I console myself with the knowledge that even if others **do** find my journal entirely uninteresting, there will be that in it which will, at least, serve to amuse **my own** after years. I flatter myself, however, that my experience will not be registered on the leaves following, altogether in vain, if succeeding ages can be induced to avoid the Scyllas upon which I may strike, and which I shall endeavour to lay down with accuracy in this **chart of my voyage of life.**

The keeping of a diary is an employment that not even the greatest of men have dispised; which fact (among many instances that I might offer) the examples of **Benjamin Franklin** and **John Quincy Adams** will suffice to show the truth of. DOCTOR RUSH, not the least remembered among **the illustrious Fifty Six,**[1] in a lecture **on the means of acquiring knowledge,** mentions, as one, that of "recording such facts and thoughts as are suggested by observation, conversation and reflection," and he adds that it serves in an eminent degree "to beget inquiry and recollection, and to create a facility of composition." So highly was this exercise considered by that correct philosopher, that he wished it could be made a **part of a collegiate education,** and introduced as an **essential part of the parental** training of Children.

But, since people are apt to augur a **bad book** from a **long preface;** and as I have said enough already to show **both cause and precedent,** I will not extend this prologue to a much greater length; but will conclude it by remarking, that when Dido laid the foundation of Carthage, she found a favourable omen in a horse's skull; and (**with all due apology for the sudden transition!**) that I begin my present undertaking with propitious signs. Sixty-four years ago from this day our forefathers declared independence from the power of Britain. They fought; they conquered; **and behold the glorious results!** To-day I profess freedom from that **Ennui** (or more candidly I might say, **laziness**) which has so long oppressed and benumbed my every energy; and after I shall have fought and conquered it, may the consequences in my case be likewise evident, likewise happy! And may I never have reason to exclaim with the good Roman Emperor, *"diem perdidi!"*—I have lost a day!

4 July, Saturday.   Columbia's Birth-day.

This eventful day was ushered in by the beams of an unclouded sun, and if we may believe the Virgilian line, that his face "reveals the secrets of the sky," the very heavens sympathized with the happy emotions felt by millions of freemen—**that they were free!** At an early hour in the morning the deep-toned thunders of many a gun that has often hurled back death and defiance to the enemies of our country and of human liberty, began the festivities of the day. Then, rallied by the soul-stirring airs that so oft of yore led our armies to glorious victory, all men met beneath the proud folds of the star-studded

1. The "illustrious Fifty Six" were the signers of the Declaration of Independence, among whom was Dr. Benjamin Rush (1745–1813) of Philadelphia.

banner, and, laying aside all minor points of difference in opinion, united with one heart in singing paeans to the immortal deliverers of the unoffending daughter from the unnatural cruelty of the mother. Orators drew, in all the strong colours of the reality, the sufferings of those who bore the brunt of the revolution and, as if inspired with the breath of Apollo himself, emulated their enchained audiences to pour out the last drop from their veins sooner than to part with the precious boon, the invaluable birth-right of freedom; until their eloquence drew a tear from the dryest eye, and forced a responsive glow of enthusiasm from the coldest breast. From the pulpit; from hills and vallies dyed purple with patriotic blood; from almost every place hallowed by the remembrance of the past, or held sacred in the present, appeals were made which not even hearts of flint could have withstood—**appeals that would have forced one, in spite of himself, to be a patriot**. So harmonious and so happy seemed the enthusiastic crowd on every side, that the lover of classical lore might have imagined that Astraea,[2] the "last of the celestials" had again asserted her benign reign over the discordant elements of man; and all, at the close of the carnival, must have been impressed with the truth, that whatever may have been the dissentions of the American people yesterday, or whatever may be the diversity in their sentiments to-morrow, there is no danger of the subversion of our national institutions **until the Fourth of July shall be blotted from the calender of the year, and erased from the memory of those who now hail it as the natal day of their country's liberty.**

As for myself—it may not be amiss to note here that I was not singular enough to spend a day in work which every body else devoted to the outpouring of grateful feelings to the statesmen who planned and the warriors who accomplished a deed whose grandeur the capture of an hundred Troys would not measure. On the contrary, in company with two friends, I set out in the morning down the Delaware, on board of my little sail boat, the *Kinderhook*,[3] and passed several hours very pleasantly at Fort Mifflin and Red Bank, places inseparably connected with the history of our Revolutionary struggle— and doomed to live in story as long as Thermopylae or Marathona.[4] On the site of old fort Mercer, two or three hundred people collected to celebrate the day with "song and dance and wine," notwithstanding

2. Astraea, a Greek divinity, was symbolic of justice.

3. Mickle, ever the loyal Democrat, has named his boat after the home of President Martin Van Buren.

4. The American victory at Red Bank (see entry for 1 January 1838), though a spur to patriot morale, was a minor affair scarcely comparable to the strategic contests between ancient Greeks and Persians.

the last of which, it is a sign of the times worthy to be recorded, that fewer intoxicated men were never seen on a similar occasion, than to day. Of fifteen thousand people who are supposed to have crossed the river from Philadelphia to Camden, it is said that scarcely fifteen were drunk; which is peculiarly gratifying when we remember the shameful orgies and bacchanalia with which the day used to be pro- faned. If any time more than another can palliate a too free lift of the elbow it is surely this; and when Temperance reformers can induce men to drink the health of "Old George" in a bumper of clear pure water on this day of the year, then indeed they will have won trophies more lasting than Egypt's pyramids, and wreaths far more enviable than those which pressed Napoleon's brows.

Towards evening, having the set of the flood tide and a light northerly breeze, we again made sail; and having beaten a dozen boats who started with us, arrived at home in good time and better spirits, with the occurrence of no accident, except that one of my companions tumbled overboard, much to the detriment of his nicely brushed clothes and sprucely starched collar. . . .

5 July, Sunday.

Not being very well to-day, I remained in my room, reading Cooper's *Naval History* and the Bible, or perhaps I had better say the Bible and Cooper's *Naval History*. In the morning, I received a visit from William N. Jeffers, junior,[5] my esteemed friend, with whom I played several games of chess, which is an amusement that cannot, I think, be objected to, even on a Sunday. It is a game that requires much thought; and the making of right moves in chess may teach a person to take proper steps in life, which is what most people go to church to learn; wherefore I spent my time as profitably as they: *quod erat demonstrandum*.

But let it not be supposed that the object of my friend's visit was nothing but amusement. He meets me every Sunday (not having any other day to himself) in my study, which we convert into a gymnasium for our mutual improvement in rhetoric, and where we take and give each other lessons in articulation, and action, a knowledge of which comes amiss in no sphere of life.

6 July, Monday.

The weather is rainy and unpleasant. I staid at home, reading Cooper's *Naval History of the United States*. This I consider a very

5. Mickle's close friend Jeffers (1824–83), sometimes simply called "Will" in the pages which follow, would soon join the navy and begin a distinguished career. Before his retirement, he commanded such ships as the *Monitor* and attained the rank of commodore.

interesting work—calculated to snatch from oblivion many a gallant though humble name, that fell for his country afar off on the boundless sea. Whatever Cooper writes, even if on a barren theme, will be long read; who then shall number the days of his present History?

7 July, Tuesday.
To day I went to the city and bought Justin's *History*. My collection now comprises most of the Roman authors of any note; and I purpose soon to prosecute my Latin studies with renewed vigor.

8 July, Wednesday.
I have nothing to record for the edification of posterity, except that last night I did not sleep a wink, owing to sundry commotions in my bowels. This may be fun for you, my reader, but be assured that it is any thing else to me.

9 July, Thursday.
William Shaw, one of my former cronies, who has been away for years, having called on me, I gave up the day to his company, and to the retrospection of many a jolly prank.

10 July, Friday.
To-day, in company with Shaw, I went a-sailing, and otherwise killed time in ways too numerous to mention. The hours are precious, but friendship's demands are imperious, and must be obeyed. . . .

11 July, Saturday.
This morning I went to market; and after my return spent the day upon the water. The weather is decidedly too warm for any mental exertion at all, which may account for my not having made any progress in my Justinus. In fact learning will spoil, like meat, if put up in hot weather, and be worse than nothing. The only science that can be successfully cultivated in summer, is the science of killing musquitoes; the only art, that of keeping cool.

12 July, Sunday.
It was really my intention to have gone to church to-day; but somehow or other, I—a—I mean—that is—a—I—ahem!—**entirely forgot it**, until it was too late. The snow of resolution too often melts before the sun of temptation; and too often, as in the present instance, am I deterred from the commission of some good act by the allurements which it belongs only to heaven-born Friendship to extend. But, as the poet says, "To err is human, to forgive, divine." I hope that the reader, however much he may censure my remissness at first, will forget to chide when he remembers that my sin sprang from a generous source just as muddy streams often arise from a pure fountain.

As usual, Jeffers and I were exercising this forenoon in elocution. What progress I may have made, I cannot say, but my partner has certainly improved a great deal. His voice, which was formerly like a noble but unbroken steed, has been rendered, by these continued gymnastics, tractable and obedient to the will, the efficient vehicle of the passions and emotions of the human breast.

13 July, Monday.

Will long be remembered for the tornado which swept over the vicinity of our very goodly city of Camden and its neighbouring little town, Philadelphia, doing some damage to the shipping in the Delaware, some to the Ridgway Ferry house[6] at the foot of Market Street, and a considerable to the fences, pig-sties and hen-roosts that fell within its desolating path. The tornado seemed to be formed by the junction of two strong currents of air, this from the North West and that from the South West; and moved with prodigious velocity in an intermediate direction to the Eastward. The clouds were whirled about, in every way, commoving and conflicting with each other in a manner at once beautiful and sublime. The water in the river was scooped up and whizzed to an immense height, in sheets of foam and spray; while the unsuspecting vessels, making storm sails, attempted to weather off from the Jersies, or else, stripped of all their canvass, madly scudded before the gale, to oppose which were worse than vain. During the thunder storm which immediately preceded the blow, a house in Fetterville was struck by lightning, and a woman, who was in it, in the act of dancing, was immediately killed! Several others, who were either in or near the house at the time were severely shocked; and the building itself was shattered in a wonderful manner by the subtle and terriffic agent of Omnipotence.

Many ludicrous incidents are said to have occurred in Philadelphia, owing to the recentness of the great tornado in Natchez, and the report that Professor Espy,[7] the meteorologist, had predicted a similar one to be about to visit these parts; a report which though attributed to a scientific gentleman, gained only with the ignorant and credulous. Persons began to think of going to the other world in earnest; and so great was the general depression, that—that **sundry Bank men and Brokers were willing to jump accounts with the devil, without insisting upon the customary ten per cent discount on their sins.** Verily, the times are improving!

6. The damaged ferrying concern was owned by Jacob Ridgway of Philadelphia.
7. James Pollard Espy (1785–1860) was a meteorologist for Philadelphia's Franklin Institute, and, after 1842, for the War and Navy Departments. A tornado had devastated Natchez in May 1840.

14 July, Tuesday.

The work of this day was indeed short and sweet, for it was as follows, that is to say: taking a boat load of ladies to Gloucester Point and back again. My precious cargo was landed "in good order and well conditioned" as the merchants say: and so well did all parties enjoy themselves, that a pic-nic was resolved upon for next Friday.

15 July, Wednesday.

To-day I read Juvenal's first Satire in the original Latin, preparatory to beginning a Hudibrastic doggerel, which I have been meditating upon for some time past.[8] The times are such that one might truly exclaim with the bitter bard of Aquinum, *"Difficile est non Satiram Scribere."* In morals, in politics, in manners, in every thing, how many are the short-comings of man! But yet those very persons who give the most throat to the trite cry of *"O tempora! o mores!"* are the very persons, in many cases, who have chiefly contributed to the degeneracy of the age. It is my intention in the rhymes that I purpose, to show the evils that really cry for reform, and to hold up to just ridicule, the labours of certain over-weening philanthropists and busy-bodies WHO WOULD BURN ROME FOR THE SAKE OF ILLUMINATING A SINGLE HOUSE.

16 July, Thursday.

Went to Woodbury this afternoon, by the Rail Road; or as some better grammarians than I, would say, **"took the Rail Road to Woodbury"** which the reader may suppose was about equal to Sampson's toting off the gates of Gaza, or Hercules' scooping out the straits of Gibraltar. I found my aunt and cousins well, and had much ado to avoid promising them my company to the sea-side, where they will start in a few days.

The evening I passed very agreeably with some young ladies in Camden, with whom I arranged the particulars of the pic-nic, *quod lege infra.* These ladies in the course of my visit, let me into **the arcana of woman-nature** to a degree that I never was before; and I say but the truth when I aver that some of their **double-entendres** and innuendos brought a blush even to my very forehead. This levity of conversation is one of the pernicious fruits of following the fashions of the French, which is fraught with DAMNING MISCHIEF to every woman that indulges in it. **Indecency of expression leads as certainly to indecency of action, as the road to Tyburn leads to the gallows.** A woman who of her own accord takes the first step towards prostitution will not need much persuasion to be induced to take the last.

---

8. Mickle plans to compose a poem in the style of Samuel Butler's (1612–80) *Hudibras,* a satiric romance.

17 July, Friday.

At about nine o'clock, this morning, on the last quarter ebb, two boat-loads of us started from Camden to spend the day in a kind of *féte champêtre* at Red Bank and the interesting localities in its vicinity, as agreed upon on last Tuesday, and ratified last evening. **It were a wilful neglect of the benefit of posterity** (for whose especial edification, I repeat, this book was begun) **to omit a fully-detailed account of this very important transaction.** So having replenished my ink-horn, and invoked the appropriate deity, in the true imitation of the best ancients, I now begin as follows.

In the wherry, commanded by Captain Job Wilkins,[9] were his son, Bill, **and that which was far more essential to our enjoyment,** a basket full of provisions. In the *Kinderhook* skiff, commanded by my consequential self, were four ladies and one gentleman, Samuel Spicer Eastlack Cowperthwaite, who was obliged to do all the talking while I did the steering. We had a light breeze, at starting, from South West, and owing to the great advantages which the wherry had over the skiff, she beat us a good deal in sailing to Greenwich Point; for while the passengers and two fifty-sixes for ballast, brought us down to our gunnel-streak,[10] she was comparatively light and entirely managable. Captain Wilkins, however, heaving to, or running free off the wind occasionally, we kept within hailing distance and preserved the unity of the party.

At the Point House we stopped and procured some refreshments, which we were so long in discussing the merits of, that the tide was slack before we re-embarked. At this place, Captain Job lightened me of my ballast, and of two of the girls; which change enabled me to leave him nearly half way in beating down against the wind and the current. After a long and tedious voyage, at one o'clock I made Eagle Point, and in another half hour landed at the foot of the steps at Red Bank. The sun was shining in full glory; but the breeze having freshened with the flood, and considering the smiles of the **beautiful** Mary,[11] and the sweet music which Sam's flute discoursed, we altogether had a very delightful run of it.

When the other boat arrived, as it did *remis ac velis*, we had a collation spread upon **old Earth's broad table**, of which all partook with an appetite sharpened by the ride, and to which I did ample

9. Job Whitall Wilkens was Mickle's great uncle, his paternal grandmother's brother.

10. Mickle probably refers to two fifty-six-pound sacks of sand, which helped bring the vessel down to the stripe on its gunwale.

11. Mary Taylor, a native of Bridgeton, New Jersey, was visiting Camden briefly.

justice out of respect to the fair hands that prepared it. Then came the swing, and dance, and song; the walk among the dark clustering pines; the more than affectionate squeeze of the soft, voluptuous hand; the more than friendly press of lip to cheek, and so forth, and so forth, in all of which however, I took no part, as listening with more pleasure to the narratives of Uncle Job, whose ancestors lived on this very spot, and handed down to him many a thrilling legend and many a curious anecdote of the memorable twenty-second of October, Seventy Seven. He showed me the house, nay the very room, in which his wife's grandmother sat a-spinning on that immortalized day, until a cannon-ball whistling through the hall induced her to take her wheel into the cellar, where it is a matter of historical fact, that she spun undisturbedly during the whole engagement although the house was struck several times by the shot from the British fleet playing on Fort Mercer![12] This is but a specimen of the Spartan firmness of our Jersey dames of Seventy-Six. They cared no more for the crack of a cannon than our modern belles do for the crack of a kiss.

Thus we passed our time very pleasantly until about six o'clock, when, as the heat of the day began to subside, it was proposed to shift our quarters. A slight misunderstanding occurred, by which Master Cowperthwaite, the pretty flirt Mary Taylor, and another lady were left at Red Bank, while Captain Wilkins took Bill and the remaining two girls over to Fort Mifflin[13]—I following, by myself, in the skiff. A considerable span was consumed in reviewing the military precautions at the fortress, during which the wind had hauled to South East, and freshened into a stiff breeze, that, since all my ballast and cargo had been started as aforesaid, was as much as I could carry without shipping a good deal of water. Running ashore at the stairs at the Bank, I hallooed as loud as I could for our lost companions, but obtained no answer; and then, beating down at the imminent peril of my life (for strange to say! I cannot swim) I found them at the mouth of the Creek, as angry as it is possible for one to be without choking to death, at the "mean trick" which they alleged I had played them in going off without their precious company! The display of temper made by Mary on this occasion convinced me that "all is not gold that glitters," indeed; and I resolved—but it is none of the reader's business what.

All having again started in company, we stemmed the ebb tide

---

12. Historical evidence suggests that Ann Cooper Whitall, wife of James Whitall, remained in her house during the battle for Fort Mercer. Whether she calmly attended to her spinning is not known.

13. Fort Mifflin, on Mud Island in the Delaware, had been a vital link in Delaware river defenses during the Revolution.

home, with a stiff South Easter, and ran the distance, not without some danger, in the space of an hour and ten minutes, to Camden. Owing to the darkness of the night and the roughness of the water, the girls were not a little timorous; and more than once, as my boat raised by the stern on one sea and seemed about to pitch headlong into another, they would scream in strict accordances with the latest Parisian fashions. At a little after nine o'clock we were all safe ashore and (the danger passed) were unanimous in agreeing that we had spent a pleasant day very pleasantly. And in conclusion I will add that this pic-nic will serve the double purpose, of supplying matter for a page or two in my diary, and a subject for the tongues of certain old gossips and over-careful maidens; who, forgetful of the days when they, themselves, were young, seem to think that the youth of modern days cannot attempt to enjoy themselves together, without the commission of some folly or perhaps, sin. Well! let them gad over the town and gossip about it as much as they please. I only despise and pity them, from my deepest soul. "*Loquaces, si sapiet, vitet.*"

This morning when first I woke to consciousness, I involuntarily exclaimed "Praised by Fortune that I have no pic-nic to attend to day, *cum talibus sociis*, at any rate!" Now this thing of pic-nicing is not exactly what is supposed to be. The poetry of the affair soon vanishes, like the effervescense on a glass of mineral-water, and leaves nothing but the sad reality of the head-ache; as in my case.

A man named Baer lectured this afternoon in the woods near Camden, on the subjects of hard cider and hard money.[14] He calls himself the "Buckeye Blacksmith," and succeeded in convincing all that he could make a horse-shoe or an ox-chain much better than he can make the chain of an argument. Being in the city opposite, I lost the opportunity of hearing him; but it is said that he amused the Whigs exceedingly, and proved beyond a doubt that Harrison ought to be elected President of this country, simply by calling the friends of Van Buren a set of loafing rascals, and graceless Swartwouters, without either shirts or characters, brains or honesty; all of which was very well said by this immaculate man, who, it has been shown by thirteen witnesses, is himself a horse-thief, an absconding debtor, and an outlaw from the Buckeye State of Ohio, where he would be imprisoned, were he to return![15] When will the days of Humbug cease?

14. Newspaper accounts of Baer's visit to Camden do not provide his full name. Baer appears to have been a Whig party regular. He spoke in Camden in behalf of that party's candidates during the 1844 election campaign as well.

15. Martin Van Buren's campaign for reelection against William Henry Harrison had been hurt by revelations about Van Buren appointee Samuel Swartwout's theft of public funds.

19 July, Sunday.

To-day (*credite posteri!*) I went to church; where, I am bound to say, I fell asleep, just as the reverend gentleman was entering into the eleventh grand argument to prove the somewhat ambiguous position taken in his text, namely, that, as all men in all former generations have died, it is probable that all men in all ensuing generations will die. I suppose he settled this point at last, to his own satisfaction, if not to his hearers'.

20 July, Monday.

Was spent in washing out my boat, in reading, and in the still harder occupation of thinking. Does the reader smile? Perhaps he has never engaged in connected, systematic thought with the thermometer at ninety above zero.

21 July, Tuesday.

I called this evening upon Miss Taylor, to pay her a philopoena which I lost on last Friday. Masters Cowperthwaite and Jeffers were also there on similar errands, I suppose. My present consisted of Mrs. Hemans'[16] *Poems,* in two volumes, in which I wrote "To Mary A. Taylor, from a friend." So ended my acquaintance with this girl, whom I expect never to see again, as she will leave Camden in a few days for her home in Cumberland County. Though I had tears I would'nt shed them now!

22 July, Wednesday. Salem.

At ten o'clock this morning I began to commence to get ready to think about going to Salem. At twelve o'clock, had my mind fully made up to go. And at two, started on board of the Steam Boat *Pioneer,* in company with two of my cousins and Miss Little.[17] At seven o'clock we landed at Salem the Peaceful, and having seen the two ladies safely to their quarters, my cousin and myself took board at Sherron's Hotel[18] for the time being. After a good supper of fish and coffee, I took a stroll over the town—looked at all that could be seen in the dark—returned—went to bed—and spent the night very agreeably in fighting the musquitoes and bed-bugs. A little after daylight, having forced the aggressors to come to some terms and raise the seige, I took a short nap, and was awaken'd by the ringing of the breakfast-bell on the morning of

16. Felicia Dorothea Hemans (1793–1835) was an English poet.

17. Mickle may be referring to the daughter of Archibald Little, a chronometer maker, of Federal Street, above Second. The *Pioneer* was a paddle steamer built in 1835.

18. Sherron's Tavern, at the head of Market Street, had not been operated by members of the Sherron family since 1799.

23 July, Thursday.

After a hearty breakfast I went a-fishing in Salem Creek, and had my usual luck, which is none at all. I then lounged about until dinner time, which did not come a bit too soon. In the afternoon promenaded over the town again and saw nothing worthy to be commemorated; heard nothing worth the rememb'ring; learned nothing that I did not know before.

On the arrival of the boat at Salem from Philadelphia, (having first, however, been so unfashionable as honorably to pay our tavern-bills) we started off in a four-horse stage-coach for Bridgeton. Before we had left Quinton's Bridge far behind, it begain to rain; and as I sat on the front seat in order to make room inside for the ladies **and their hand-boxes**, I got completely drenched to the skin. Between seven and eight o'clock in the evening, we reached out port of destination, and having freely partaken of a warm supper, I lost no time in getting to-bed. "And the evening and the morning were the second day" of this delightful trip!

24 July, Friday.   Bridgeton.

Brought much to my joy, a clear day. My clothes, however, as I had but one change, (not expecting to remain so long,) looked rather the worse for their washing, yesterday. In the forenoon I took a stroll over the place, and was agreeably disappointed in my expectations. It is a much larger, more pleasant and more business-like point than I had any idea of; and the people are generally shrewd, and intelligent, and converse with much force, although perhaps with little elegance, on any of the great questions of the day. The spirit of party politics I soon observed to run very high; and not the least gratification of my visit, was to hear the original arguments and modes of argument adopted by some of the Cumberland politicians to prove that Martin Van Buren is, or is not, the man of a million most fit to preside over the destinies of our common country. Among these logicians I found one prototype who shall be the Samuel Luke to my Hudibras.[19]

During my walk I saw, (and was surprised at seeing) Mary [*Taylor*] Oftmentioned-before; but (I hope the reader will pardon my want of gallantry) I gave her the cut direct and turned up another street. I had a much better reason for doing this, than bashfulness; but what it was I do not choose to say.

In the afternoon, I looked at the iron-works, the paper-mill and whatsoever besides presented any interest to my eyes; and on the whole, acquired much useful knowledge that I lacked before.

19. Sir Samuel Luke (d. 1670) may have been the model for Samuel Butler's Sir Hudibras.

25 July, Saturday.

Arose at three o'clock and returned by the stage to Salem; from which place I started at seven in the *Pioneer* for home. Arrived about noon, pleased with my journey, but glad that it was over.

26 July, Sunday.

Being much fatigued with loss of sleep, I devoted this whole day to that necessary business, but was waked several times by the ringing of friends who "had just dropped in, to inquire if I saw the charming Mary?" The dunces did not meet with a very cordial reception of course.

27 July, Monday.

Went a-sailing and did several other things too unimportant to be particularized; among which, however, I will mention that I read the first Book of Caesar's *Commentaries* over, merely to keep my hand in at translating. Every person should occasionally review what he has read, especially in the memory-slipping classics.

28 July, Tuesday.

When I say that this was a pleasant day, and that there was a fine breeze on the Delaware, I need not add that I went a-sailing; for this, of course, I would be understood to have done.

In the afternoon I went to see the ruins of a house in Kensington, which was burned last night by an infuriated mob of fishermen and fishwomen; of whom the inhabitants of this district are principally made up. The building, a hotel, was owned by the President of the Trenton Rail Road Company; and was totally consumed by the mob, because that Company insisted upon laying rails down Front Street, to the great jeopardy of the limbs of the children resident thereabouts. Now, although an Act had been passed by the Legislature of Pennsylvania authorizing the laying of the road as aforesaid, yet it was wrong and improper in a narrow and thickly inhabited street. But this does not palliate a resort to tyrannical Mobism, at all. In a democratic government like ours, nothing can palliate it. By our constitutions, every evil and nuisance is capable of being reached and reformed, or removed, in a legal manner, and without the intervention of self-instituted judges. Whatever cannot be amended by law, needs no amendment at all: but of this fact, all democracies seem determined not to see the truth.

29 July, Wednesday.

This afternoon, having read all morning, I found myself "once more upon the waters, yet once more!" as a certain Bard has it, who was detested when living and who is immortalized, now dead.[20] When opposite to the lower end of Windmill Island, a squall struck my skiff and caused her to luff sharp into the wind. I put my helm hard up to keep her away, when lo! both gudgeons came out of the stern post, and left me in a ticklish craft, in a dangerous squall, without a sign of rudder! I quickly lessened sail, however, and steered safely home with an oar. This incident I have recorded not because of its supposed interest, but because, (for want of a better reason, I will say) of such stuff are journals made.

30 July, Thursday.
Remained in the house, reading and laughing over the adventures of doughty Hudibras.

31 July, Friday.
To day, I ended the month by ending for the third time, Butler's witty, but too little relished Satire, of *Hudibras*; which is a work not without its faults, but one which may be read often, and read every time with increased pleasure. The faults of this book, or at least what seem to me to be faults, are firstly, the obscenity which disfigures its almost every page; secondly, the confusion of bastard, with real wit; and thirdly the discordant and unmusical doggerel of the measure which the author has adopted. . . .

I have signified elsewhere in this book, my intention of a Satire in imitation of *Hudibras*, being written by me, to be called the "Adventures of Scrapio." I have made considerable progress within a few days, in this work; and have got that most difficult part, the beginning, done in a manner that entirely suits myself. In writing peices as well as in travelling the circuit of the sun, *"prima via ardua est,"* and when **that** is overcome, then indeed as Ovid says, *"Ultima prona via est,"* and easy to be passed. I find the **quadrameter** very natural of execution, and think I can compose at least thirty lines of it a-day, even in this hot weather.

1 August, Saturday.
This month comes in with remarkably fine weather—that is, to those who admire the fact of the thermometer's standing at ninety degrees, which is about three lines short of the insupportable.

In the forenoon I went to Philadelphia; in the afternoon I was reading; and in the evening reviewed Ovid's beautiful fable of *"Phaëthontis Mors,"* all of which I could translate very readily, except the passage *"Alma tamen mater,"* and so-forth, which held my wit and

20. Mickle misquotes the opening lines of John Milton's "Lycidas."

perception at bay, until, completely tired of the unequal warfare, I closed the book and—**went to sleep!**

2 August, Sunday.

Spent the day chiefly in reading *The devil on two Sticks,* and was much impressed with the philosophy contained in some of the odd little gentleman's remarks.[21] Jeffers paid me a visit, and we continued our exercises in elocution, not, I trust without mutual improvement.

In the evening feeling somewhat stupid, I adopted my usual remedy with the usual success; and drove the blue-devils entirely away by calling upon the Ascrian Nine. . . .[22]

3 August, Monday.

This would have been an interesting day for the contemplation of Professor Espy, or any other meteorologist; inasmuchas it presented the phenomenon of three separate and entirely distinct gusts, from the same quarter, and divided by pleasant weather, and a clear sky. Each gust was attended with thunder and lightning, and heavy rain; and each passed from the South-West to the north-east.

The weather being thus uncertain, and the world out of doors uninviting, I remained in the house, reading and overhauling the pidgeon-holes in my writing desk. . . .

4 August, Tuesday.

Brevity is always good; but most especially is it admirable in a writer who has nothing to say. Therefore I will sum up this day's work in two words: Did nothing.

5 August, Wednesday.

This morning I took two of my little cousins down the river to Red Bank and Fort Mifflin; and explained to them so far as I could the nature of the engagements that occurred at those places. Young as they were, the poor recountal of the valiant defence made by Greene, caused their eyes to flash rays of patriotism, and their breasts to beat with renewed love of liberty. Who indeed can recur to those days and those deeds without similar emotions?

6 August, Thursday.

The "Washington Library Society" met this evening; but there being no quorum present, we adjourned for a se'ennight; and took an evening sail in my skiff. The moon was shining very brightly; the wind

---

21. Alain René Le Sage's (1668–1747) *The Devil on Two Sticks,* first published as *Le Diable boiteux* in 1707, was a satirical view of Parisian customs as seen by a devil-like old man.

22. Mickle refers to the nine Muses.

was blowing very briskly; the company laughed very heartily; and on the whole the time passed very agreeably.

7 August, Friday.

The weather being somewhat doubtful I did not (*mirabile dictu!*) go a-sailing; but spent my time with less pleasure than profit, and with no profit at all, in reading Duncan's *Logic.*

Master Edward Wilkins[23] spent the evening with me, and seemed to be much pleased with some portions of this Journal which I read to him. At ten o'clock I went to bed, and had a curious dream, which even now, twenty four hours after, is so strangely blended with reality, or rather, which so much seems to be real, that I cannot rid myself of the disagreeable sensations which it produced. My uncle being gone to New York, left my mother and myself in charge of the house. And as lately there have been burglaries committed in Camden by persons evidently acquainted with the houses which they robbed; and as it is well known that my uncle is the receiver of the money taken by the Ferry Company, I deemed it best to hold myself in readiness to meet any advantage that might be taken of his known absence, to purloin it. Accordingly, charging a brace of pistols, I placed them, together with a small dirk, underneath my pillow, which covered twelve bags of silver, containing fifteen hundred dollars, and a sum of about five hundred dollars in Bank Bills, being in all, two thousand left in my charge, to be defended in a community that contains some individuals who would cut a man's throat and suck his blood, for the amount of "thirty peices," aye, or the half of it. I went to bed with a little fever, which was perhaps increased by a knowledge of the responsibility of my peculiar circumstances; and falling several times into a doze, I was suddenly awakened by some horrid object appearing before my half dreaming eyes. Two or three times, as the alley gate beneath my window swayed to the wind, on its discordant hinges, I would start up, grasp the deadly firelock which I bought for higher game than mere robbers, and listen attentively until my fidgetty ear was satisfied that the noise boded no harm; then I would lie down again, more than half out of humour that my alarm was causeless; for though it may be a savage confession, yet it is a true one, I could have pinked any man who might have attempted to break into the house, with a feeling of indifference, bordering on delight.

Well—So passed the night until twelve o'clock, when I fell for a moment into a sound sleep. Presently a figure, all muffled in white, of course, according to the usage of all bona-fide ghosts, stole softly into

23. Wilkins, a boyhood friend of Mickle, was now a local mason.

my room, and approached my bed. I leaped upon the floor, seized a pistol, cocked, and fired it full at him. He gave a hideous yell, an unearthly shriek, staggered, and fell. I hastened to pluck the disguise from his face; but with what a cold rush did my blood find my heart, as I recognized the features, stiff in death, of one of my earliest, one of my truest friends!

Now, though I think I am as free from foolish superstition as any one; and though I as little regard the airy visions of a dream, as any being can, yet I must confess this last night's passage rides my soul like a nightmare. Boo! I can hear that shrill, quavering scream still tingling in my ears! I can see that beloved and familiar face turned up in the beams of the pale moon, in all the ghastliness of death! I still feel the soul-sickening emotions that I felt as I bent over the prostrate form of him who was the victim of an innocent prank!

8 August, Saturday.

This morning as I was going to the Post Office the first person I met was the very one that in my dream I shot. We had a hearty laugh over the incident, but somehow or other my laugh was rather forced. I felt something akin to a doubt as to whether my eyes told the truth. After returning from market I sailed to Gloucester and back two several times, with a fine westerly breeze. In the evening "The Washington Library Society" of which "I have the," and so forth, to be President, held a Meeting and transacted some unimportant business.

9 August, Sunday.

My good friend Will spent the forenoon with me; and we passed the time in diverse occupations, such as reading one to the other, criticizing each other's original essays, playing chess, and so forth, and so forth.

10 August, Monday.

I accompanied two ladies, to day, to the Brandywine Chalybeate Springs in the State of Delaware, about five miles from Wilmington; which is a sort of second Saratoga, where people resort, to dance half the night, and sip the mineral tinctured water, marry, for the sake of their health. Now as for the dancing, I do hold it to be a fact that all are fools (the ladies of course excepted) who engage in it; and as for the water, were it not fashionable to drink it, persons would just as soon gulp down the contents of a blacksmith's cooling tub, as it. I fancy there can not be much difference in the flavour of the two, but which has the advantage it were hard to say. . . .

We arrived in time to partake of a sumptuous dinner, and had a very favourable afternoon in which to look at whatever was interesting in either nature or art, in the vicinity of the Springs. There were about eighty persons sat down at the dinner table, among whom I looked in vain for a pretty woman, or a polite man. All were in their bearing cold and uninviting, and each seemed to be occupied with thoughts of himself and of no one else; the common fashion of those who come from Philadelphia, which is a city celebrated equally for two things, *"omnibus in terris quae sunt a Gallibus usque Auroram et Gangen,"*— namely, for **the right angles of its streets**, and —THE HOGGISHNESS OF ITS INHABITANTS.

Were it likely, that the romantic scenery of Red Clay Creek will meet a fate similar to that of Sodom and Gomorrah, or were it probable that it will disappear like Pompeii and Herculaneum, I would enter at length into a description of its **transcendent beauty**, for the special edification of posterity. But as the chances are that the scene will last so long as there is any body on this ball of ours to see it, I will forbear, and bid the reader for the present, **Good Night!**

11 August, Tuesday.

Having seen all that was marketable to the eyes, and not exactly relishing the idea of paying two dollars a day even for such good living as was to be had by staying, we to-day left Brandywine, and returned home by the rail-road through New Port, Wilmington, Chester and Philadelphia.

12 August, Wednesday.

I employed this day in fixing and overhauling my boat—"my blithe, my bonny, bounding boat." In the evening attended a Temperance Convention, but very unfortunately fell asleep during the delivery of a narcotic exordium by one of the speakers, whereby I am assured I lost a most excellent peroration.

13 August, Thursday.

There is nothing to record to day, except that the rain fell in torrents.

14 August, Friday.

The registry of this day is "short and sweet." Went a-sailing.

15 August, Saturday.

Having nothing to say for myself, I will just jot down that my good friend Will started this morning for Bridgeton, whence I suppose he will return in a couple of weeks, bewitched by the charms which the wily Mary so well knows how to set off. *"Amor vincit omnia; et* Billy *cedet Amori."*

16 August, Sunday.

I was busied all day in writing for my uncle, relative to an extensive purchase about to be made by the Ferry Company of which he is Secretary and Treasurer, of Mr. Jacob Ridgway,[24] the most rich, renowned and respected skinner of fleas, and doer of other small matters, by way of turning an honest penny. I made amends however, by going to church in the evening to hear Mr. Tyndale deliver a sermon in his usual straight forward, unembellished style.

17 August, Monday.

From eight o'clock this morning till eight o'clock at night have I been a-sailing with Robert W. Ogden, Jr.[25] in my skiff; and a violent head-ache attests the truth, that "Pleasure is ever bought with pain." We took a long cruize down the river, yea, even unto Woodbury Creek; and outsailed every thing near our own dimensions that we came across.

18 August, Tuesday.

Well! *Semper ego lusor tantum?* Shall I ever be a player only? Shall day succeed to day and week follow at the heels of week, and months glide noiselessly away—and I have no better account to render of myself than that I went a-sailing, or worse still, that I did nothing?— No: God and my good resolution prevent it! The Heavens forfend it. From this day forth, while my body is being invigorated by healthful exercise, let me not forget to strengthen and improve my mind also with useful knowledge. To-morrow then, hey for Sallust![26] Hey for the turning over of a new leaf in my life! I will portion my day off as follows: From morning till noon, severe study; from noon till supper, lighter studies and recreation; from supper to bed time, composition; all other time not appropriated, close and systematic thought.

Under this arrangement I think I can make out better than I have done to day; for being in doubt this morning whether I had better go to reading Latin or go a sailing, I was so long in making up my mind which to do that evening found me still undetermined.

19 August, Wednesday.

Agreeably to my Resolution formed yesterday, I got up earlier than common, this morning, and slipped from my bed-room into my study, where I attacked Sallust with as much energy as the old Roman

---

24. Jacob Ridgway (1768–1843), a native of Little Egg Harbor, New Jersey, was one of Philadelphia's most prosperous citizens, having acquired a fortune in shipping and real estate. John W. Mickle's Camden and Philadelphia Steamboat Ferry Company hoped to buy Ridgway's ferry interests on the Delaware. See entry of 22 August 1840.

25. Mickle's friend Ogden was the son of an official of the Camden Bank.

26. Mickle is about to begin reading the works of Roman historian Crispus Sallust (86–c. 34 B.C.).

gladiators used to attack the Numidian lions withal. Before and after breakfast I translated one page; and upon **this short** acquaintance I think I may venture to predict an **agreeable** acquaintance in old Crispus. He certainly makes some very good remarks in the beginning of his book, as, for instance, that "the powers of the body we possess in common with beasts; the powers of mind, in common with the gods. Wherefore it seems to me more proper to seek glory by works of the genius than by works of physical strength."[27] The opinion of Sallust upon the relative merits of *"actores et scriptores rerum"* would seem from this to differ from that of Themistocles;[28] who being asked whether he had rather be Achilles or Homer, replied "Hadst thou not rather be the victor announced, than the announcer of the victory, in the Olympic games?" For my part I think the glory of the *Iliad* should be equally divided between the bard and the characters; for Homer is indebted to Achilles and Hector and the rest of them, for his theme, and they are indebted to Homer for the glorious execution of that theme. . . .

In the afternoon I went to a Regatta on the Delaware at Greenwich Point. The race was for four and six oared boats; and the prize which consisted of a suit of colours, was taken by the barge *James Page*, pulled by the brawny arms of Kensington fishermen, each one of whom is a very Charon. The boats rowed down to Howell's Cove and back.

20 August, Thursday.

This morning, opened Sallust again and translated some of him. But my mind has been so long at rest, that I can not start it off again as quick as I could desire. If the same principle applies metaphysically as physically, my mental rigging must have amplitude enough; at all events, as with very large material bodies, it takes a tremendous force to overcome its *vis inertiae!*

21 August, Friday.

. . . This afternoon a certain young man with whom I went to school two or three weeks at Burlington, and who seems determined not to let me forget our acquaintance, called upon me.[29] He makes it a point to bore me with a visit about once every fortnight—hang him—and really I dont recover from the effects of one call before he makes

27. Mickle paraphrases the opening lines of Sallust's *Conspiracy of Catiline.*
28. Themistocles was an Athenian statesman and general of the early fifth century B.C.
29. Mickle attended Burlington High School, a private institution, operated by Baptist clergyman Samuel Aaron (1800–65), from March to December 1839. His fellow student was John Hinchman, a distant relative, who was to die in a boating accident in 1841.

another. Now this young man, like many other young men, cannot perceive the truth of which every one else is so sensible, namely that he is so near a fool that it were hypercritical to quarrel about the application of that epithet to him. Oh no! This young man is wise in his own conceit. He occasionally writes in humble prose for the edification of unmusical mortals, although his chief forte lies in making, perpetrating, or doing, if you please, certain compositions, the enigmatical nature of which he himself clearly solves by calling them "poetical effusions." He can accomplish any thing in this line from a doggerel up to an epic; but it mostly delights his Muse to celebrate the charms, hidden and revealed, of certain wenches and pot-slewers; which he does in true Byronic style, albeit, instead of those stale rhymes "breeze" and "trees" he uses by way of original beauties— "knees" and "sneeze," and instead of "rise" and "skies" his fertile and fervent imagination has hit upon the far more poetical words "lies" and "thighs."

Now this said young man was entirely ignorant until a twelve month ago, that the Pierides[30] had entrusted his odd-shaped head with the poetic spark; and used to be satisfied to walk in the humble path of prose. It was left to Fowler,[31] the great humbugger, to be the Columbus of this glorious discovery; it was left for him to ascertain by actual feeling that the bumps of imagination, sublimity, ideality, and all others necessary to the constitution of a first rate poet, were "prominently developed" upon the cranium of this young man. The scientific phrenologist imparted this important fact to his patient; and soon after, **the price of old shirts advanced ten per centum!** Ever since then John Hinchman has been numbered among those whom Juvenal hits off in the following lines: *"Tenet insanabile multos Scribendi cacöethes—."* Said John, since that glorious era in his existence, has done nothing but invoke the propitious Muses; and he never fails to carry his pockets full of Sonnets and so forth, with which to entertain those whom he visits.

22 August, Saturday.

'Tis seventeen years ago to day since my dearly beloved, although disremembered father left this world, where he was respected by all who knew him, for "another, and a better sphere." He died in the prime of his life, leaving behind him a young and affectionate wife, and a reputation which even family enemies admit was spotless.

---

30. The Pierides are, simply, the Muses, so named in Hesiod and other ancient Greek writers, from their presumed home in Pieria, a part of Macedonia.

31. Orson Squire Fowler (1809–87) was the leading popularizer of phrenology in the United States.

Decended from one of the oldest and most respectable families in West Jersey, the honorable and honest career of his life, though short, has contributed in no small degree to that noblest of the nobility of which I can claim my ancestry to have been. Beloved at home, and respected abroad, his loss was regretted every where—to me it was a bereavement of which I am not able to conceive the greatness. Light be the sods upon his grave! It is my happy privilege to hope that I may show in another state, that love to him which fate forbade me to express in this.

At sunset this evening the Steam-boat *William Wray* passed through Windmill Island Canal; to signify that the long-pending and celebrated bargain, between Jacob Ridgway and the **Odious Monopoly** had been consummated.[32]

23 August, Sunday.

To day I commenced reading the Bible; and intend to go through it to the end. It is a large book, truly, and would do much more good in the world were it but quarter so big; but nevertheless I intend to see what good it will do me to read it entirely over again; for verily what little gospel was driven into my head when I went to school to that primp old dame, Mary Barton, seems all to have leaked out and fled through the chinks in my memory. It is very unlike to Sir Hudibras his wit, which lasted so amazingly, considering its quantity; although had he used his wit as much as I did my gospel, I cannot but think it, the former, would have worn out too.

24 August, Monday.

I read and reviewed a little in Sallust, to day, and find his history of the *"res gestae"* very interesting; but the chief charm of this writer is, that his style is simple and easy. He does not delight in those complicated constructions of phrases, and those *"sesquipedalia verba"* which we meet with in Cicero, and in some of Cicero's apes in modern times. Sallust has the credit of having been a shrewd fellow; and he certainly does say some things that entitle him to that appellation. . . .

This afternoon there is to be a great political meeting held by the Democratic party at Woodbury, the shire-town of this county. General Wall, Peter D. Vroom and Colonel Page are expected to speak.[33] Dont like it—too much of it. A bumbailiff cant be elected now-a-days with-

---

32. The Camden and Philadelphia Steamboat Ferry Company, a tool of the Camden and Amboy Railroad, had sought to reduce competition by buying Jacob Ridgway's ferry houses, boats, and equipment (centered at Federal Street) for $300,000.

33. Vroom (1791–1873) had been governor from 1829 to 1832 and from 1833 to 1836 and was currently serving in Congress. James Page (1795–1875) was a prominent Philadelphia lawyer, currently serving as postmaster of the city.

out there being a dozen or two stump meetings on the subject. It is well enough for every man to be a politician in a certain measure; but party politics run too high; party spirit and factious zeal go too far. The liberties of our country I fear will be like the egg; in the squabble of the two political parties to protect them, the object of such protection will be cracked. It has been said that wine makes fools of one third of mankind, and that women make fools of another third. In these times of "hard cider" it may be added that politics completely befools the remaining third.

Tom Paine's—that name unmeet to Christian's ears!—I say Tom Paine's noble Vindication of the *Rights of Man* served to fill up a vacant hour this evening very well. It would be unfair to venture my humble opinion in relation to this work, until I have completed it; especially as I opened it pre-determined to find it, as all the other effusions of this black-souled or no souled, writer (if you please) are, a monstrous heap of hellish infidelities, an Augean stable of atheistic dung, a vile tissue of most damnable lies—a book, in short, prompted by the Devil himself, and executed just as the Devil would have it, by the Devil's cheif scribe, Tom Paine! Such, pictured in my imagination as reflected from the pulpit, are all the works of this writer. But I must confess that the first pages of his *Rights of Man* do not savour quite so much of hell as I was led to expect. How the others may be, time, which reveals all things, even an old maid's gray hairs, will show.

25 August, Tuesday.

In the morning I was busy at Sallust; in the afternoon at Paine. I translated the incredible amount of five lines in the former, and read a dozen pages of the latter.

26 August, Wednesday.

Not feeling very well this forenoon, I have not looked into my old friend Crispus to-day. I hope his manes will pardon me for going a-sailing during the hours allotted to him.

28 August, Friday.

To make up for time lost yesterday, this morning I read upwards of four pages of Sallust, "*de conjuratione Catilinae*;" and this is but a small lesson, compared with what I might do, if I were to try. Last winter when I studied under Mr. Aaron at Burlington, I used to recite between six and eight hundred lines a day in Caesar's *Commentaries*; and after I came home I read Ovid's *Metamorphoses* in three weeks. Nor did I go **over** these authors merely; I went **into** and **through** them. Then, as now in reading Sallust, I never gave up a passage until I had a clear idea of the sense and a perfect knowledge of the grammatical construction of it.

After having translated what I considered enough for one day, I went a sailing, and took with me my cousin and namesake, whom I initiated into the science and mystery of navigating a boat.[34] He seemed very apt in learning the different manoeuvres and I may venture to predict that he will not after a little practice, disgrace his tutor by any lubberly, awkward blunder of helm or sheet.

29 August, Saturday.

Although it is an undoubted fact that the high destiny of man's advent into this sub-solar and sub-lunar sphere, is to benefit himself and not to harm others; and although it is a point conceded on all hands that, to date the deluge prior to the creation of the terrestrial orb, upon whose circumference we exist and ambulate, were a most egregious anachronism: yet I challenge all the sophistry and logic extant, to prove this position, namely, **that I have looked into Sallust this day**. Now the reader may laugh at this queer mode of reasoning; but I assure him that it is the way in which about one half of the lawyers and two thirds of the politicians make up their arguments. "Inasmuch as a dog's tail" says the disciple of Cicero, with all the forencic gravity of which he is capable, "Inasmuch as a dog's tail, your honor, is always located, situated and positioned near his, the said dog's hind, after or posterior extremity; therefore it follows, your honor, that the defendant John Smith is guilty of the alleged enormous offence of stealing his bed fellow's pen-knife." "Whereas" thunders the political orator—"Whereas Sam Swartwout run away with the public money, therefore Harrison ought to be elected President of these United States!"

But to leave quibbling, and go to the record of stubborn fact: To day—not being very well—I made no further progress with Sallust; and went a-sailing, not so much for pleasure, as for medicine. As I passed the wharf I saw my good friend Will standing thereon; but I had no time then to stop and ask him the particulars of his visit.

30 August, Sunday.

To-day I read a considerable in "the good old book," and translated five pages of Sallust, to say nothing of what I perused in Tom Paine's *Rights of Man*. In the afternoon I went a-sailing an hour or two with Will Jeffers; and afterwards played a game of chess with him, and was beaten. This is a strange **ollapodiana** [*hodge-podge*] for a Sunday, truly!

31 August, Monday.

Mr. Joseph B. Cooper, an esteemed friend of mine, asked me about a week ago to set some day on which I could take him to Fort Mifflin,

34. Isaac W. Mickle (1827–62), son of Isaac's Uncle Benjamin, was later a lawyer, an editor of the Camden *Democrat*, and an army officer.

a place that he had never seen, and at which he wished to procure a humming bird for his ornithological cabinet. Well, as ill luck would have it, I appointed to day; and true to his promise, Mr. Cooper was on the wharf at nine o'clock, ready to start. The morning looked threatening, I had a headache, and to cap the climax, before the third one of the party was ready to go down the river, the tide was nearly ready to come up it. At ten o'clock, however, Mr. Cooper and Mr. Lehr,[35] and Masters Cooper and Lehr, and myself were all afloat, and had fairly weighed, before a light northerly breeze.

As we passed the buoy off Howell's Cove, it was very evident that the ebb was much slackened, and before we doubled Eagle Point, it was certain that we were stemming the flood. It was now twelve o'clock, and our port of destination seemed but a little way ahead, when the wind shifted to South West, bringing with it a heavy shower of rain. Putting back, we landed at Eagle Point, and went into an untenanted fish cabin, where we feasted on those fruits and provisions which we had brought with us. At about one when the storm seemed to have passed over, we again made sail and beat down to Red Bank. Here we were overtaken by another shower, which we received, however, with that fortitude which a consciousness that we cannot better ourselves, always inspires. After this had passed away, we found ourselves in the middle of the river, in a powerful flood tide, without any wind, two miles from where we wished to go, and with only one oar, which, too, was broken nearly off in the middle! . . .

At last it was resolved to carry our object, although it took a week to do it, and so we rowed as well as we could with our broken oar, and arrived at the Fort at four o'clock, just as the tide began to fall. Mr. Cooper went ashore and examined the works, while I remained in the boat and whistled for a wind to carry us back.

At half past four, the weather being extremely pleasant, and the wind blowing pretty freshly from South West, we started for home, and arrived at Camden a little after high water.

So passed I the last day of the summer of Eighteen hundred and forty!

Both political parties are busy at work—holding conventions, having parades, and so forth. The Whigs are resolved to elect their candidate by a system of electioneering which, however much decent men may be disgusted, is sure not to fail with the lower orders.[36] Their motto seems to be "*Sit Harrison electus, ruat coelum!*"—in accordance

---

35. Jacob W. Lehr sold patent medicines from his residence on Market Street, Camden.
36. The Whigs, in the election campaign of 1840, tried to win votes for William Henry Harrison by the use of placards, slogans, parades, rallies, and false claims about their candidate's humble origins (a log cabin) and simple taste (hard cider).

wherewith they countenance drunkenness, lies, slanders, the singing of indecent and scandalous songs, and the doing of any meanness whereby they can get the strong-smelling huzza of the lowest vagabond that wallows in the gutters. This too is done by a party that professed but a year ago to have "all the talents, all the respectability of the country" in its own ranks, and that affected to regard its opponents as without shirts or character!

But how miserably do they contrast with their opponents now! **They** appeal to the most sordid appetites of their fellows; **the others** to their reason. **They,** taking back the sneers they once cast upon "the vulgar herd," now demean themselves into apes and parrots to make that very herd laugh; **the others**, saying now—as they ever have said—that "all men are equal," treat them as equals, and as men. **They** may triumph for a while; but the success of dishonour and dishonesty cannot abide long: it vanishes like the dew of the morning. But the principles contended for by their opponents, defeated or delayed as they may be for a time, will finally triumph, and triumph for ever. For, in the beautiful words of Bryant,

> "**Truth,** crush'd to earth, will **rise again;**
> **Th' immortal years of God are hers!**
> But error, wounded, writhes in pain,
> And dies, amid her worshippers."[37]

1 September, Tuesday.

To day I am able to report five pages progess in Sallust, besides having gone a-sailing, paid a visit to a sick person, and received one from another who is hale. This is not bad for the first day of fall, is it, reader?

2 September, Wednesday.

I have nothing to record to day, except that I filled a sail-boat, and had liked to have left "the glimpses of the moon," for a while, at any rate. She fell upon her beams ends, and I jumped overboard and held on to her keel, until she drifted ashore. I did not get much wet.

3 September, Thursday.

At six o'clock this morning I started in the Steamboat *Pioneer*, along with my uncle and several others from Camden, for a Democratic Convention which was held in Salem, New Jersey, for the purpose of undoing what the opposite party may have done at the same place, at their meeting, a week ago. We arrived at Salem about

---

37. A slightly incorrect version of a passage from "The Battle Field" by William Cullen Bryant (1794–1878).

eleven o'clock, and I was lucky enough to get a seat at Hackett's[38] first table, where I did ample justice to his excellent dinner. About one o'clock I walked out to the place where the meeting was to be held, and found a great concourse of people and carriages already assembled. Upwards of three hundred vehicles came from Cumberland County, not less than one hundred and ten from Bridgeton alone. The people were chiefly composed of honest, hard-working men, the producers, and not those who live by the productive labours of others; the real poor men, and not the pseudo-poor, who use log cabins for traps by which to catch unsuspecting votes; in short, the bone and sinew, and not the dropsical flesh, of society, as was the meeting held at the same place last Thursday. The line of demarcation between the present Whig and the Democratic parties of this country is as strongly defined as the contrast between poverty and riches, honesty and knavery can make it.

The meeting was organized by the appointment of Richard P. Thompson as President; and was addressed by General Wall, Ex-Governor Vroom, James Page, Charles Brown, and Mr. Kelley, with much effect.[39] Governor Vroom's speech, in particular was excellent. In relation to the New Jersey Congressional Fraud it was unanswerable. Page was, as usual, witty and sarcastic; at times energetic, and always interesting. He exploded the Whig Humbugs with an ease that showed him to be entirely familiar with the business; and told his stories with his wonted flippancy. "The Whigs themselves" said he in conclusion, "have saved me the trouble of exposing their hypocricy." Then, pointing to a log-cabin which the friends of Harrison had erected hard by, "Yonder" he continued, "is the proof of it. Yes, poor men! those logs are more eloquent than my tongue can be, in appealing to you to crush a party which can stoop to such means of obtaining your favour!"

Every thing passed off quietly and orderly; and the convention adjourned at six o'clock, with nine thundering cheers for "Van Buren, Johnson, The Sub-Treasury and Columbia."[40]

38. Isaac Hackett was proprietor of Salem's Union Hotel.

39. Thompson (1805–59), a Salem lawyer, later served as attorney general of New Jersey. Charles S. Brown (1797–1883) was a radical Democratic state senator from Philadelphia, later a congressman. William D. Kelley (1814–90), currently a student of law in Philadelphia, would soon begin a distinguished career as a lawyer, judge, and fourteen-term congressman, 1861 to 1890.

40. Richard M. Johnson (1781–1850), of Kentucky, was running for reelection as vice-president. A law establishing a subtreasury, or independent treasury, had passed Congress in June 1840. Under the law, the federal government could establish its own subtreasuries, entirely independent of state banks or private banks, in various cities. The act was repealed in 1841.

We got to Philadelphia about midnight, and by one o'clock I was fast asleep.

4 September, Friday.

Just two months have now passed since I began to keep this diary; and instead of tiring with it, I find the slight labour more than rewarded by the pleasure of turning over its pages and retrospecting its records. And I intend henceforth to take more pains in its composition; to take better care what I write and how I write it; and to endeavour to make it more worthy both of myself and of those to whom, a half century hence, I may give it.

To day I read a good deal in Sallust, whom I find to be, as I prophecied him, to be about to be found, an agreeable, a very agreeable acquaintance.

Will Jeffers spent the evening with me, and we resolved to institute among the Democratic young men of Camden a political club, for the furtherance of sound Democratic principles. I hope the idea may succeed as well as he wishes it to.

5 September, Saturday.

Seeing Gideon V. Stivers[41] and Samuel Cowperthwaite, to day, I proposed to them the founding of the Democratic Club which I mentioned as having suggested itself to me, yesterday. They are both not only willing to aid the scheme, but are almost enthusiastic for its success. Huzza!

This evening The Washington Library Society met, and transacted some important business; among which, was the expulsion of John Clement and John Ballantine,[42] for delinquency in paying their dues. Being in the chair, I had not an opportunity to helping them out of company which they have disgraced so long; which I very much regret.

6 September, Sunday.

Remained at home, reading Sallust, and framing a speech for a future occasion.

7 September, Monday.

Did nothing worth recording. There are times when one's brains and energies go, as the saying is, "a-wool gathering," and such a time has this day been to me.

41. Stivers, a young carpenter, remained friends with Mickle even after his removal to Brooklyn, New York, in 1842. His father, of the same name, was a highly respected Camden carpenter and bridge-builder.

42. Clement (1818–94), son of John Clement (1769–1855) of Haddonfield, followed his father's career, becoming a surveyor and later a judge. Ballantine was a Camden coachmaker.

8 September, Tuesday.

All this forenoon I was busied in writing. After dinner I sailed with Job Wilkins down to the armed Schooner *Flirt,* just arrived below the Navy Yard.[43] She fired a salute of thirteen guns while we were close under her quarter.

9 September, Wednesday.

Besides studying a little, the only thing that I have done to day was to go to the upper part of Camden to see the wreck of a brig which was towed up yesterday by a coasting schooner. She is clipper built, and hails from Baltimore. Her name is illegible, more than "*Willi*——." Her masts had been cut away by the board, and her larboard side is covered with barnacles and sea grass. Her boats being still with her, when she was picked up, as well as her charts, compasses, and other movable furniture, it is likely that her crew were all lost.

10 September, Thursday.

The weather being extremely rainy and unpleasant, I remained in the house, reading, reflecting, and writing. I make it a point to write more or less every day, for I am convinced that the mind is improved if the pen makes nothing but strokes and pot hooks.

11 September, Friday.

One of the steamboat men this morning caught a humming bird, the wings of which had become so entangled with cob-webs, that it could not fly, and gave it, as a kind of present, to me. Putting him into a cage, I fed him on stershen—if so it is spelt—on stershen [*nasturtium*] blossoms, and had a good deal of sport with him, no doubt, at his expense. Two or three times as the cream of human kindness would overflow my heart at witnessing his desperate attempts to escape through the slats of his prison, I was almost induced to let him go, to sip the nectar from his chosen flowers. But as at length he began to become reconciled to his captivity, I held on to him.

12 September, Saturday.

This morning I fed my little prisoner, and left him in high good cheer, while I went a-sailing with Bob Ogden and Will Jeffers. After describing a spider's web on the Surface of the Delaware we came ashore and took a walk. About noon I returned, and alack-a-day! found my poor little humming bird dead! I had strewed its cage with the sweetest and the gayest flowers; but liberty—liberty was not there! and who would live where liberty is not? What a lesson might not

43. The *Flirt* was a 150-ton navy ship, built in 1839.

some of the craven dastards who can smile in golden bondage learn from the great spirit of this little bird!

13 September, Sunday.

I have felt unwell all day, and have kept in the house. Reclining on what Cowper found to be so prolific a theme,[44] I almost forgot my bodily ailment in reading and laughing over the doughty exploits of La Mancha's Knight. *Don Quixotte* is a book that can be read a dozen times, with increased delight at each perusal.

14 September, Monday.

My indisposition still increases. At the present writing, which to commit a bull, is at one o'clock tomorrow morning, a hot fever riots through my veins. Last night, I had a chill after going to bed.

15 September, Tuesday.

Again last night (or rather this morning, for I did not retire till early) I had a slight touch of the fever and ague, after crawling between my sheets. I am not so sick to-day however but that I can read. Sitting up in an easy chair made by my uncle when at sea, I have read a hundred and fifty pages of the life of Samuel Drew, the Cornish shoemaker and metaphysician. Will Jeffers spent the evening with me.

16 September, Wednesday.

Sick! Sicker!! Read a little, eat a little, puked a little, and maledicted Adam a good deal for bringing upon us poor mortals, among other curses, the headache.

17 September, Thursday.

To-day I took two calomel powders, one pill, and some fever drops, prescribed by Doctor Mulford. These had their intended effect. In the evening I attended an assembly of the Washington Library Company which is under my presidency. Important business relating to the recent expulsions required me to commit this imprudence. As the rules of decorum demanded that I should sit uncovered, and as the room was not heated, I suppose I shall to-morrow have an addition cold.

18 September, Friday.

Tolerably sick, and intolerably angry; to which latter cause it may be owing,

19 September, Saturday.

—that I am well.

44. Much of English poet William Cowper's (1731–1800) poem "The Task" is devoted to a sofa.

20 September, Sunday.

Inasmuchas it is a false modesty which deters one from penning his own praise in a case where he feels that praise is due to him: and inasmuchas I have neither played chess, gone a-sailing, nor whistled songs this day, but on the contrary have remained at home reading the Bible and performing other commandments; which acts omitted and committed are equally, in my estimation, laudable:

Insomuch is the reader expected not to laugh at this monument of my praiseworthy self-denial.

21 September, Monday.
Brevitas est pulchra. Sallust—hundred lines—gratified, and instructed.

22 September, Tuesday.

To day I added to the already great number of irons which I have in the fire, by commencing an Essay Metaphysical. *Eheu!* I have work enough cut out to last me a year! There is a grand heroic poem to be called "The Humorous Adventures of Scrapio," of which there are two hundred lines finished; and a speech or two, nearly completed, to be delivered the very next time I have the honor to be invited to make a fool of myself, or rather, to show that I am one already made; and a Biography of the Washington Library, of which the first paragraph is actually in a state of great forwardness; and a Memoir of Myself up to the time of commencing this Diary, which I have not yet set a pen to; and lastly an Essay on the Relations and Duties of Man! *Mehercule!* as a Roman in my case would exclaim; that is, being interpreted, "I wish I were Hercules," that I might accomplish these six labours!—the translation being somewhat liberal, of course.

But I have not mentioned one curious task that I have to perform. Some time ago a friend of mine, being smitten with the charms of some neighbouring humble copy of Venus, and finding prose entirely too feeble a medium for his impetuous thoughts, and supposing me, I know not for what reason, to be a poet, applied to me to execute him an amorous ditty by which he might hope to soften the obdurate heart of his Dulcinea. I laughingly agreed to set upon the work instanter, bade him good by, and, as is my custom, never again thought of my promise until, several days after, I met him in the street; when—the usual salutations being over, "Have you finished" asked he, "my verses yet?" I gave two or three ahems, and pulling my handkerchief out of my pocket, began very industriously an operation upon my olfactory organ which precluded the possibility of an immediate reply. During the time thus gained, if I have any powers of doggerel, they were certainly busily at work, as the peculiar dilemma in which I was placed required that they should be. At length after stretching my invention and my Corydon's patience to their utmost tension, "Well, really," said I, "I owe you a hundred apologies for my remissness in not having them entirely done. I have made a beginning however as the following lines testify:

> Thy charms, dearest Ella, I long to embrace:
> They pervade thee all o'er from thy feet to thy face;
> But these all combin'd
> Can't compare with thy mind,
> Any more than a melon's core can with the rind!"

"Excellent! excellent!" exclaimed my friend, rubbing his hands with satisfaction at my impromptu. "But when can you finish it?" "O, I will do it immediately—right off—certainly" I replied; and so we parted.

But I find it is harder to perform than to promise; and besides, I shall want all the absurdity that I can think of for my own use the next time I fall in love. . . .

23 September, Wednesday.

To day I made a dive into the bottomless pit of metaphysics. If I come up light-handed—

Why then I will do exactly as most other metaphysicians have done!

24 September, Thursday.

The weather being pleasant, I went a sailing for an hour or two this forenoon, and circumnavigated Petty's Island for the gratification of Uncle Job, who was with me.

25 September, Friday.

A few days ago I mentioned that I had begun to dabble in metaphysics; which step I was led to take most by a desire to see if their real was as great as their apparent dryness. I found that it was not; and by degrees have become so enamoured of my subject that it is the first thing in my head on getting up and the last on going to bed. In my dreams, as in my wakeful hours, it is the uppermost in my mind. This enthusiasm will continue for a few days, and then, if I know myself, my "Essay on the Relations and Duties of Man" will be laid up in a pidgeon-hole in my writing desk, among many of its kindred, while I start in chase of some other project. I have the misfortune to be one of those who begin every thing and finish nothing—and a great misfortune it truly is; one that I would give the very shirt of my back to get rid of, and be the richer by the operation. But it lies in my nature, in my blood and marrow; and I might as well try to alter the colour of my eyes, or the shape of my skull, or the length of my legs, as to get rid of it. Can the leopard change his spots? Can the giraffe shorten his neck? Can the peacock alter his feet? No more can man, or what is much the same, a boy, wipe out the lines which Nature has drawn in his disposition.

26 September, Saturday.

So intently engaged upon my Essay that I could hardly find time to go after a suit of new clothes which were to be done to day, albeit my old ones began to look pretty venerable. The following bill may throw some light upon the obverse of the Spanish proverb, "Were it not for the belly the back might wear gold."

> "John W. Mickle, for Isaac Mickle,
> To Enoch Allen,

To one Super Blue Cloth Coat,	$23.00	
" one pair Super Buckskin Cashmere pants,	9.00	
" one black cloth vest,	4.50/	$36.00"

Who, after looking over the above bill will deny that were it not for the back, the belly might eat—terrapins and frog's hind quarters? Or who but will be convinced, that, how many tailors so ever it takes to make a man, but one is necessary to make a rogue?

27 September, Sunday.

I went over the river this morning to look at a collection of Curious Coins owned by a certain John Kane who is a complete original in the great family of fools. He carries his love for his hobby to such a length, that while he has medals and coins to the value of an hundred, nay, a thousand dollars, he has hardly a crust of bread for his children or a whole shirt for himself. Judging from his house and the appearance of every thing in it, you would suppose that poverty could make him no poorer; but judging from the Cabinet of Coins which he exhibits to you, you would take him to be some princely antiquarian and connoiseur, to whom the riches of Potosi[45] would be no object. Such are the eccentricities of man!

28 September, Monday.

As I was lying in bed this morning, taking a logical view of all the reasons that presented themselves to my mind why I should or should not get up immediately, and ere I had yet decided the nicely balanced question under consideration, who would pop in but Will Jeffers, my delectable chum, and what should he hold up before my half doubting

45. Potosi, a Bolivian city, was famed for its silver mines.

eyes but a letter from the author of the *Dutchman's Fireside,* now the Secretary of the Navy, acquainting him of the fact of his appointment as a midshipman in the service of the United States? I knew long ago that Will had an inclination that way, and he confided to me the Secret that measures were being taken to procure him a commission; but I never believed that he would get his desire, and consequently, was not a little surprised when he removed all of my infidelity by exultingly showing me the signature of James K. Paulding to a paper which invests him with the oak wreath and anchor. Jumping upon the floor at hearing this news, I congratulated my friend for his good luck with all the formality of which I was capable; but I suspect my bows and flourishes were more polite than elegant, considering I performed them in my shirt and nightcap.

I attended a sale of some curious coins to day, at Birch's Auction Room in Second Street. A "Washington Penny"[46] brought three dollars and a half, and the whole collection sold high. There seems to be a spirit of curiosity in the matter of Coin, which if carried much further, will make it worth some Yankee's while to set up a manufactory of Hebrew shekels, Greek oboli, and Roman denarii; and perhaps, if he be a Yankee out and out, it would not be an unprofitable speculation to coin a few copies of the original and identical "thirty peices" for which Judas betrayed Christ, or of the medals which Moses caused to be struck, or struck himself, in celebration of the exit of the Israelites. Gullible as the world is, it would require a thorough Yankee to give such peices an air of genuineness that none could doubt.

My uncle is gone to Bordentown to day, upon business relating to the recent purchase of the Ridgway property. And now while upon this theme I will mention an incident connected with it, which although not remarkable in itself is yet so as showing a trait of the richest man's character in America. The negotiations between Messrs. Ridgway and Stevens[47] concerning the above property were conducted throughout with great courtesy and generosity. It was with uninterrupted good feeling that steamboats, rows of houses, wharves and fixtures were sold and bought, to the amount of three hundred and two thousand dollars. The richest man in America congratulated the richest man in New Jersey, and the latter returned his congratulations to the former, that the bargain was made. But in the height of their bowing and scraping, it occurred to Mr. Ridgway that there were seven dollars taken on board of the steamboat *Hornet* the very day that she was

46. The Washington penny was one of a variety of coins struck during the period 1783–95, bearing the portrait of George Washington.
47. Robert Livingston Stevens (1787–1856) was president and a major stockholder of the Camden and Amboy Railroad and a leading naval architect.

sold to the Ferry Company, and at the same moment it occurred to Mr. Stevens that the proceeds of that days work, whatever it was, belonged to him; which thought was diametrically the opposite of the one just then passing in the mind of Mr. Ridgway.

After a few more bows they understood each other perfectly. They both insisted on having the seven dollars, and neither could think of allowing the justness of the other's claim. The bowing process of course stopped, and each stood start upright in the conciousness that his quarrel was fair. High words ensued. One would be damned and the other would be ditto, if the money did not belong to him; and this logic was rendered more powerful by prodigious knocks with their hands upon the neighbouring table. After a deal of loud talk and hard thumps, however, the richest man in America, finding that his proposition for each to take half would not succeed, reluctantly consented to pay to Mr. Stevens the disputed sum.

This incident I have from my uncle, who was present at its occurrence.

29 September, Tuesday.

I have been reading Locke's *Essay on the Human Understanding* for the most part of to-day. I also translated some of Sallust, and nearly finished Catiline's Oration to the Conspirators. Whether this be the production of the author or the actor of the History it does its producer honour.

30 September, Wednesday.

Engaged in reading Locke's *Essay*, and in writing my own. In the morning I went to Philadelphia and bought Beloe's *Herodotus*. I have now a pretty complete historical library. Let me not forget, though, that he is more learned who understands one book thoroughly, than he who dabbles in a dozen, and never goes further than the first leaf, or perhaps only looks over the title page.

1 October, Thursday.

Who can say that I am not studious and perservering after he shall have learned that I never put a boot on my leg this whole day; but sat in my slippers reading Sallust from morning till night, and almost till morning again? Who, I ask, can deny that I have begun the new month auspiciously?

2 October, Friday.

Imitated yesterday's industry.

3 October, Saturday.

This evening I attended a meeting of the Washington Library Society, and made an attempt to get rid of the trammels of my office.

My resignation was accepted by a majority of one, and I began to congratulate myself on my escape. There are however among our members some pretty astute tacticians, and they evinced something of their generalship in the manner which they adopted to keep me in the presidential chair. After two or three ballots for a successor, which I suspect were intentionally futile, one of the rogues whispered in my ear that as there was going to be a great difficulty in getting another officer, he hoped I would agree to a measure which he was about to propose, to insure the success of the next ballot. He then moved the following resolution: "Resolved, that the member who shall have the highest number of votes on the next balloting for President, shall receive, and fulfil the duties of, the office to which he is elected, under a penalty of one dollar." Hereupon an obstreperous debate arose, which seemed to spring from a sincere difference of opinion, but as I afterwards learned, was only a part of the preconcerted plot. After many words pro and con, I proceeded to take the final vote upon the passage of the resolve. There were four in the affirmative and four in the negative; so that I, as President, of course had the casting voice. Suspecting no snare, I decided affirmatively, and announced that the house was ready to enter into another ballot. While this was going on, I could almost have jumped for joy at the thought that my official career was so near a close; For I assure the reader that even this humble station is not without the thorns that ever lurk in the seat of power, and an escape from it was an escape which I most devoutly wished. Imagine my surprise, then, when the tellers announced that "**Isaac Mickle is** UNANIMOUSLY **elected** PRESIDENT **of this Society.**" That I was chagrined at this trick I will not pretend to deny. That I was out of humour, every member can testify; for when they saw their plot consummated, they all set up a laughing chorus, for which I did not neglect to fine them to the utmost of my power. Some who were uncommonly merry were fined four or five times.

As I am determined not to pay the dollar, I must serve to the end of my term; but I will play the Dionysius with them till they heartily wish their trick undone.

4 October, Sunday.

This morning I took a walk for my health, which for want of sufficient exercise is not very good. I am in the habit, too, of going to bed very unseasonably, and of rising proportionably late. These things must be looked to. . . .

In the evening I went to the Baptist church, where some stranger was inveighing against the custom of breaking the Sabbath in a strain of the most complete nonsense that I ever heard. The following specimen which I give from memory is nearly literal: "There are many Sabbath breakers in the world, my hearers! and perhaps some of you who sit before me are sabbath-breakers too. [Here he let his uplifted fist fall with tremendous force upon the open bible that lay on the desk for the purpose, as I suppose, of waking up those whom the narcotic qualities of his previous logic had put to sleep.] Yes, [he mournfully continued, after a long pause, thrusting his thumbs through the buttonholes of his coat] Yes! many in the world, and I fear not a few here! Some of you I have no doubt offend in this way without thinking. [Then assuming a look of mathematical wisdom,] You spend **one** quarter of God's day in sleeping, **another** quarter in eating, and **another** quarter in dressing; and then you only have **one half**, or at least **two thirds**, of it left for prayer and worship. [Now up-raising both hands and bending eagerly forward,] But the commandment is, "Remember God's sabbath day"—mind, **God's sabbath day**; it dont say a half or a quarter of it, "and keep it holy." [Here hooking his two fore-fingers together,] Dont you see then the truth of my proposition?" Now this is no exaggeration; and it cannot be denied that very many of the sermons of our day are made up of just such stuff.

5 October, Monday.

I was under a promise to John Kane, the antiquarian . . . that I would call upon him again to day to look at the remainder of his coins. But I forgot it until an hour after the time appointed, and so put it off, *sine die*, or *ad infinitum*, I dont much care which.

At ten o'clock I went to Woodbury, dined with my aunt Mary, returned at half past two, as I went, for nothing, and made two acquaintances and four dollars by the process!

There being a fine breeze when I got home, I jumped into my skiff, loosed the lines, hoisted sail, and sped away for Richmond. . . .[48]

6 October, Tuesday.

Read a little in Sallust and walked for exercise to Kaighn's Point and—back again, of course.

7 October, Wednesday.

Let people say what they will against the habit of lying in bed late in the morning it is not without some redeeming qualities—it is not a habit altogether evil. For my part it is the only time in which I can philosophise respectably. Then (and except then, never,) can I take a comprehensive view of a subject; and **trace** effects **to** their causes, and

---

48. A part of Northern Liberties Township along the Delaware River just north of Philadelphia, Richmond became a separate district in 1847 and part of Philadelphia in 1854.

hypothecate effects **from** given causes; then, and only then, can I unravel logical problems, and see through opaque syllogisms; then, in short, I can do any thing, but get up!

Well, as I lay in bed this morning according to my custom, the following preposition suggested itself: **A long lived blockhead is happier than a short lived Solomon**. From this foundation I raised this logical superstructure: It being self evident that health without Latin is preferable to Latin without health, and as it is utterly impossible that I can contribute any thing to my mind to day without defrauding my body in proportion—**Therefore the devil take Sallust while I go a-sailing**.

Having arrived at this very satisfactory terminum, I jumped out of bed, got my breakfast, and was soon away on the waves of the noble Delaware!

8 October, Thursday.

To night I attended a political meeting at Elwell's hotel,[49] where my uncle and a better orator made speeches. I was here informed that **John K. Clement** has turned political spouter also; and when I returned I wrote a short notice of boys intermeddling with such things—for the *Democrat*.[50]

9 October, Friday.

I was received very politely this morning when I took the notice alluded to yesterday, to the office. *Ille qui edit* said *se facturum* as I wished.

This evening, being at Doctor Mulford's, I borrowed Drews *Essay on the Soul*, a book which I have often wished to get hold of.

10 October, Saturday.

Began to sit with Dickinson[51] for my miniature. He told me it would require six more sittings to finish. Should I ever somerset into any degree of fame I will leave to the curious world two portraits—the one aforesaid of my features, and this diary of my mind, the former perhaps the most flattering, the latter the most faithful.

The *Democrat* contains my notice. Lawyer Croxall, I was told, is also going to have a hit at John.

49. James Elwell was the current proprietor of the Railroad Hotel at the foot of Federal Street.

50. Twenty-five Gloucester County Democrats bought the *Village Herald and Gloucester Advertiser* in 1840, moved its offices to Camden, and renamed it the *West Jersey Democrat*. The first issue appeared on 15 April 1840, with Isaac Bullock and William Johnson listed as publishers.

51. Daniel Dickenson (1795–?) was a portrait painter from Connecticut who moved to Philadelphia around 1820 and painted there until 1846. He lived in Camden from 1847 to at least 1866.

11 October, Sunday.

Instead of going to church to day I staid at home and read three verses of the Bible.

12 October, Monday.

At ten o'clock this morning I sat again for my likeness, which if Fame does not lie about the artist, will be an excellent one when finished. I observed among the specimens in his studio a miniature of himself, executed before a mirror; in which any one who had ever seen the original would at the first glance recognize Dan Dickinson. For my part I could have told whose likeness it was, if all the picture, except one eye, had been covered—so faithfully had he copied the peculiar expression of that organ.

13 October, Tuesday.

The election for State officers begins to day in New Jersey, and will be contested with a violence uninstanced perhaps since the days of Jefferson. The Whig party will, I expect, increase their majority; for acting upon the assumption that most men are fools, they have adopted a manner of electioneering at once insulting, unfair, and efficient. The times upon which we of this day have fallen, are indeed remarkable. The political doings of this year will form an unique page of the history of the States. From the "loophole of retreat" I will observe, and in this book will I record, the events of this memorable age, that posterity will regard with so much interest.

An election is also held in Pennsylvania to day to fill State offices. I crossed the river to see how the canvass was managed in Philadelphia, where party spirit usually rages with more violence than in any other section of the Union; and was pleased to see that every thing was conducted with great order and decorum. There were no fights, no clamorous debates; deep interest was painted in every man's countenance; fanaticism was evinced by the words and actions of no man. Each exercised the rights of a freeman, and left his fellow freemen unmolested to enjoy theirs. So may it ever be!

14 October, Wednesday.

The Democratic party at the election in Philadelphia yesterday reduced the majority of their opponents to twenty five hundred. Much money was wagered by the Whigs that they would have four thousand, as usually they do. Some bet ten to one on that number; and their folly is paid by the ill luck of their gambling. This victory will make an offset to the Whig gain in other states.

In the city and township of Camden, the poll which closed to night shows the majority of the Democratic party to be nearly doubled, compared with the vote of any preceding year. Philadelphians and Camdonians at least cannot be convinced that Federalism is Democracy, by looking at a skunk-skin or a cider-barrel!

Benjamin Mickle, the son of my late half-uncle Benjamin, died to day, aged two or three years. Perhaps we should not rejoice that he is released from a world so full of misery as this; and yet it would not be unfeeling not to weep. He is bettered; what occasion then for tears?

15 October, Thursday.

This afternoon the little boy who died yesterday morning was buried in Newton.[52] His father's grave was opened, and his coffin placed in it, upon his father's breast. I like not this mode of sepulture. There is more of poetry than true feeling in it. The dead leave every thing they own to the living, and the living I should think might at least afford the dead a grave a-peice. But it is the fashion thus to jumble bones together; and why should I object?

16 October, Friday.

Had another sitting to day for my portrait. As my acquaintance with the artist increases, I find him to be an enthusiast in his profession, and in his manner somewhat eccentric. His conversation consists sometimes of a rich vein of humour, and sometimes of a deep burst of genuine poetic feeling; but now and then he, as well as most other men, talks the most egregious nonsense. Without understanding the ancient languages, by the means of translations he has acquired a thorough knowledge of all the classic poets; and I never saw a man who had entered so deeply into the wild, dreamy spirit of the Greek and Roman fictions and fables, either with or without an understanding of the original tongue. He showed me illustrations which he has executed of nearly all of Ovid's beautiful *Metamorphoses*; and so well has his work been done, that it seemed to me as if the very words of the poet had received colour and figure from the pencil of the painter.

As I was returning homeward I stopped at a second-hand book store in Chesnut Street, and found a copy of Livy printed in 1536, I think, and commented upon in the veritable autograph of the great philologist, Melancthon.[53] Not having enough money with me to pay for this curiosity I engaged the bibliopolist to keep it a few days in reserve for me. I am to pay him five dollars for it.

I cannot but notice the obliging civility of this bookseller. Although I had never seen him before, yet he offered to let me take what works I pleased, at any credit I had a mind to ask. He volunteered to lend

52. Newton Cemetery, on the banks of Newton Creek, was the first burial ground in Old Gloucester County.
53. Melanchthon (1497–1560) was a German humanist and scholar. This volume is now in the collection of the New Jersey State Library.

me, whenever I would call, any volume I would like to read; and really forced me to bring home with me a very valuable book which I am to return at my pleasure. Now I think he must be a great fool, or I must have an extraordinarily honest countenance. He neither asked my name, or residence, and had no reason to believe that I was not a rogue.

Having finished reading Drew's *Essay on the Immateriality and Immortality of the Soul,* I returned the book to its owner, unconverted by the arguments it contains. As the production of an uneducated shoemaker it is highly curious, but as a conclusive argument it is defective. The immortality of the soul should not be hung upon a hook so treacherous and doubtful as its immateriality; and in demonstration nothing that is not self evident should be taken for granted. These errors I consider to be the most prominent in the plan and conduct of the ingenious but unprofitable argument that I have just finished.

Now that I am upon the subject of metaphysics I will record the fate of the Essay which I commenced on the twenty second of the last month, concerning the "Duties arising out of the Relations of Man." In looking for arguments to support the position I had taken, I found insuperable objections to it, and convinced myself that it was untenable. In trying to convince others that my grounds were true, I was satisfied by my own arguments that they were wrong, and so **committed the whole thing to the flames.**

A young gentleman of the Junior Class at Princeton College called upon me this afternoon to give me some information as to the terms, rules and studies of that celebrated school, which I have thought of entering this month. After he had told me how far he had read in Greek, how well he was versed in Latin, and so forth, I asked him what was the derivation of the word "sophomore." With a pompous air of consequence founded in my supposed ignorance of Greek he proceeded to answer me that σοφος was the Attic word for wisdom, (σοφία or σωφροσύνη is wisdom, σοφος being an adjective,) which in combination with the English termination, -more, meant **more wisdom!** I thanked him for his explanation of course, but could not help thinking to myself, "Σἠ σοφία ἐστι μωρία!" The fact is, modern colleges are manufactaries of **learned fools** and wise asses, and the name of being at one is more than the reality.

18 October, Sunday.   **My Eighteenth Birthday!**

> "Eheu! fugaces * * * *
> Labuntur anni: nec pietas moram
> Rugis et instanti senectae
> Afferet, indomitaeque morti!"

Not feeling in a moralizing mood, I have to beg of the reader, to **take for granted** a very excellent sermon on the above text from Horace, concerning the lapse of time. The theme is so trite that I can think of nothing to say upon it that has not been said a dozen times before. Therefore I will merely remark that to day I complete my eighteenth year—one half of my life having been spent in sleep—one quarter in mischief—one eighth in eating—one sixteenth in study—and the balance in——vain! Could I live my years over again I would keep out of love, out of debt and **out of the newspapers**; or to say all in a few words, I would take the advice of her who has too often advised me to no purpose.

19 October, Monday.

I sat for my portrait for the fourth time this morning, and find that my opinion of the artist was not far from correct. He is a fountain of anecdotes, and has a way of telling them that dispels the tedium of sitting, and makes it a pleasure rather than a task. My picture when done will I suppose represent me laughing; for I have hardly had a grave face since I began to sit for it.

As I returned I stopped and paid the bookseller for the venerable copy of Livy which is mentioned in the entry of last Friday. The price was five dollars. It is dated 1535—and not 1536, as I thought it was; its age is therefore three hundred and five years.

The whigs had a grand fandango in the woods near Camden this afternoon. A beggar presided, a knave spoke, and fools huzzaed. I

POLITICAL DOINGS OF 1840.

went to the place of meeting to hear Samuel L. Southard's[54] far famed voice; but the reality came far short of my expectations. This much however I must say: he can lie faster than any other man I ever heard. The whole affair was conducted so indecorously that no lover of propriety could regard it with any other feeling than disgust. . . . Each one seemed anxious to out-do the rest in acting the fool.

20 October, Tuesday.

The Camden Races begin to day—and of course, it rained. I say "of course" because it **has** always rained during these pastimes, since the Races were established, and probably always **will** while they are continued. Some say this is because Heaven likes them not!

22 October, Thursday.

I had another sitting to-day in the studio of Mr. Dickinson; returning whence I bought Fenelon's *Lives of the Ancient Philosophers*, which I am going to look into when I have finished "Junius."

23 October, Friday.

Sat again for my portrait.

24 October, Saturday.

My friend Midshipman Jeffers got his orders this morning "to proceed to New York forthwith, and report himself present, on board the *North Carolina*, ship of the line, Commodore Renshaw."[55] **Well Will, God take thy senior officers to himself as soon as convenient**, that thou mayst be promoted! This is all the harm I wish thee, or them.

25 October, Sunday.

To-day witnessed the first snow fall of this season. Rather an early beginning for winter, this—but winter has charms for me, and let it come!

Will Jeffers spent the evening in my study—we both thought, though neither whispered, perhaps for the last time!

26 October, Monday.

Sat again for my portrait: which entry I am nearly tired of making; inasmuchas there was a good deal of ice this morning; because Harrison is going to be our next President; wherefore I went this afternoon to see some paintings, in oil, by my good friend Chas. Humphreys.[56]

54. Southard (1787–1842), a Whig, was former governor of New Jersey and a cabinet officer under Presidents Monroe and Adams. He had been a United States senator since 1833.

55. James Renshaw (d. 1846) was the current commander of the 74-gun *North Carolina*, a sailing vessel built in 1818.

56. Humphreys was a painter and glazier on Camden's Federal Street.

Among which was one, a likeness of an intimate acquaintance of mine, which was so remarkably well done, that after I saw his name written at the bottom I had no difficulty whatever, in recognizing it! Humphreys, however, is one of the *autodidaktoi*, and has a right to expect much leniency.

27 October, Tuesday.

Iterum sedi in studio Mister Dicinsonis, which, being liberally interpreted, imports that if the artist does not finish my miniature before long, I shall take the matter into my own hands, and finish it myself.

My uncle, Assistant-Marshal for the district of Camden, to day completed the census of his township, for the present year. He has been about eight days in making the enumeration.

Will Jeffers starts to morrow for New York, and perhaps I will go with him. It is altogether owing to the nature of the dreams which I have to-night.

28 October, Wednesday.

Although I was very unwell this morning when Will called upon me to accompany him to New York, yet I was unable to resist his earnest solicitations that I should consent. Dressing therefore with much haste and little care, as the time required, I jumped into the cars with him, at nine o'clock, and at a little after two found myself for the second time in my life, in the most considerable city in America, and the most rascally in the world. We passed through Princeton and Newark, which towns I had never before seen. I have been to New Brunswick and Elizabethtown, two or three times; and to most of the other towns through which we passed.

Having been recommended to the Battery House,[57] I went there and ordered a room. After dinner we went over to the Brooklyn Navy Yard; returned and went to see the Liverpool packet steamer, *President*; walked up and down Broadway once or twice, and returned again to our lodgings to supper. I could not help observing the great paucity of dishes on the table at this meal. Although I am by no means a big eater, yet I could have eaten half of all that was set before the fifteen of us! This, I dare say, is the fashion, but I'll be thumped if it's an agreeable one, when you are better blessed in appetite than in means.

In the evening we went to the Olympic Theatre, and staid just long enough to learn that to stay any longer would be of no use.[58]

57. The Battery House was one of Manhattan's leading hotels, located on Battery Place.

58. The Olympic Theatre was at 444 Broadway. Mickle and Jeffers either did not like, or perhaps could not get tickets to, the popular *1940!* or *Crummles in Search of Novelty*.

29 October, Thursday.

When I got up this morning I found the heavens overcast and threatening; and as I knew enough of New York to know that in rainy weather it is the last place in which one need wish to be, I resolved to depart for home. Therefore bidding Will "good bye," I paid my bill, and embarked on board the steam-boat *Independence*, at seven o'clock for South Amboy. Had the weather been clear I would have remained with my friend until he went on board his ship. It was my intention to have staid two or three days at least, and my return so soon took my mother and uncle by surprize.

30 October, Friday.

I called upon Will's uncle this morning, to say to him that I had seen his nephew safe arrived in New York, and that he was going on board the *Carolina* yesterday.

31 October, Saturday.

Spent this day in talking politics, which is a very fashionable, but also a very questionable employment. Surely such a time never was before! Old and young, drunk and sober, rich and poor, all talk of politics, and think of nothing else. The spirits of the Democratic party are raised a little to-day in consequence of their success in the Phila-delphia election yesterday. The hopes of both parties hourly fluctuate. Both claim and both doubt. All are intensely excited. A fortnight will decide whether the American people are the fools which one faction has supposed them to be, or the sensible creatures that they are treated like by the other. God save America!

1 November, Sunday.

I passed this day in reading Pitkin's *Political History of the United States.* This is an interesting work; but it bears many marks of the prejudice of the Federalist who wrote it; at least this is my impression, from a hasty glance over some parts of it.

2 November, Monday.

Began a series of political papers.

3 November, Tuesday.

The New Jersey election for electors begins to-day. The interest of politicians amounts to an agony. Even women and very young chil-dren partake of the general feeling. There never was so violent a con-test before. God save the liberties of America!

4 November, Wednesday.

Our polls closed to-night, and the Federalists have made a small gain. This was done by lying, cheating, and bribery. I know two or three instances in which poor men were bought by rich Whigs. In Pennsylvania all is doubt and perplexity. Both parties claim to have succeeded. My belief is that Mr. Van Buren cannot be elected; but the people have been deceived, not convinced.

6 November, Friday.
Cloud after cloud gathers round Van Buren's prospects. It is to be feared that both New York and Pennsylvania have spoken against him. To-morrow will decide.

7 November, Saturday.
"God pity America! America blush for thyself! ! Harrison is elected President! Error rides in triumph over prostrate truth: Fraud and deception have prevailed! Honesty has taken wing for the lost Pleiad! Intelligence is no more! ! ! If I could carry with me the graves of my father's, I would start ere to-morrow's sun for the ends of the earth!"

So said one side to day when the news arrived that New York had gone for the old ninny of North Bend. The other exclaimed something after the following fashion.

"God has blessed America! America, congratulate thyself! ! We have conquered, and the truth has triumphed. The standing army is overcome; and Matty has taken heels to Kinderhook! The Sub-treasury shall be no more! Hurrah! hurrah! Were heaven to open to me, I would not leave this happy land! ! !"

The battle is now decided, and I can sleep again with some soundness. The result is disgraceful to the intelligence of America, rather than dangerous to her liberties. The man who has been chosen has neither the brains to conceive, nor the courage to carry out any project for great good or evil. Still he may be made the instrument of others more dangerous than himself; therefore I repeat God save the liberties of America!

The tide in the river was two feet higher to-day than I ever saw it before.

8 November, Sunday.
The mails that arrived last night confirm the election of the very valiant old soldier who had the extraordinary good luck to fight a hundred or more battles without ever having received a wound!

I spent the whole of this day in the house, writing industriously; but when I had finished all, I had done nothing, and so burnt the result of my labour.

The tide in the Delaware, is as high to day as yesterday.

10 November, Tuesday.
The whigs in Philadelphia are making a great noise about their

victory. Cannons are firing in several places, and have been all day. They had better save some of their powder to keep up their spirits in November, forty-four.

Two men who had made a bet of twenty five hundred dollars on the re-election of Mr. Van Buren, came to see me to-day about it. The bet was made about six weeks ago, on this side of the river, in order to avoid the Pennsylvania laws on the subject; and I was present at the time, and consulted with on the preliminaries. The two Philadelphians who had lost called upon me to-day for my advice. I told them that by our New Jersey laws they could recover their share of the money from the stake holder, but advised them to give it up, like men of honour. "But" said they "it is our all; if we lose it we are ruined." "Why then" I asked "did you risk it upon so uncertain an event?" "Because," they replied "we were certain of winning." "And if you had won, you would have demanded to be paid?" I continued. "Yes." "And now you do not mean to pay?" "No." "Well then," said I, "there is no more to be said about it. Yonder door-hinges were oiled yesterday!" Taking this moderate hint, they departed.

11 November, Wednesday.

There is a great rejoicing among the whigs about these times, and a corresponding elongation of countenance among the opposite party. The poor devils have the chance to rejoice so seldom that I cannot find it in me to envy them. As to the democratic party, this defeat will be their salvation. Their principles must last as long as the republic, and the Waterloo of this fall will make the party purer, their union firmer, and their future success surer. . . .

12 November, Thursday.

The whigs still keep up their firing. It makes no difference however how much powder they shoot away, for now that they are in power they will rob the government of enough to pay for it. There is some talk of their having a great illumination in the city of Philadelphia; but they are somewhat afraid it would lead to a riot.

I got through Fenelon's *Lives of the Ancient Philosophers* to-night; much instructed.

13 November, Friday.

My mother went to-day on a visit to her sister in law Mary M. Haines and I remained at home to keep house. I passed my time very agreeably in reading Pitkin's *Civil and Political History of the United States*. I also read in Sallust the speech of Caesar, and the reply of Cato before the Roman Senate on the Conspiracy of Catiline. Cato insinuates that Caesar knows more about that business than he cares for telling. On the whole this is to me the most interesting part of Sallust.

14 November, Saturday.

There was a violent thunderstorm to-night. The season is late for such a phenomenon in this climate. I wonder what harm to the state this prodigy forbodes?

15 November, Sunday.

I would have gone to church to-day, but unfortunately as I was pulling on my breeches—my best ones—this morning, I tore them just in the place where a rent is most evident. As it would not have been compatible with my dignity, especially as I am President of a literary Society, to appear in public in such a plight, I staid at home and printed on my little press some notices for "a meeting of the young men of Camden" on next Tuesday night.

16 November, Monday.

Read a good deal in Pitkin's *History*, and distributed the notices that I printed yesterday. Moreover I took my press apart and made some alterations in it. This is the only toy I have; and considering I never let the girls trouble my head I think I may be allowed to enjoy it. I always had a great admiration of the mechanical operations of a printer, and two or three years ago I procured this miniature engine to be made, and bought some old types, ink and so forth, and commenced business for my own amusement. It prints very neatly and expeditiously, and I often find it to be handier than the pen for making several copies of the same thing.

17 November, Tuesday.

I have been acting the part of Solon and Lycurgus to-day; that is drafting a Constitution for the proposed debating Society that undertook to meet to night. I got my task nearly done, but from some cause or other only four of my acquaintances met at the hour and place mentioned, namely Samuel Cowperthwait, Gideon Stivers, Lemuel Davis[59] and Edward Porter. We adjourned therefore to meet on Monday night next, *codens loco.*

18 November, Wednesday.

I began to-day to write an essay, on what subject I cannot exactly tell until I get it done. My pen is like a ship without a rudder—it goeth whithersoever it pleaseth. Sometimes when I start out with the intention of enlightening the world on some occult theological point I

59. Davis was a very close friend of Mickle (their common date of birth helping to unite them), who currently worked in a bookstore.

unconsciously get to talking about Martin Van Buren and William Henry Harrison; and sometimes when I aim at astonishing and delighting every body with a grand profound elegant and learned treatise on politics I find myself suddenly making . . . rhymes. . . .

It has been snowing incessantly all day; and now that I am writing I hear the jingle of the merry merry sleigh-bell as some company of *bon-vivants* are dashing past my window.

19 November, Thursday.

The old woman's feather-bag was not quite emptied yesterday, and so this morning she turned out the remnant upon our fields and roofs. It is a fact worthy of remark that I can always study best when it is snowing. Why it is I know not, but that it is, I can swear. I read some to-day in Sallust.

20 November, Friday.

To-day: Twas ten before I left my bed, soon after which I breakfasted, and having then in Pitkin's read a page or two, I put my hat upon my head (as most men do) and sallied forth to hear the lies, called news, which every day arise and fly, like fleetest lightning flies or comet in the distant skies; or which like snow-balls on a hill roll on and roll and roll, roll still, and gather as they roll, until at length they break. In this expedition I learned that the victorious Whigs are already quarrelling among themselves about the spoils of office. Some are modest enough to ask for only one half of the offices in the country, but the great majority would like to have all. Their present victory will be like those of Phyrrus—the fewer the better.[60]

21 November, Saturday.

This evening I began to write an oration to be delivered next Monday evening—if sooth my nerves hold out when the time comes.

22 November, Sunday.

I have been hard at work all day in what is for me a new branch of business—speech-making. And it is a reflection drawn from experience, that Demosthenes and Cicero deserved all the fame they attained to. If I may judge of their sweat by my own their labors produced more than enough perspiration to quench all the fire their eloquence could kindle.

23 November, Monday.

This morning I finished my speech in great haste and without following the advice of Horace; "*Sape stylum vestas.*"

60. Greek general and statesman Pyrrhus (*c.* 318–272 B.C.) is famous for the remark, "One more such victory and I am lost."

In the evening Messrs. Cowperthwait, Baxter, Sage, Ogden, Stivers, McKnight,[61] and another young man besides myself, met in pursuance of the . . . notice, which I had printed and circulated. . . .

Here then is the result of all my harangues and placards and circulars! Only seven young men out of a population of between three and four thousand, who are ashamed to be asses! Fie on the blackguards! I am done with them.

The speech which I had written with so much pains never left my breeches pocket; and all the fine gestures which I had rehearsed before the looking-glass were in vain. But "better luck next time" as the fellow said when the halter broke!

24 November, Tuesday.

Nothing of great moment occurred to-day. I spent an hour or two in Philadelphia; but saw nothing that is not always to be seen in a city full of fools, as what city is not?

25 November, Wednesday.

This evening the Course of Lectures before the Washington Library Company, was opened by David Paul Brown,[62] on Eloquence; and though the weather was exceedingly unpleasant, the streets extraordinarily wet and muddy, and the chances altogether against us, we had an uncomfortably full house. This lecture was gratis—therefore the good people of Camden would have turned out in a Greenland night to patronize us. The next lecture is not gratis, and the good people of Camden, therefore will see us hanged before they attend, although the night be as balmy as Cuba's, and as free of clouds as the summit of Mont Blanc, on a midsummer noonday.

Mr. Brown is a good orator, a tolerable scholar, and a very vain man. He has a costly finger ring and a pearly set of teeth, which he delights to display. His voice now resembles a hoarse whirlwind, and now the thin, sweet notes of the Aeolian harp. He looks what he speaks, and addresses our eyes and ears at the same time. His forehead is high, and his eye is keen and expressive; his nose is flattish, his nostrils large, and his lips thick and heavy, which features have led some to suppose that he is partly a Negro. In short, he is a man to whom we might listen for a week, and learn nothing at last. His manner pleases; but his matter is either borrowed or stolen from the Latin writers, with whom he appears to be perfectly familiar. His style is zig-zag and incoherent; with some beautiful expressions, more

61. John Baxter was a tailor at Third and Federal Streets, Miles Sage a carpenter, and William McKnight a coach-trimmer.
62. Brown (1795–1872), a prominent Philadelphia lawyer since 1816, was a highly regarded orator, noted for his florid style.

mere commonplace, and many, entirely in bad taste, for in his speeches, as on his person, he is too fond of tinsel.

The lecture was very well received; and, to the infinite horror of the deacons of the church in which it was delivered, some carried their admiration so far, as to clap and stamp! This was especially the case when he illustrated the power of eloquence by saying that "had any merchant a Cicero for a salesman, he would sell all the merchandise in Market Street in a half an hour," adding in a jocular tone a pleasant satire on the times, "but I would not like to say that he could induce people to pay for what they bought, so easily."

In the course of a conversation with the committee which waited on him, he said he had a young man to come to his house every evening, with his pen and inkhorn, who took down his words as he delivered them, walking about the room. In this way, he told them, all his lectures and court-speeches were manufactured, without any labour to himself.

Mr. Brown is a Jerseyman by birth, but practices law in Philadelphia.

26 November, Thursday.

What a wonderfully grateful people we are! We will see the few old veterans of the Revolution, who still survive, starve in unhonoured poverty before us, nay we will throw them, all hacked and scarred for our benefit, into an ignominious prison for a paltry debt; but after they are once dead we scratch up their bones, and place them in a coffin, the cost of which would make the declining days of a dozen old soldiers, cheerful and comfortable; and after carrying them through the streets with a long parade of fifes and drums and banners, bury them again, with a grand oration, amidst the roar of artillery, the peal of chimes, and a discord of all horrible sounds; with a great ado of praying, and psalm-singing, and paeans, and all that sort of thing; and finally end the farce by placing over them a splended monument, carved with quotations from Homer, Saint Paul, Don Quixotte and Botta's *History,* and conclude the whole by having a splendid frolic, with abundance of dancing, and singing, and a superabundance, of course, of rum.

These remarks are elicited by having seen the second funeral of the gallant [*Gen. Hugh*] Mercer (who fell at Princeton) which was celebrated to-day in Philadelphia with great ceremony and folly. He had been buried in Christ Church yard in Second Street, and I have no doubt slept there in peace. But a certain Saint Andrew's Society must needs anticipate the Judgement day, and bring to light again all that time and the worms had left of the old General. He was dug up, and carried through the town, followed by his son and the Governors of Pennsylvania and Virginia, and a long train of military, to **Laurel Hill Cemetry**, where he was again buried, not forever, but until such time as the eccentric gratitude of this great nation shall again call him to resurrection, and carry his ashes thro' the streets, to the infinite merriment of the delighted boys. . . .

28 November, Saturday.

This morning I went to Philadelphia; in the afternoon, I staid at home, reading. My cousin and namesake paid me a short visit towards evening, and I find he is a pretty intelligent lad. He has read more books than I; and understands them, it is no compliment to him to say, quite as well. . . .

29 November, Sunday.

I have been employed to-day in writing a Code of Laws for the Debating Society that is, or is not to be, as to-morrow night will decide. I had one advantage in composing my laws which Solon had not in composing his: there was no bore at my elbow, tearing me with silly questions, and telling me that I was spinning spider-webs.

1 December, Tuesday.

Old Winter, like all other tyrants, begins his reign with a wonderful mildness. One might almost be led to suppose, by observing the weather to-day, that rough Boreas, forgetful of his ancient pranks, lay among the glens of the Alleghanies, sleeping the sleep of death. This is a suspicious circumstance, however; and should rather put us upon our guard against frozen noses and frosted feet, than lull us into a false security. The ominous crows are flying to the generous south: and a threatening ring has encircled the moon for several nights. Unpleasant prognostications, these, for the woodless poor—whom, with all my heart I pray, God protect!

Notwithstanding the severity of the circumambient atmosphere, and the seducing allurements of Terra's physiognomy, seducing at least to all who are predisposed rather to peregrination, than a sedentary application to intellectual pursuits; notwithstanding, all this, I say, I staid at home, and read a dozen pages in——the adventures of *Valantine and Orson!*[63]

I translated, also, one, or nearly one, of Cicero's *Orations*. Then eat my supper—And went to bed!

2 December, Wednesday.

Samuel S. E. Cowperthwait, being by me to day fully and duly

---

63. *Valentine and Orson* was a French romance first published in English in 1550.

questioned, deposeth and saith: That John K. Clement, of the city and township of Camden, in the county of Gloucester and state of New Jersey, saith: that on Monday night last, he heard Isaac Mickle, also of the city, township, county and state aforesaid, read a speech before the assembled young men of the said city; and that in his opinion, the same was very—that is to say—quite—he meant, tolerably—passable. . . .

This evening, the Reverend George Chandler[64] delivered the Second Lecture of the Course, before the "Washington Library Society," President of which, I have the honour and so forth to be. There was a better attendance than I expected; but a far worse speech than I had looked for. In short, like many of his reverend brethren, Mr. Chandler's more than half an ass!

4 December, Friday.

It has been snowing nearly all day; and I have been meanwhile "taking my case in mine own inn," now reading the odes of Horace, and, anon, looking out at the window upon the tempestuous weather, with a thought and a sigh for the cheerless poor. Charitable wishes are cheaper than charitable deeds, but pass in fame on a par with them. Therefore, consulting both economy and glory, I wish as follows: May no lazy loafer freeze to death in the midst of Loco-foco matches and a pine forest.[65] This reminds me of the mooted question in moral philosophy, as to whether a man is justifiable, who steals to preserve life. These are my sentiments upon the subject: To die when it is in one's power to live, is suicide. Suicide is always a sin. To freeze to death when your neighbour has a pile of wood next door, is, to die when it is in your power not to die. Therefore it is suicide. Wherefore to steal so much of that wood as will keep you alive, is not only a justifiable act, but one which is your duty to do.

5 December, Saturday.

The snow still continues to fall and drift in huge banks.

6 December, Sunday.

All day to-day has it been snowing incessantly. The house I live in is built, like, in a measure, to Hodge's razors—**to rent.**[66] The snow leaks in under the door and around the windows; and there are great banks

64. Rev. George Chandler was pastor of the First Presbyterian Church of Kensington.

65. Loco-focos were originally self-igniting matches which soon would give their name to an equal rights faction of the Democratic party and later would become a nickname for Democrats in general.

66. Mickle puns on two of the meanings of the word "rent." The identification of "Hodge's" is obscure.

and hills of it in every room. With my whole corpus stowed into the fireplace I spent the day in reading Pitkin's *History*.

7 December, Monday.

At the meeting of the Henry Institute to night, there were present: John H. Baxter, John K. Clement, Lemuel Davis, Elwood Fortiner, Samuel Fortiner, John Hazard, Isaac Mickle, Mr. Mulford, George Ostler, William Rogers, Miles Sage, Henry Samuels, and Gideon V. Stivers....[67]

8 December, Tuesday.

This morning I set up and printed two pages of the Code of laws of the Institute; taking the responsibility of amending it wherever I thought it needed amendment. In the afternoon I read some of Sallust and a good deal of Pitkin.

9 December, Wednesday.

The weather is mild; and the snow fast disappearing. In the evening Mr. Chauncy P. Holcomb[68] lectured before the Library on the "Fine Arts." The discourse in matter was excellent, in manner, contemptible. Among many striking passages I remember only the following: Speaking of the neglect which the arts meet now-a-days, he said, "in this money making age, people had rather have the lands of their friends than their likenesses; and if they had the latter, some would pawn them away to see Fanny Ellsler!"[69] Again, "We know more of the character of Washington from his pictures, than his biography." This last is perhaps more original than true.

10 December, Thursday.
Staid at home, reading.

11 December, Friday.
Printing.

12 December, Saturday.
In the morning went to Philadelphia; in the afternoon, reading.

13 December, Sunday.
The registry of this day is negative: I did not go to church.

67. Mickle's efforts to found a new debating society for young men had met with considerable success. "The Code of Laws of the Henry Institute," dated 1 December 1840, lists the names of thirty-two members. Of those mentioned for the first time here, Samuels and Rogers were local carpenters, Hazard a map-engraver, Samuel Fortiner a stone mason, Elwood Fortiner a saddler, George Ostler a laborer, William B. Mulford a cooper, and Davis a student.
68. Holcomb was a Philadelphia attorney with offices at 91 Walnut Street.
69. Fanny Ellsler (1810–84), an enormously popular dancer, had performed in Philadelphia's Chestnut Street Theatre in November 1840.

15 December, Tuesday.
To day I staid at home, reading.

16 December, Wednesday.
This evening Mr. Morris,[70] a late traveller in Palestine, lectured before the Library on Petrae, the doomed city. His discourse was very instructive, and entertaining.

17 December, Thursday.
I finished my book this evening, and bound four or five copies. It is the Code of Laws of the Institute; was written, set up, printed, bound, and published by my own unassisted labour. The pages are about two inches square, and there are twelve of them. No regular printer could have done it much better!

18 December, Friday.
Finished Pitkin's history; and regret to find that a careful perusal only strengthens the impression which I expressed of it, on the first of last November. . . . Towards the end especially his kink is very evident.

19 December, Saturday.
Mr. David Paul Brown lectured to-night in the Methodist Church, on the Human Passions. He was eloquent, as usual; but his wit was most intolerably stale. When a man begins to crack jokes on the respectable fraternity of bachelors, you may set his wit down at a pretty low ebb.

20 December, Sunday.
To-day I finished Sallust, and began Virgil. In the latter I read just one hundred lines. I am convinced that the classics are productive of not a great deal of good: but since I have undertaken the job, I intend to go through with it. It is about a year since I began to read Caesar with Mr. Aaron, in Burlington. At that time I could scarcely parse *"terra est rotunda."* Since then I have read a good deal in Ovid, several of the Satires of Juvenal, all of my friend Sallust's *Catilina,* some of Cicero and Horace, and now am about to begin Virgil. There has not been much method to my studies; but this much I can say with a clear conscience: Whatever I have read, I have understood. As for my graecism—alas! my Greek, like the woman's butter, when she stopped churning, has all gone back. And my French too! Three years ago I could read French like a veritable Gaul: now, I have to scratch my organ of concentrativeness (if that is what the phrenologists call it) before I can translate even the trite *"nous verrons."*

70. Edward Jay Morris (1815–81) was a Philadelphia legislator, diplomat, and author.

21 December, Monday.

I read to-day to the end of Virgil's Second Eclogue; having before me the translation of Dryden; which, while it does not help the reader to go right, prevents him from going wrong. . . .

22 December, Tuesday.
Read the third Pastoral of Virgil, and—

23 December, Wednesday.
the fourth, and—

24 December, Thursday.
the fifth.

25 December, Friday.

I went a-skating a little while this morning, then returned home and read Virgil's sixth Eclogue, sat down and ate a Christmas dinner with my own little family, although I had four invitations to dine out; and after that went to Philadelphia, for the same purpose for which most people go, "to see and be seen."

26 December, Saturday.

To-day I performed my task, and read *Virgilii septimam eclogam.* Maro's[71] verse, after all, is not so difficult as I was induced to believe it.

27 December, Sunday.

. . . I . . . read my portion of Virgil, to wit, the eighth eclogue, marking with a pencil, as is my custom, all the passages remarkable either for poetry or sense.

28 December, Monday.

Read the ninth eclogue, and half of the tenth. After which I went to the city, and bought a New Year's Present for my cousin Anna Mulford, to wit, one of Peter Parley's interesting little books.[72]

29 December, Tuesday.

Half an eclogue more, and I will be through Virgil's pastorals! That—ahem!—that half, for some reason or other—ahem! I did not get through to day.

30 December, Wednesday.

My industrious fit has left me, and I am, what nature made me— lazy. I tried three times to-day to finish Maro's tenth eclogue, and each trial put me to sleep, sound and snoring sleep! Well, did not

71. Maro was Vergil's cognomen.
72. Peter Parley was the pen name of Samuel Griswold Goodrich (1793–1860), who wrote about 170 "little books."

Goldsmith use to throw his slippers at his candle, to put it out? All genii are lazy—aye, say you, but all the lazy are not genii! Be this as it may—I sometimes feel most inexpressibly languid; which is the effect, I dare say, of too hard study! Sometimes after I have been reading too closely for an hour or two, when I rise from my chair, my head swims around, my eyes fail, my steps totter, and I hardly know where I am, or where I want to be.

Mr. Chauncey Buckley[73] lectured to-night before the library Company, on "Spain, under the Moors." Were Mr. Buckley an intimate friend of mine I would hint to him, very modestly, that when a person attempts to teach others what he does not know himself, he generally manages to make himself appear very like an ass. The manner and matter of the lecturer was (excuse the number, grammatical reader!) very un-oratorical.

31 December, Thursday.

With a desperate resolution I attacked the remaining half of Virgil's tenth eclogue, to-day, and conquered it! As my learned friend, Mr. Cox, *Bachelor Artium*, would say, *"Nil desperandum!"* By the by, this same Cox is one of the most eccentric fellows that I ever saw. He was born in "the fast anchored isle," and educated at Cambridge, where he took the degree of A.B., which he never fails to attach to his name. What citizen of Camden has not read at the end of some pompous Circular the still more pompous "O. Cox, A.B.?" But to proceed with my narrative. Being an ardent lover of liberty, and of a temper, withal, somewhat romantic; as soon as he left his Alma Mater he bade adieu to the fogs and royalty of old England, and sailed to this, our western world, in search of that liberty which he had read of in the classics, but could not realize at home. By what means he reached Monmouth Court House in this state, deponent knoweth not; but certain it is, he there married a blowsy, barbarian looking woman, not the smallest of whose charms, perhaps, was, that she owned the farm on which the celebrated battle of Monmouth was fought, during the Revolution.

After carrying Virgil's *Georgics* into practice until he was well nigh starving to death, he emigrated again, and, as they say at the west, "hung out his shingle" in Camden, as "an instructor of youth;" stating in a very pompous circular, over the very pompous "O. Cox, A.B." (O! Phoebus, what a name!) that he took that step not from any pecuniary motives, but merely with a desire to afford himself amusement.

I entered his school and staid three years. My chief employment during this time was writing letters to a little girl who lived next door.

73. Chauncey Bulkley, a Philadelphia attorney since 1822, had offices on Prune Street.

This brought me into many scrapes, and collisions with my potent rival, Frank Browning;[74] and often, I ween, did I belabour him for undermining me in her affections! The worms now crawl in and out of his once beaming eyes—peace to his ashes! I loved thee, Frank, e'en while I beat thee! May I hope that though I have a friend less on earth, I have an angel more in heaven? If I persue this digression—but no matter!—**weep** for a friend? Pshaw! the callous world would call it childish.

But though I learned nothing else under the guidance of Mr. Cox, he at least gave me a relish for composition. Somebody has said, "it is a pleasing task to teach the young idea how to shoot." Mr. Cox was doubtless influenced by this poetical proverb when he commenced keeping school for amusement! But he must have been reminded that "all general rules have exceptions" when the first of my ideas that exploded shot **him**! I was aware that abuse is the easiest of all tasks, and consequently in my first theme, made a rude but severe experimental charge on schoolmasters in general, and English schoolmasters in particular. Though this excited his British spleen at first, we were soon reconciled; and passing a compliment on my composition he ironically advised me to give my thoughts to the public, through the press: another mode of "amusement" which he occasionally resorted to, when his other resources failed.

Well, time passed on, and I continued to submit my weekly essays to his eye; but I had not forgotten the ironical expression of his face when he advised me to print. At length the opportunity for retribution came. In one of his newspaper peices Mr. Cox had violated one of the rules of English Grammar. Taking his irony literally, I **did** print, over an anonymous signature, a crude but bitter notice of my learned tutor's blunder. Soon after this, in another of his articles, the printer made him blunder most egregiously in a Latin quotation. Little as I knew of the language at that time, I discovered the error, however, and seizing upon it, imputed it to the ignorance of the author, and trusting to my mask, dealt some pretty spiteful thrusts. He, being so intimate with my style, could not fail to know where these firey squibs came from; and the consequence of his knowledge was, that we again were, to use modest words, two persons. When I look back at that period of my life, I cannot imagine how I escaped the birch which I so richly deserved.

"It's a long lane" says the proverb, "that has no turn." There was a Waterloo for Napoleon, and I too met a reverse. Flushed by these

---

74. Benjamin Franklin Browning (d. 1839) was a close boyhood friend of Mickle's who had died of scarlet fever in his late teens.

successes, and fancying myself gifted with the armour of Achilles, I plunged into a criticism of some miserable trash which a certain Priscilla Budd[75] had served up to the public; and prefaced my critique with a quotation from that egotistic ode of Horace, wherein he promises himself immortality, with so much candour. By some unlucky oversight, however, I copied the very first word of it wrong. This brought on a newspaper war, in which I, attempting to defend my blunder, was murdered without quarter. Mr. Cox, over the signature of "Beta," John Clement, . . . over that of "Timotheus," Mrs. Budd, herself, as "Q," and the Editor of the *Republican*, overwhelmed me with dictionaries and doggerel, and drove me entirely off the field. The editor of the *Mail*, Mr. Gray, being unacquainted with Latin, misprinted nearly every quotation which I dug up, and scattered in the air that I might retreat with a better grace. I quoted from half the authors in the language, and at the same time could not have conjugated *amo*, had it been for my life!

But hark! the old clock below me announces with all its tongues the approach of a stranger.

One! two! three! four! five! six! seven! eight! nine! ten! eleven! twelve! !

Year of our lord, One thousand eight hundred and forty, farewell!

Reader! whether friend or enemy, I wish thee many, many happy days! Fare thee well! **Fare thee well!**

The principle events of the year which has just ended, have been as follows: In our own country: the defeat of the democratic party, by a system of electioneering that never has been equalled, and I hope never will; and the visit of the celebrated dancing-girl, Fanny Ellsler. This woman was the mistress of young Napoleon, and once, it is said was most beautiful. The excitement which her coming among us caused, exceeded anything that the reader can imagine. Poor devils who could hardly procure bread to eat at common times would manage by hook or by crook to purchase a sight of the environs—of what was significantly called "Napoleon's grave," and in some cases as much as ten dollars was paid for a seat when she danced. She exhibited at Chesnut Street Theatre in Philadelphia, and the good people of that quiet city almost went crazy on the important occasion. In Baltimore, to the everlasting glory of the Monumental city, some dandies who could not jam into the Theatre to see her legs, adopted the only expedient that was left them, and harnessed themselves to her carriage and actually pulled her to her lodgings! For once, at least, the asses

75. Priscilla B. Budd (d. 1866) was the wife of Paul C. Budd, a house painter and coach painter who later served four terms as Camden's mayor.

were in their proper places! This harlot has gone from one end of the country to the other, cutting pidgeon-wings and showing her limbs to crowded houses, for which she receives five hundred dollars a-night; while a virtuous woman in the exercise of any honest and honorable calling, might toil long years without receiving an equal sum. As Sallust says of Sempronia, so it might be said of Fanny Ellsler, "*Saltare elegantius quam necesse est probae.*"[76] Indeed, her exhibitions, as I have been informed, transcended all modesty, even that which Shakspeare speaks about, "the modesty of nature," for if she had merely exposed her naked charms without the inflaming addition of voluptuous music, her visit would have exerted less bad influence upon the minds of young men.

The Census of the United States was also taken this year for the sixth time. The population of the country is not yet published by the officers at Washington. I will guess that it is sixteen millions.

In the world, the following are the great events: the Chinese war: the birth of a princess royal in England; the removal of the ashes of Napoleon. The Americans burn with indignation at the first of these; joke about the second; and are glad at the third. The universe condemns the wrongs practiced upon the Chinese by the English: and every admirer of the genius of Napoleon is glad that his bones repose once more in the bosom of his "*belle France.*"

The boundary question, between Maine and New Brunswick is about as near settled now, at the end of the year, as it was at the beginning of it.[77]

76. Mickle knew this quotation from his reading of Sallust's *Conspiracy of Catiline*. Sempronia was the wife of Decimus Junius Brutus and the mother of Decimus Brutus, one of Caesar's assassins.

77. The boundary had been in question since the Peace of Paris in 1783. War seemed probable in 1838–39 when Canadians refused to leave the disputed Aroostook region. A truce, declared in March 1839, remained in effect until the Webster-Ashburton Treaty established the present boundary in 1842.

St. Mary's Hall, and Bishop Doane's Residence, Burlington

1841

1 January, Friday.

I begin with the new year a new volume of my Diary; convinced by the experience of six months that a little time can be spared very well out of every evening, for the recording of things done, sights seen, news heard, emotions felt, and thoughts occurring, during the day. . . .

The weather has been remarkably fine all day. But nevertheless, being resolved to make an industrious beginning of the new year, I remained in the house, reading Anthon's *Blackstone.* In the evening I stepped around to John Baxter's[1] tailor shop, which is the head-quarters of a clique of young men of a certain class, with whom I choose to become just so intimate, and no more. Most of them belong to the Institute . . . and one of them, a Welshman, named Henry Samuels, is certainly an extraordinary fellow. He is stout built, and stumpy, as to his frame—his forehead as high as Daniel Webster's, his eye keen as the eagle's. In debate, his voice is flexible, although his pronunciation is a little faulty; his gestures vehement, and his percep-

1. Mickle's friend Baxter ran a tailor shop on the corner of Third and Federal Streets.

111

tion of the weak side of his adversary's argument, instantaneous. Although he planes and bores from sunrise to sunset, yet when he rises on the floor of the debating society to speak, he often shames those who have all the time to read, and as many books as they can ask for. To obtain a victory over "little Samuels" as he is called, is a matter not easily to be boasted of.

4 January, Monday.

The intense cold still continues. The Delaware is fast "in icy fetters bound," this morning for the first time this winter. Consequently I left Virgil and Blackstone to themselves for an hour or two this forenoon, and went a-skating. One of my comrades broke through, and came near being drowned; and after that I thought it prudent to return.

In the evening the Institute met and discussed the following question: In which history are the more admirable characters to be found, the history of Greece or that of Rome? It fell to my lot to open, on the side of Greece. I spoke twice, about ten minutes each time; but as I have no notes of what I said, I cannot recal my words to memory. The council gave the decision in our favour, for which compliment I thanked them; and then we adjourned.

5 January, Tuesday.

I ventured on the river again this morning, and skated till noon. The remainder of the day I passed in reading.

6 January, Wednesday.

William N. Jeffers, Esquire, lectured to-night before the Library Company upon the "Judicial Office." The lecture was interesting enough, but the attendance, owing, as the speaker observed in his introduction, "to the warring of the elements and the bad walking," was slim. It has been raining all day, and the streets be literally flooded. . . .

8 January, Friday.

The tide in the Delaware, at one o'clock, POST MERIDIEN, is uncommonly full. The ice in the channel is all afloat, in consequence of the warm rains which have been falling for the past two days.

I spent an hour or two with Doctor Mulford, this evening; and I could not have otherwise passed the time more instructively.

9 January, Saturday.

Will be long remembered for a fresh in the Delaware, a greater than which has never occurred in the recollection of the oldest men. The tide was at its maximum at two o'clock this afternoon; at which time a wherry loaded with passengers was rowed from Kaighn's

Point up to the Amboy Rail Road, directly over the highway; which was submerged to the depth of three feet. Houses in Fetterville were entirely surrounded by the invading water, and their occupants were obliged to get one pair of stairs higher in the world. In Philadelphia, boats might have been rowed straight up Market to Water Street. The New York cars returned to Camden this morning, having been stopped by a breach in the road at Rancocas Creek, across which the conductor borrowed my skiff to ferry the passengers. This fresh has been caused by the melting of the snows to the northward.

I never changed my slippers to day; but remained at home, reading Virgil's *Georgics*. I made out to get through a hundred lines.

10 January, Sunday.
Accounts of the destruction caused by the late freshet are hourly arriving. Ruins of bridges, cabins, and what not, are drifting with the rapid ebb down the river. Some of these come from fifty miles above Bordentown. There was no perceptible flood at all, in the river, to day—the fresh, discharging itself very rapidly down the stream, overruled the influx from the ocean altogether.

11 January, Monday.
The extraordinary mildness of the weather for a week past, still continues. A week ago I was skating where now vessels of all kinds are sailing about with nothing to hinder their progress. Even in my recollection, no such weather as this was experienced in January. And as civilization fells the western forests, our winters will continue to decrease in severity, until they are as moderate as in the corresponding latitudes of Europe. Boreas, passing now over millions of smoking chimnies, does not feel so piercing, as when he met nothing in his path but snows, from which the ancient forest trees kept the genial sun. . . .

13 January, Wednesday.
. . . There was no lecture to night, in consequence of Mr. Job R. Tyson,[2] (the lecturer intended) having a nervous wife! A pretty excuse, forsooth, for a man of business! Men should promise slowly but perform surely.

15 January, Friday.
To-day the Philadelphia Banks resume specie payments. The "United States" was in particular pushed.[3] The crowd of applicants reached clear into the street.

2. Tyson (1803–58) was a Philadelphia lawyer and historian, and later a Whig congressman.
3. Nicholas Biddle's former Bank of the United States, now operating under a Pennsylvania charter, had insufficient specie to meet the demands of its creditors.

16 January, Saturday.

The run upon the United States Bank still continues. Mrs. Scull,[4] our landlord and next door neighbour was over this morning, to get some of her promises redeemed; and says that the applicants at her counter formed a line as at the elections in great cities, the last comer taking the last place, and waiting till all before him had been accommodated. The people have been robbed and tantalized by the rascally Banks to such a degree that I for one would not have wondered if they had served it as the Frenchmen did the Bastille—meaning by it, the dam of all the thousands of villian spawns which curse our country, "the United States."

18 January, Monday.

Laying aside Scrapio, at which I had been industriously at work since breakfast, I pulled on my boots after supper, this evening, and went around into Front Street as usual, with the intention of hearing a debate before the Institute. But when I arrived at the hall, lo! the door was shut and the interior dark! The committee had changed the place of meeting without notifying us. After some trouble, and having nearly perished with the cold, I found the Society at Miss Turner's school room,[5] nearly ready to proceed with the discussion.

The question was: Which have suffered more by the discovery of America, the Indians or the Negroes? In the affirmative were Messrs. Elwood Fortiner, Cowperthwait, and Baxter; in the negative Messrs. Garwood, Stivers, Samuels; in the chairs, Messrs. Samuel Rogers, Josiah Rogers, and George Spain;[6] in the house a full attendance.

Mr. Fortiner said he had come unprepared, but still he would say something. He said the very ground we stood on was once owned by the Indians; and after drawing a brief picture of the Sufferings which that unhappy race have suffered from the cupidity and cruelty of the whites, remarked that he was "spun out," and sat down.

Mr. Garwood followed—all gesticulation, all blunders, all nothing at all. This gentleman is one of those who can say anything very well, when luckily he has anything to say, which, owing to his having a dull fancy and a scanty library, does not often happen.

Mr. Cowperthwaite advanced this syllogism: "A being that has no brains can feel no sufferings; a negro has no brains; therefore a negro can have no sufferings." The other side had admitted the premises of no brains no pains. He was labouring with some chance of success to demonstrate the second member of his proposition, when the speaker

4. Merchant Joab Scull and his wife lived at the corner of Second and Federal Streets.
   5. Turner's school was on Camden's Third Street, between Market and Arch.
   6. Hamilton C. Garwood was a local dry goods merchant, Josiah Rogers a carpenter, and George Spain a cooper.

tapped his watch to signify that the allotted time had been taken up. . . .

Mr. Stivers next rose. With his foot on the bench and his elbow on his knee, he went to work at the last gentleman's sophistry slowly but surely. After quoting abundantly from Abolition pamphlets, he gave room to Mr. Baxter, who whispered an excuse for having nothing to say, and resumed his seat.

Mr. Samuels followed brilliantly, with a stirring account of the wrongs of the red man. His speech, which I saw him composing at night in a carpenter shop, with one dim light set upon the best desk he could procure, to wit, a workbench, was a surprizing effort for one in his circumstances. To assist such as he was always to me a source of pleasure; and I have the satisfaction of knowing that though I myself neglect my books too much, more than one friendless carpenter boy has had easy access to them.

After the six debaters had spoken in replication, the reader's humble servant rose and said, that he had listened attentively and with no less pleasure than edification to the eloquent debate just closed. He felt assured that while so much spirit was evinced in the discussions on that floor, tomb-stones and epitaphs would be articles for which the Institute would have no demand. He then reviewed the arguments pro and con, and dwelt especially on the ingenious sophistry of Mr. Cowperthwaite. He said it was his unprejudiced conviction after what he had heard, that the negative side, whether they got the reward, or not, deserved it; and having recited Cowper's well known "Negro's Lament,"[7] took his seat, after speaking fifteen minutes.

Mr. Davis had been led to a different conclusion from me; and was in the act of showing why "by sines and tangents straight" when he was called to order.

The Council decided unanimously in the negative.

19 January, Tuesday.

Read a volume of Walter Scott's *Tales of Scotland*. Elwood Fortiner called upon me this afternoon, to borrow a book. He is a pious young man, and has some pretension to Biblical learning. To find him something to do therefore, I pointed out to him [2] Chronicles, 21:20, and *ejusdem*, 22:2, and asked him to reconcile the two texts.[8] He read

---

7. William Cowper (1731–1800) wrote "The Negro's Complaint," an anti-slavery monologue, in 1788.

8. The first passage relates that Jehoram began his reign as king of Judah at age thirty-two and ruled for eight years. The second passage says that his son Ahaziah succeeded him, beginning his reign at age forty-two. Thus the son appears to have been two years older than his father. Modern biblical scholars believe that the author of this passage meant to write Ahaziah's age as twenty-two when he became king.

them over, and was surprised he had never noticed the unaccountable paradox before. He said he would ask the minister about it, and tell me how he clears up the thing. It is strange to me that so palpable a mistake should have slipped through the paws of so many learned translators and revisers.

20 January, Wednesday.

Mr. Sullivan[9] lectured this evening before us, upon the "Scenery of Switzerland." His youth was passed among the eternal Alps; and his lecture was of great interest and beauty. His manner was tame—his matter, "prose run mad." Much of it was of that kind of sublimated nonsense which nine out of ten love to listen to, once in a while. . . .

21 January, Thursday.

I read a hundred lines more of Virgil to-day. In the evening I called into a shoemaker's shop, where about a half a dozen men resort nightly to spend an hour or two, in telling what wonders they have seen in their past lives. John Potts, a blacksmith, has travelled a good deal in the southern states. He was saying to night that he had seen the Natural Bridge in Virginia, and gave me a full account of it. It is, he says, a hundred and twenty or thirty feet high; its thickness about thirty feet. Cedar Creek over which it passes, is fordable. There is a hole through the bridge, close to the wagon track, through which a horse might very easily fall into the water below. On the steep sides of the rocks of which this natural convenience is made, are sundry boards with the names of persons painted on them. It is a matter of dispute with the neighboring swains, who can affix his name in the highest and most difficult place. "The highest name, the greatest fool," we all exclaimed at this point of the narration. He says he rode over the bridge without knowing he had come to it. So did Bruce at the cataracts of the Nile. In the case of our traveller, it was owing to bushes which prevented him from seeing the water. Swallows skimming along below, look like flies. Water is continually oozing out of the "belly of the bridge," by which he meant its under side. And lastly, he says that the pictures in the geographies are pretty, nay, very, good representations of this great wonder. I often pick up in my wanderings about town, items of information, in this way. A shoemaker's shop sometimes holds more than lasts and awls.

25 January, Monday.

I finished to-day the second chapter of Gillie's Greece. In the evening I attended the meeting of the Institute, and was almost **forced**

9. John Turner Sargent Sullivan (1813–48), a native of Boston, had been educated in Germany and was currently practicing law in Philadelphia.

into reading my doggerel of Scrapio. I read three hundred and twenty five lines of it, somewhat to their diversion, as it would seem by their peals of laughter. . . .

26 January, Tuesday.

The sky was so clear and the atmosphere so spring-like, this morning, that I could not resist the temptation of a walk into the country. Sallying forth therefore from my narrow little study, and having stopped on my way at the bookbinder's in Fetterville, I went along the river-road through Kaighn's Point, down to my father's farm, and around home again by the Woodbury highway.[10] When fatigued, and more than half disgusted, with books, and tired of looking at the sameness of bricks and mortar, and displeased with myself and every body else; nothing does me so much good as to see the wide fields, and breathe for a little time the pure air of the country. The footage to-day was excellent. The farmers were employed in mending their banks and fences, singing as they wrought, some rustic ditty that showed their hearts light and their lots happy. The distant river seemed as if asleep, and the surrounding fields and meadows seemed about to wake, from the torpor of January, to the bloom and verdure of May. All that I saw and felt, tended to put me in a better humour with myself, my books, and the world; and so I returned about noon, not the loser by my ramble.

27 January, Wednesday.

Doctor Moriarty,[11] a Catholic priest from Philadelphia delivered the lecture before the Library Company to-night, upon Patriotism. Many pious Protestants were led to attend out of curiosity. They had an idea that a Roman Catholic was something like the devil. The house was crammed. The lecturer spoke in a very loud voice. When he began he almost frightened me off my seat. Among many new things he said that no state ever prospered when once the *novi homines* had got the rule. He recommended to all young men to study the classics, especially Demosthenes, Virgil, and Livy. He rebuked the new way of electioneering adopted by the whigs, in a most pointed manner, and concluded with a superb compliment to women in general, but American women in particular. The Doctor is an Irishman; about the middle stature, but very fat. He has a way of twitching in his right eye which one can never forget. He has gesticulation enough, such as it is; but on the whole is an eloquent man.

10. Mickle had walked to his birthplace, the farm called Walnut Grove, near the Delaware in what is today South Camden.

11. Patrick Eugene Moriarity (1804–75) was an Irish priest and temperance reformer, who had just settled in Philadelphia in 1839. A fine speaker, he soon became the most prominent priest in the area.

29 January, Friday.

To-day I have read fifty lines of Virgil, half of Cicero's oration against Caecilius, and two chapters of Gillie's *Greece*. Three cheers for—myself!

31 January, Sunday.

I spent the chief part of this day in reading Gillie. This learned volume has been laying for four years upon my shelves in *otio cum dignitate*; for I, terrified by its huge size, have never until recently opened it. I was under the impression that all big books were dry and wiredrawn; but this, I find, is an exception. I bought this and many other historical books with the sum of twenty dollars, which my respected mother gave me first and last for taking medicine. "In the days of other years" I would never swallow pill nor powder till I had received a Spanish dollar in my hand. Who but a bad boy would have asked, who but a kind mother have granted this?

The past month has been one of most remarkable mildness. In the memory of no one now living perhaps, was there ever a January so much like May. Since the freshet on the 9th the river has been clear of ice; and the thermometer since the 7th, has scarcely for an hour been below thirty-two degrees. . . .

1 February, Monday.

. . . *Sub Vesperâ*, as the ancients would say, I attended the Institute meeting; and had the honour of being called to preside, during the discussion of the following oft-discussed question: Should the slaves in these States be immediately emancipated? The matter was debated very ably by both sides, with the exception of what was said by a Charles Stone,[12] on the negative. He seemed to have thrown the alphabet into a bag, and shaken it up, and then brought out the words, syllables and letters, just as they came. He talked such prodigious nonsense, and made so many and so ludicrous gestures, that the whole house was in a peal of laughter; and none more than, reader, your humble servant, myself, albeit, I was in the chair.

2 February, Tuesday.

I began my task about ten o'clock this morning, and got through the hundred lines about two. After I returned from the meeting last night I read one of Scott's *Tales of a Grandfather* through, before I went to bed—which event, indeed did not happen until three o'clock this morning. I feel of course not a little drowsy.

In the evening I dropped in at the shoemaker's. The tale upon the

---

12. Stone was a Camden flour merchant.

tapis was of a cow in Newton township that used to stop at a certain place two or three times every day, while a very large blacksnake, obeying the signal which she gave, would come from his hiding place, and suck her dugs dry. I have heard of cows sucking themselves, but never before of their allowing a snake to do it. William Caum was the narrator; others present said they had seen the same thing. "Live and learn" is old advice, and good.

3 February, Wednesday.

Need I mention "a hundred lines" again? Hereafter I will record when I do not translate my tasks, not when I do.

Morton McMichael[13] lectured to-night. His subject was National Vanity. He drew the defining lines between pride and vanity, and gave the preference to the former. True pride is noble; the most pardonable vanity is degrading. Of the ancient world, Persia was vain, Greece proud; of Greece, Sparta was proud, Athens a little vain. Vanity was evinced when Xerxes cast his ridiculous fetters into the laughing sea; pride, when the Spartans offered retribution for the two heralds they had slain.[14] France is vain, as the late exhumation of Buonaparte will show, England, proud, as all her past history attests.

The lecturer now drew nearer home. The Americans he said are a proud people. They inherit it from their Saxon ancestors, and the tale of seventy-six fans the noble flame. They are proud of their glorious past, proud of the prosperous present, proud of the promising future. He then attempted to lift the veil of time, and show us what would be our condition in two centuries. Civilization then will have blent its tide with the wave of the Pacific. Three hundred millions of inhabitants will sing paeans to their national father, Washington. The fertile plains of Texas and Mexico will be ours. Our capital will be on the banks of the Mis'sippi. The Alleghanies and the Rocky Mountains will teem with an iron race of freemen warriors, panting for conquest and glory. Every sea will groan with our commerce; and at last the country from which we claim our origin, will become a province under the most mighty and splendid of republics, our own already invincible Columbia!

I accompanied Mr. McMichael to his lodgings, and in reply to a

13. McMichael (1807–79), a native of Bordentown, New Jersey, was a prominent Philadelphia newspaperman and later would become a leading Whig and Republican politician.

14. The historian Herodotus relates (7.35) that Xerxes, angry at the sea for interfering with his plans to invade Greece, ordered his men to whip it and throw a pair of fetters into it. The Spartans had killed Persian messengers sent to them by Xerxes' predecessor Darius, but offered atonement by sending two young warriors to offer their lives to Xerxes (Herodotus 7.134).

question I asked him, he said he was confident he had not overdrawn the picture.

4 February, Thursday.

. . . It is a strong argument against reading the classics in the original, that they all have been translated by such men as Pope, Dryden, Gifford and Moore.[15] I have sometimes doubted indeed whether the excellent translations which have been made of all the principal writers in Greek and Latin should not **altogether** supercede the study of them in the original. The Saxon, I am sure, would more become the decendants of Saxons.

5 February, Friday.

The moon to night at about nine o'clock, was in total eclipse. The sky was clear, and those who were in the open air had a fine view of the interesting phenomenon. For myself, I did not see her until she had nearly emerged; since I attended a lecture on Astronomy in the Baptist Church. . . .

6 February, Saturday.

In company with Edward Cole and Master Ogden from Philadelphia, I rode out to Joseph B. Cooper's this afternoon, to see his cabinet of coins and medals. He has a fine collection, worth perhaps eight hundred or a thousand dollars; and is a genuine virtuoso. He showed us also his galvanic battery, for copying medals, and gave me one, just taken out. We had a muddy ride and a pleasant visit. Mr. Cooper lives in Newton township, about two miles and a half from Camden.

The Library Company met in the evening, and re-elected me President. And when I declined the honour, they resolved to have no President during the present half year. Gideon V. Stivers is Vice President.

8 February, Monday.

My task in Latin to-day contained some excellent prescriptions for planting and cultivating trees. It will require more than Virgil's sweetness however, to persuade me to be a farmer. I would not wish, now, to disparage the rural life at all: it's the rural labour that I object to; and my author in the following lines does not tend to allay one's apprehensions on that subject: *"Redit agricolis labor actus in orbem Atque in se sua per vestigia volvitur annus."* **Liber II, 401.** . . .[16]

---

15. Alexander Pope (1688–1744) and John Dryden (1631–1700) are well known. William Gifford (1756–1826) and Thomas Moore (1779–1852) had published successful translations of ancient authors.

16. Mickle quotes Vergil's *Georgics*.

10 February, Wednesday.

As I was going to market this morning, I saw some men catch a miserable looking fellow who had stolen a shovel from Dock Street wharf. At the corner of Dock and Front, one of the men borrowed a cart-whip and slashed the poor devil over the face and eyes with more than a dozen violent strokes. The blood flew from his shirtless body at every cut, and at every cut the barbarous lookers on laughed immoderately. After the process was over, the loafer confessed the theft, and said he would steal again at the very first opportunity. They called him "Yach" and he is well known along shore. I learned from the bystanders that he was formerly a smuggler, and that he was only yesterday released from the Moyamensing prison.

Mr. Sullivan . . . lectured again this evening. His subject was The Secret Tribunals of Europe, during the middle ages. . . .

The lecturer speaks rapidly, has no action, is a fine looking young man, and pleased the ladies vastly.

13 February, Saturday.

The weather yesterday was intensely cold. The thermometer at nine o'clock, ANTE MEREDIAN, was at 6° only above zero. At the same hour at night it was still lower. At about four o'clock yesterday afternoon two men started in a batteau from Philadelphia, to go on board a sloop that lay off Cooper's Point. The river was full of drifting ice, and the crossing difficult even to the steamboats. Having broken one oar, our two men were left in a bad predicament. They became entangled among the floating cakes; drifted down to Fort Mifflin; turned, about midnight, and drifted up again with the flood; and were taken off by the steamboat *State Rights*, at nine this morning, opposite Windmill Island. They were temperate men, and well clothed, or else they must have perished. As it was, they say they several times despaired of ever seeing the end of the tedious night. By jumping, and swinging their arms violently, they were preserved. One had a pair of mittens, one of which he generously lent to his companion in distress. The unglov'd hand of either was very severely frozen.

I read a little in Gillie.

16 February, Tuesday.

I walked about two miles this forenoon, to arrive at some good skating: in which employment I amused myself till sunset.

18 February, Thursday.

There was a Concert this evening at the Baptist Church—admittance 25 cents—in aidance of their new house which was opened on the third of January. There were about thirty performers, instrumental and vocal, males and females, Jerseymen and Pennsylvanians, good and good for nothing. They sung Glory to the Highest on pianos, bass drums, violins, flutes, bugles, *et multa plura*; rather an odd medley for such a purpose.

Let me not forget to record *me fuisse captum amore manus puellae, tenuis, gracilis, voluptuosissimaeque.* I could not see the owner's face; but I **did** see her elegant hand, playfully dandling her bonnet string, and having seen I could look forever! My heart can resist the charms of the sweetest face; but such a hand as **that**—with its tapering, regular fingers, its clean, transparent and just-of-the-right-size nails, its snowy, dimpled back, its soft palm, its plump wrist—such a hand as that, I say, unmans, conquers, and leads me captive!

19 February, Friday.
My disease (*malum amoris*) begins to wear off. How happy is he who can love when he pleases! how much happier he who can stop loving when he has a mind to!

21 February, Sunday.
I wrote out a speech to-day, to be delivered to-morrow evening. I have deferred this business to the eleventh hour. But two or three paragraphs were finished, when I took it up this morning.

In the evening I went to the Baptist church; and had another glimpse at the pretty hand of the fair unknown. "Again the fires began to burn."

22 February, Monday, the Birthday of Washington, A.R. 65.
Master Cowperthwait and myself, having been appointed at a recent meeting of the Washington Library Company, to get the said Company incorporated, went this morning with that intent and purpose to the clerk's office, at Woodbury. The business was done "according to Gunter,"[17] and, having paid the fees, to wit, twenty five cents— how cheap are incorporations now-a-days!—we went to my Aunt Haine's, and dined. We returned at two o'clock, and I went at work at my speech. . . .

In the evening of this memorable day, I delivered . . . [my] Address. The gentleman, Mr. Cowperthwait, and the member, John K. Clement, who were to have spoken also, from some cause or other, did not do it. My feelings when I mounted the forum on this occasion were free from any thing of trepidation; which is more than I can say of any of my former attempts at rhetoric. There was a full attendance of the members in the house; and I have no doubt there was a considerable

17. "According to Gunter" was a nineteenth century equivalent of "according to Hoyle."

number of the public, **out** of it. At all our meetings, there is a gathering at the door to listen to us; but the mob never ventures to molest us. . . .

23 February, Tuesday.

The venerable Joseph Kaighn,[18] of Kaighn's Point, died this afternoon, about four o'clock. He was hard upon three score and ten; and his long life has been irreproachable. All symptoms of pain had left him for some time before his death; and, as his physician, Doctor Mulford, says, he died of pure exhaustion. He was perfectly aware that his end was approaching, and he met it, like a man, as emphatically he was.

I did nothing to-day, but rest from the effect of my last night's speech. In the evening I stopped at Heyl's Billiard Rooms.[19] The tables were full; but I know nothing of the game, and want to know nothing.

24 February, Wednesday.

William D. Kelly delivered the lecture to-night. He was given to metaphysics, and consequently the audience was given—to sleep! . . .

25 February, Thursday.

I went to town this morning, and bought the Comedies of Terence. In the evening I called at Weatherby's, and heard some queer ghost stories told. . . .

26 February, Friday.

Joseph Kaighn was this morning buried; and his funeral was very numerously attended. I did not go. I showed him all the respect I could, while he was alive, and while he was sensible of respect; and that is surely better than attending his funeral, as I have no doubt many did, to see how his parlours were furnished. The flags on the ferry-boats were at half-mast all day, as a token of regard to the departed Ferry President.

28 February, Sunday.

Two married ladies called upon me this afternoon, and found me with an open collar, and no boots, writing in my study. I promised to my literary friend, Mrs. Budd, a copy of my Oration for the Twenty Second. I felt not a little ashamed of being caught by such company, in such a plight; but nevertheless I was, and they seemed to be, grati-

18. Kaighn had been one of Camden's most prominent citizens, an early advocate of railroad construction, a prosperous ferryboat owner, and a popular Whig politician and legislator.

19. Elizabeth Heyl had now replaced Nathaniel Edmonds as proprietor of the Columbia Pleasure Garden.

fied by the visit. There was also a single lady present—to wit, my cousin Mary Mulford.

In the evening I went to hear Mr. Sparry[20] abuse the Roman Catholics at the Methodist Church. The house was perfectly crammed; for abuse is always relished. The man, in my opinion is either a fool or a lunatic—he talked utter nonsense.

1 March, Monday.

The weather with which Spring commences is fine, and the same adjective will apply, upon the whole, to the season which yesterday joined the eternity of the past. I do not remember of any winter less mild, and my oldest acquaintances say the same. The Delaware was only closed, opposite Philadelphia, for one night and a day; but this may be owing in a measure, to the continual efforts of the ice boats to keep it open.

I was chiefly employed, to-day, in writing. I follow this amusement, I fear, more industriously than is good for my health; but the days are now approaching for sweet walks among budding flowers and bubbling fountains, for sails and serenades, moonlight rambles with the girls, and other employments which I shall not fail to grasp—provided I don't begin the study of law before that happy time.

2 March, Tuesday.

. . . The day has gone, and how have I employed it? Certainly not with any profit to myself or my fellows: excepting that I payed an instalment of one shilling on a debt of two and sixpence which I owed the oysterman at the Railroad ferry. I am relapsing, I see plainly, into my old habits of laziness. To morrow, unless my resolution evaporate in the night, I must begin to read of "Arms and the man, who first from Troy"—[21]

Since I have nothing to say of myself to-day, let me record what I omitted in yesterday's entry: that I called upon Mrs. Budd, and gave her the promised copy of my speech. The news of her visit has flown like lightning, and I was told by my cousin this evening that three young ladies of Camden have expressed a wish to see my sanctum— What, tell me, o Fates, Muses, or Graces, or whoever can! what is coming? Is my little study, covered over as it is, with bachelor notions, to be an exchange, in which all the women of Camden, old and young, married and single, pretty, and ugly as the devil, are to meet to talk scandal? Forfend it! Are my books, my curiosities, my medals, my

20. Protestant minister Charles Sparry, an agent of the Protestant Reformation Society of New York, had recently been mobbed by Philadelphians enraged by his anti-Catholic diatribes.
21. Mickle quotes the first words of Vergil's *Aeneid*.

portraits, my drawings, my essays, and more than all, these, my precious diaries, to be overhauled and criticised by those most unfair critics, the ladies? Forfend it! I will put a bolt on my door, and enter and exit by the chimney first. I will—that's flat!

3 March, Wednesday.

. . . To-night, at twelve o'clock, the democratic administration of our government expires, and William Henry Harrison, whose laurels at Tippecanoe throw into the rear, all that Alexander reapt at the Granicus,[22] comes into power, followed by a set of brainless, characterless, dinnerless office-hunters, eager for the spoil of a battle, that is a disgrace to America, and, I fervently believe, the greatest triumph that the foes of America could have wished. And what a spectacle for the world! To see a consummate statesman, whose conduct has never been attempted to be impeached, discarded by an enlightened republic, in an enlightened age, to make room for a man whose services consist in having done for his country——God knows what! a man whose military reputation is most suspicious, whose civil talents are most debatable; a man whose only recommendation, (so far as I have been able to hear during the hot election of November) is, that he is a "General," that he lived in a log-cabin, smoked common cigars, and drank hard cider! What miserable appeals were these, to the most miserable weaknesses of Columbia's most miserable sons. And what complete success has followed such disgraceful means. . . .

But Martin Van Buren will have more friends in a month hence than he ever had before. They will be friends of interest according to their principal, I own; but these will count as much as any, in eighteen hundred and forty four, when, from present indications, the man of Kinderhook will enter the lists with Clay of the West. Meanwhile we who are out, will have the 'vantage-ground. They who oppose measures have that end of the pulling rope which has the knot at it; while the others hold a tapering extremity well greased, and hard to retain.

As it is our duty to love our country, in whatever hands her destinies are placed, may Harrison have the wisdom and firmness to govern her prudently and honourably! With this wish, I return my pen to the pidgeon-hole of my desk.

4 March, Thursday.

This is an eventful day for America! A misguided people have to-day entered upon an experiment fraught with weal or woe to the happiest land under the sun. It is an evil time to change, when there

22. Mickle sarcastically compares Harrison's victory over the Indians near the Tippecanoe River in Indiana, in 1811, with Alexander the Great's monumental defeat of the Persians in Asia Minor in 334 B.C.

is a good pilot at the helm, and nothing but rocks and whirlpools ahead. The prospect of a war, and a bloody one, with England, grows stronger every hour. The monetary embarrasments of our country increase every day. There is nothing but anticipations of the future, more unpleasant than the realizations of the past. General Harrison was elected as the dweller in a log-cabin. His friends, during the electioneering campaign cried loudly and piteously for a retrenchment of the presidential expenses; he himself on the hustings promised to "clean out the Augean stables." He is elected; but already has he asked for six thousand dollars to buy extra furniture for the White House! His friends cried unremittingly for the barring of Members of Congress from executive appointments. Their cry was heard by thousands of poor jackasses: but his Cabinet is chiefly composed of those who but yesterday sat in the legislature. If these be specimens of the promised "reform," what may we expect before his term shall have expired? If these things be done to day, what will the morrow reveal?

It is a curious fact, that on the day Mister Harrison entered Washington City, the hand of the goddess of liberty which bore the scroll of the Constitution, before the Capitol, fell to the ground. The *"E Pluribus Unum"* also fell from the talons of the eagle over the Vice President's chair in the Senate Chamber. Other strange things are said to have happened, among which, however, there was none that Harrison's friends dared to claim as an omen of any "consummation devoutly to be wished." It may do no harm to note such incidents as they occur. In other days, the hearts of patriots would have been grieved at even these trifling signs.

From this day forward, I will be a politician. From this day forward, I will oppose with my pen, my tongue, and all the brains I have, that miserable horde of beggarly gamblers in politics, who have sung and fiddled and lied and swindled themselves into power, for the sake of fingering the public purse. From this day forward, may I have the independence to attempt, and the ability to accomplish, a vindication of whatever I believe to be the good of my country, and a reprobation of all that I conceive to be her bane!

At the breakfast table this morning, I opened to my uncle my intention of studying law. He asked me if I had a wish to spend some time first at a College. I replied I had not. It was then settled that I should read in Philadelphia, and board at home. My respected mother fully consents to my choice of a profession; and for this, and for countless millions of other kind indulgences to the whims of her son, May God bless her! for He alone can requite a mother's love.

The President's Message was delivered to day at 12, and reached Philadelphia at 6 o'clock, E.

5 March, Friday.

I have done nothing pretty industriously this whole day. I lolled and gaped an hour or two in Heyl's billiard saloon, paid a visit to Doctor Mulford, and eat two pounds of figs. Beside this all I have done is to compose . . . [a] speech for Weatherby, my friend the shoemaker. I stopped at his shop to-day, when he told me that there was to be a caucus meeting at Elwell's in the evening, at which he wished a certain ticket to be taken up for the town election next Monday. But he anticipated objection to his nominations, to quiet which I gave him a "Speech." . . . I wrote it on his lap-board, not with an awl it is true, but with a thing that was but little better. He was perfectly satisfied with it, and promised to learn it by heart, and deliver it by mouth if one fellow dared to hesitate at his candidates. This is the beginning of my politics—humble enough, to be sure. . . .

6 March, Saturday.

To-night the first meeting of the Washington Library Company was held, since the same has been a corporate body. The following are the Trustees, elected on the twentieth day of last month, according to law: John R. Andrews, M.D.,[23] S. S. E. Cowperthwait, Edward Cole, Robert W. Ogden, James Ballantine, Gideon V. Stivers, and Isaac Mickle. These trustees have the power "to sue and be sued," to hold property, have a seal, and so forth, and so forth. . . .

Weatherby's ticket, I learn, was, sure enough, taken up last night, at the Caucus.

7 March, Sunday.

Samuel S. E. Cowperthwait and I hired a horse and vehicle this morning to go to Haddonfield to see our old acquaintances, the Shiverses.[24] Owing to the snow which fell yesterday morning and was melted by a rain in the afternoon, the roads were in a bad condition, in some places almost impassable. We got there however about eleven o'clock, and as the visitees had gone to meeting, we put up our horse and took a stroll over a portion of the ancient fields of the Haddon family. This town was occupied by detachments of both armies in the Revolution——the Americans evacuating at the approach of the British.[25] There is a member of our Institute, named Miles Sage, a carpenter by trade, whose grandfather was an American dragoon through

23. John R. Andrews (1818–64) had just graduated from Jefferson Medical College in Philadelphia.

24. Probably the Isaac Shivers family, who lived in Haddonfield from 1837 to 1842.

25. British forces occupied Haddonfield for one day during Donop's advance on Fort Mercer in October 1777 and again for two days in February 1778. American commanders stationed temporarily at Haddonfield included Gens. Nathanael Greene, "Mad" Anthony Wayne, and the Marquis de Lafayette.

all the war. He was among those who were stationed at Haddonfield, and had been sent into the country by his officer just before the British entered the town. The dragoon transacted his business, whatever it was, and gallopped back to Haddonfield, as he supposed, to his friends. The American "gridiron" still waved from the colour pole; and as he passed it, he huzzaed for "Washington and Independence." The sound had scarcely died away, when he was surrounded by Englishmen, who dragged him from his horse, stabbed him in fourteen different places with their bayonets, and left him for dead, in the middle of the main street, on the hill, near the south branch of Cooper's Creek. He was taken into the house by a kind old lady, who doctored his wounds, and at last effected a perfect cure. Sage lived to fight for his country in many another battle, and to tell the tale of his scars to his prattling grand children. Such incidents as these are worth preserving.[26]

Between twelve and one we dined at Shivers's, and afterwards took a walk to the house of Some of Cowperthwait's cousins. They are neat, jovial quaker girls, with soft hands, and open ears. Sam, presuming on the right of relationship, stole a handkerchief from one, and a kiss from another, the latter of which I confess I envied him more than the former. Their names are Eastlacks, and they are well-educated girls, with rosy cheeks, round breasts, and susceptible hearts.

At about four o'clock we started, in a shower of rain, for home; coming, for the sake of variety, by way of Mount Ephraim. The road was good enough until we came to the causeway over the Newton Creek meadows, about a mile west of the Mount, which, owing to the breach in the dam at the mouth of the creek, was covered with water. The tide was running out with great swiftness, foaming and splashing over the road in a manner by no means pleasant to me, who am unable to swim, even in summer time when the water is warm. We had driven so far on the narrow isthmus, that we could not turn our wagon, without getting off into deep-water. After deliberating awhile, we espied a house, not a great way off, upon our right; and began to cry "Murder! Murder" with all our lungs, hoping thereby to bring some one to the spot, of whom we might ascertain if there were any gullies in the causeway which it would be dangerous to attempt to pass. I remembered that Joseph Githens,[27] my uncle's tenant, had nearly drowned himself and two women by passing such a place at Kaighn's Point after the freshet in January; and so thought it prudent not to try the invisible track.

---

26. No record of military service exists for Miles Sage and the story of his wounding lacks documentation.

27. Githens rented one of the Mickle family dwellings at Poplar Hill.

Finding our cries unanswered, Cowperthwait proposed to wait until the water ran off; but I objected to this, since it was already growing dark, and since the horse's patience might be exhausted by standing with his feet in water of a temperature of not more than forty degrees above zero. Should he become restive, we were certain to be backed off into the creek. It was agreed that one of us should wade across to the other shore, and try the depth of the water. We cast lots, and the business fell to Sam's share. He stripped, therefore, like a man of honour, jumped into the almost freezing cascade, and sounded across it. Then, coming back, he led the horse to the other shore, and jumped aboard, benumbed, and blue all over. The water was up to the wagon body two or three times, in places where the road had been carried away; and once the vehicle swam, rather than ran upon the earth.

Sam had liked not to have got dressed again before we got to Camden; and the best of the joke was, we met a carriage load of girls, before he even had pulled his pantaloons on. He crept into the bottom of the wagon, of course, and lay there until the fair eyes were left astern. This was an adventurous ride, and I want no such again. At one time I really expected never to see the morrow, but still I could not help laughing at Sam's ridiculous plight. . . .

8 March, Monday.
Town-meeting was held to-day in Camden; and the ticket for which Weatherby, the shoemaker, caucased so industriously, was elected. I discovered this afternoon that the men for whom he has electioneered so hard, pledged themselves, that if elected, they would license the house which he keeps, in Bridge Avenue, to sell rum. He has kept a tavern for five years, in defiance of the license laws, and in the summer time does a good deal of business in his "Rail Road Garden"; in the winter he makes shoes; and contrives machines. On the whole, he is a clever fellow and a good citizen, and (the rum aside) a pious Christian.

Owing to the protracted meeting at the Baptist Church, there was no quorum to-night at the Institute.[28] Sam, however, was present, and I was glad to learn, had caught no cold from his yesterday's bath. We had a hearty laugh over our odd adventure. . . .

9 March, Tuesday.
I read about thirty lines of the third book of the *Georgics* this afternoon, which is the first interview I have had with Virgil for some

---

28. Evangelistic sects in the 1830s had developed the idea of the protracted meeting, a period of several days or longer when all the energies of the church—sometimes the entire town—were devoted to revivalistic activity.

time. O neglected poet! O lazy student! I doubt whether my Latin is learned as fast as it is forgotten. . . .

Tom Gray[29] informs me that his father has gone to Washington, to procure the office of Collector of the Customs for this district, which is now held by Morris Croxall, a dying man. Before the election, Gray's paper was loud in maintaining that a Collectorship was altogether unnecessary, at Camden.[30] But now that the scales are turned, he is the most eager of all the pigs to suck this teat of Uncle Sam's. "O consistency! thou art a jewel!" It is also rumored that the new administration will make John K. Clement postmaster at this place— "Betty! my hartshorne!"

Since I have touched the subject of politics, I will mention that people regard Harrison's Inaugural as a well-written thing; but they award the credit of it to Webster, his Secretary of State. It is different from the General's speeches delivered before the election; they are to it, as Hyperion to a Satyr, I mean as Satyrs to a Hyperion.

10 March, Wednesday.

It has been snowing all day; and I have heard those who keep account say this is the fifteenth snow of the season. The weather now is less like spring than a good many days that we had in January.

But I have other things to write about than the weather. I gave a needy man to day some clothes, and other things of which he was really in want. When he thank'd me with tearful eyes, and said he would do any thing for me, "night or day, sick or well, fair or foul" I realized that "Charity blesseth him that giveth and him that receiveth." I would not exchange the happiness of that moment for any sensual pleasure I have ever known.

There was no lecture to-night. Recorder Rush of Philadelphia (a son of the illustrious Benjamin Rush, the Signer)[31] was to have edified us as to "the value of the law," but the snow storm deterred him from crossing the river. Mistress Budd was among the disappointed audience, and we exchanged civilities. She told me my Address was in active circulation among her friends. I made the best bow I could, but felt in no ways flattered.

11 March, Thursday.

. . . It was rumored to-day in Philadelphia that two Senators, King, of Alabama, and Clay of Kentucky, were about to have a hostile

---

29. Thomas M. Gray was the son of Philip J. Gray, publisher of the Camden *Mail.*

30. Camden had been designated a port of entry in 1834.

31. Samuel Rush (1797–1859) was the son of Dr. Benjamin Rush, a signer of the Declaration of Independence.

meeting.[32] This is unimportant to the country at large; since if both fall, there will merely be two fools less in the world. There was also a report that Fox, the British minister had demanded his passports, owing to a correspondence with Secretary Webster, upon that sore subject—the burning of the steamboat *Caroline*.[33] There are several unsquared accounts between this republic and England, which sooner or later, must lead to a rupture. Things at present look squally; and most with whom I have conversed consider the day to be close at hand when the storm shall burst.

12 March, Friday.

This has been a horrid day! Snow, rain, hail, sleet, and hurricanes have alternated, and now (about midnight) they all come at once. Detained by this war of the elements from going abroad, I read considerably more than a hundred lines (or, as I will say hereafter, to gratify my learned readers, *hecatonstich*) of Virgil. He is now laying down rules *de equis*, from which the best of our jockies might profit. But his description of the war-horse, fine as it undoubtedly is, falls infinitely behind that of Job. . . .[34]

The celebrated Thomas P. Hunt, the Cold water Champion,[35] lectured this evening at the Methodist Church; and notwithstanding the tempestuous weather, there were two hundred and two persons out to hear him, among whom I was one. He took the position that the business of rum-selling was worse than counterfeiting, and fully proved it; after which, he asked with great emphasis, "Now gentlemen, is it consistent with common sense to punish the counterfeiter for doing a little injury, and, at the same time, license the rum-seller to do a great one?"

This great apostle of Temperence is a broken-backed, contemptible looking individual enough. He stated that for the last thirteen years he had lectured on an average twice a-day, in thirteen states of the Union; and that he had an army of cold water boys and youth, who numbered a million and a half strong. In many of his expressions, he

32. Henry Clay had lashed out at Sen. William R. King (1786–1853) of Alabama on the Senate floor and avoided a duel with him only by apologizing publicly.

33. The *Caroline* had been a private American vessel, used by American supporters of Canadian insurrectionists in 1837. In December of that year, some Canadian militia entered the United States and set the boat on fire, destroying it and killing one member of the crew. The incident led to virulent Anglophobia in the United States, but British minister Henry Stephen Fox (1791–1846) did not leave the country at this time.

34. Job 39:19–25.

35. Hunt (1794–1876), a clergyman, was a renowned temperance lecturer, originally from Virginia, but now living in Pennsylvania. He argued, of course, that cold water was a superior drink to spirits.

was absolutely indecent; and indecency on such a theme as he had, indeed "admits of no defence." He abused Weatherby and Weatherby's Council candidates most unmercifully, and had a word for a good many more of our citizens. His speech, for a little doubtful good, will do much of certain harm.

13 March, Saturday.

After my return from market (and I always go to market twice a week, in the great city, to buy provisions for our family)—after my return, I say, I accomplished my *hecatonstich* in two hours, and spent the rest of the forenoon in reading one of the Comedies of Terence.

The tides to day are unusually high—owing perhaps to the torrents of rain that fell yesterday.

I looked in, this evening, at a company of little girls who were met at Doctor Mulford's to celebrate his daughter Emma's twelfth birthday, which comes to-morrow. They were enjoying themselves vastly, and it did me good, too, to look at them in their innocent mirth.

14 March, Sunday.

I read a hundred lines of the Sweet bard of Mantua [*Vergil*], this morning; and employed the remainder of the forenoon in drawing and writing. Since I have never studied the art of drawing, my attempts are but rude and unsightly things. . . . I have been assured, however, by painters that I might be able to handle the pencil pretty well, if I should apply myself to it. . . .

16 March, Tuesday.

Further than that I translated my allotted portion of Virgil, I have not much to say of myself to-day. . . .

Sam Cowperthwait, my chum, and I, went to Baptist meeting this evening, and heard a sermon by John Hall,[36] from the text, "Adam, where art thou?" He divided the subject into three heads: I, What was the condition of Adam and Eve after the fall? II, How has the fall effected mankind in general? III, O citizens of Camden, where are you? . . .

17 March, Wednesday.

Had I a dollar for every Irishman that will be drunk to-night, I would have before next week the finest library in the Union. Father Matthew[37] will have work enough in the Emerald Isle to day, to keep

36. Hall lived on Chestnut Street, Philadelphia, but did not have a pastorate in that city or in Camden.

37. Theobald Mathew (1790–1856) was an Irish Capuchin priest and social reformer noted for his temperance campaigns.

his converts to temperance from backsliding. If he can keep them sober on Saint Patrick's day, I will stand for their sobriety the rest of the year, and stand too, with no fear of the responsibility I take.

Isaac Hazlehurst[38] lectured this evening on "the empire of the Moors in Spain," and an able lecture did he give us. The decline and fall of the Crescent, and the rise and triumph of the Cross, in enchanted Grenada: the learning and piety of the Moors, and the ignorance and bigotry of the Christians; the love of justice in the one people, and the disregard of it in the other; were painted with a master hand. . . .

Mr. Hazlehurst is a lawyer from Philadelphia, where, I think, his reputation is unequal to his merit. . . .

After the lecture, I had a short chat with two of the Cooper-street constellation—and the prettiest two, in the bargain.[39] There are four sisters of them, and upon my word, were I fool enough to fall in love at all, I cannot tell which one of the lovely band I would choose. They are all well-educated, all well-formed, all well-countenanced, and, seventhly and sixteenthly, they all have elegant hands. But . . . I defy the arrows of the little god. . . . I am too independent to give way even to a woman. . . .

I spoke to one of the above girls to night by mistake. I have never been introduced.

18 March, Thursday.

A week ago from this day I began at the third Book of Virgil's *Georgics*, reviewing then the thirty lines which I read on the Tuesday before. This morning I stopped at the two hundredth line of the fourth book—having read in seven days, seven hundred and sixty five lines. And I do not hesitate to say, that I have as clear a conception of the sense, and as accurate a knowledge of the construction of what I have gone over, as I would have had, had I read the same quantity in the same time at old Nassau Hall itself. I want to get into the *Aeneis* next week.

In the evening I met at the Library room (in my uncle's old counting house, at the corner of Bridge Avenue and Second Street,) Messieurs Cowperthwaite, Ogden and Ballantine, and we **all four** amused ourselves till after ten o'clock, in a manner not to be told, though it may be guessed.[40]

19 March, Friday.

After I finished my lesson to-day, I walked down to the book-

38. Hazlehurst had been a Philadelphia attorney since 1831.
39. The stars in this constellation were the girls of the Sheppard family, Phoebe, Mary, Hannah, and Josephine.
40. Mickle and his friends were playing cards.

binder's (Wannan's) in Fetterville,[41] and paid him a balance of fifty cents which I have owed him for some time for binding this, my diary. The only debt I now owe is twelve-and-a-half cents to the oysterman, for refreshments, and (I had forgotten!) about a dozen philopoenas to the girls, for that "melting bliss," 'yclept a kiss, which, as some poet has said, with a peculiar sweetness, doubtless inspired by his theme, "never comes amiss, Not even when we steal it.". . .

My uncle was at Woodbury to-day, concerning the road which is proposed to be opened from Newtown Meeting-house to the Public ferry, at the foot of Bridge Avenue.[42] The Coopers and the Brownings oppose it heartily.

Samuel Cowperthwait spent the evening in my study, and I began to give him lessons in playing chess. We played a more reprehensible game last night; but I trust we are both sufficiently firm to resist the fascinations of the round table. As we were in the height of moving and countermoving, to-night, Weatherby the shoemaker, was ushered into my sanctum. He said he had often wished to see my "shop" and that now he had come to gratify that wish. I tried my best to amuse him, with pictures, music, anecdotes, and curiosities; for, notwithstanding his calling, he is a clever little fellow, and I know he would do me any favour in his power. . . .

20 March, Saturday.
The weather to-day, for the first time this spring, is so mild that people are sitting with their windows up. The flower roots in our garden have been sprouting for a fortnight. "The spring time o'year, is coming, ah ha!" And why should I not fall in love with some bright-eyed girl, with whom I might walk abroad in the blooming fields, and enjoy this balmy season? Yes, why? I will take the expediency of this thing into consideration at the first leisure moment I have—perhaps when I shall have finished Virgil's *Georgics,* and *Eclogues.*

The mention of the Bucolics, by the by, calls to my memory the following undeniable fact, to wit: I have not read a line of Latin to-day. I have yet a half of the fourth book of the *Georgics* to translate, and the *Pastorals* to review; but if the weather be always as pleasant as *hic dies,* I know not when my task will be finished. I went, this forenoon, to Philadelphia; in which goodly city I called first at Mr. Dodson's engraving office in Minor Street, to see Cowperthwaite; next I went with Sam, and engaged a seal to be made for the Library Company; thirdly, we dropped in at a Jewish painter's to see a pic-

41. William Wannan had established his bookbindery in Fettersville in February 1839.
42. No such road was constructed at this time.

ture of *Antony haranguing over the body of dead Caesar;* and
fourthly, I stopped at a tailor's in Chesnut Street, and got measured
for a pair of trowsers.[43] "Further than this, deponent saith not."

Item extraordinary! Being at Weatherby's this afternoon, meddling
with his sharp tools, I cut nearly half the nail off the forefinger of my
left hand, and with the nail, a portion of my finger end. I own the
hurt is bad enough, but am thankful it is no worse. What would have
become of my dear diary, had the cut happened on the right hand?

21 March, Sunday.

I neglected to state yesterday that my uncle called upon ex-President
Van Buren, who is now in Philadelphia, on his way to Kinderhook. He
drank a glass of wine with him, and says he is in good spirits and fine
health. My uncle aforesaid has dined with Mr. Van Buren at the
White House, on several occasions; but he says he never saw the
President so happy as the **Citizen** appeared to be yesterday. He carries into retirement with him the best of all consolations, an approving
conscience; and he is not unaware of the fact, that the future will do
his administration that justice which a popular phrensy, in the present,
has denied him. . . .

This morning I made up for yesterday's neglect of Virgil; and
arrived to within one day's journey of the end of the *Georgics.* I went
to church this evening, and heard Mr. Tindall preach. Six of the
choristers out of thirteen were asleep!

22 March, Monday.

At last I have finished Virgil's *Georgics!* and my perseverance was
about as near being run out, before I got through, as Maro's subject
was to being exhausted when he introduced the fable of Aristaeus, to
swell out his fourth book. At some other time (when I shall not be so
sleepy) I will speak more at large concerning the poem I have just
read; and, that Virgils' manes may comprehend the import of my
discourse I will speak in Latin. . . .

23 March, Tuesday.

It is my intention to take two or three holy-days before I commence
the *Aeneid,* amusing myself in the meanwhile in drawing and painting,
reviewing Virgil's *Pastorals,* and reading Shakspeare. To-day I have
done something at all these.

I was at the house of Doctor Mulford an hour this evening, when,
after our conversation had turned upon law and lawyers, he told me

43. Mickle's stops included one at the office of Richard W. Dodson and one
probably at the home of Solomon Nunes Carvalho (1815–94), a South Carolina
native, who had begun painting in Philadelphia in 1838.

the following incident; "I was once summoned as a witness on a trial at Mount Holly. It was just after I had got my diploma, when I was young in years and looks. The opposing Counsel, to invalidate my testimony, resorted to the following mode of questioning me: "Young man, can you read?" I replied, "Yes, I can read." "I suppose you can write?" "Yes, I can write." "Well, here, take this pen, and write some word." ["] I took the pen" said the Doctor; "and wrote in large characters, the word IMPERTINENCE. The lawyer, in a kind of abstraction, read what I had written, aloud, and the Court was convulsed with laughter— He coloured up to the eyes, and told me he had no more questions to ask. After the Court rose, he came to me, and apologized for his conduct. Since that time we have been well acquainted." The moral of this anecdote is, "Answer a fool according to his folly," and deal with an impertinent man according to his impertinence.

24 March, Wednesday.

The *Mail* of this morning contains a notice of Hazlehurst's lecture on the Moors in Spain, which does some honour to the writer of it, I must own, although that writer is John K. Clement, the only enemy I have in Camden. He is a most remarkable imitator; he catches the ideas and words of another, in a trice; and sometimes he carries the indulgence of this, his peculiar talent, to an excess.

Samuel M. Rush, Recorder of Philadelphia, lectured this evening upon "the value of the law." His essay was an elegant peice of composition; but his manner was rather tame, owing, perhaps, to the meager attendance with which he was greeted. Public Speakers say they cannot do well when empty benches are grinning in their faces; but I am sure I could make out much the better for the house being empty, or very nearly so. Mr. Rush is a son of Doctor Benjamin Rush, the Signer, and is a remarkably fine-looking man. His lecture entirely removed from my mind all those little prejudices which I had formerly entertained against law and lawyers, and finally settled the fluctuating needle of my determination to the profession of the green bag.[44] May that hereafter be the north-pole towards which all my energies (if any I have) may point!

For a week or two back there has been an indication in Philadelphia, among the democratic press and party, to nominate Commodore Stewart[45] for the next Presidency. Immediately after the result of the

44. English lawyers often kept documents and papers in green bags, thus lending a nickname to the profession.
45. Charles Stewart (1778–1869), a native of Philadelphia, had become a national hero during the War of 1812 when he commanded the famous *Constitution* during several triumphant cruises. He was currently in command of the Philadelphia Navy Yard.

last election was generally known, the whole party in the west, seemed inclined to renominate Mr. Van Buren for their candidate. I saw several papers from that quarter of the country, and they were unanimous in supporting his interests. Thomas H. Benton, Senator from Missouri, wrote a letter to one of the Cincinnati papers, declaring himself in favour of taking up the faithful and patriotic, although defeated, New-Yorker. Since then the current seemed to set for a little while in favour of Colonel Johnson, and John C. Calhoun's name was whispered, **and whispered only**.[46] Stewart's name is now the favoured one, with the democrats of Philadelphia; and very strong articles in furtherance of his nomination appeared in *The Spirit of the Times*[47] every morning during the sojourn of Mr. Van Buren in that city. Who will be the one **selected**, I dare not yet predict; but let it be whom it will, it is conceded on almost all hands that he will be **elected**. It is thought that Clay will be the federal candidate; and he is the most proper one in the country to be taken up when defeat is expected, because of his having been defeated so often that discomfiture has ceased to mortify him!

25 March, Thursday.

This day of the year has been, almost from time immemorial, the *dies movendi*, in this section of the country. In New York city, I believe, the most general moving day is the first of May. In Philadelphia I know from observation there is a class of movers who shift quarters punctually at a certain time, as often, too, as that time comes—to wit, the day before their rent becomes due. Nor is this class, by any means, small in number; nor have they the politeness in all cases to inform their sometime landlord into what dark alley they have migrated. On such days as this, when all is commotion and jostling, there are many ludicrous sights to be seen, and one of these I saw this morning. The "Odious Monopoly," of which my uncle is Secretary and Treasurer rented, some months ago, the Ferry-house at the foot of Federal Street in this city, to Mr. Cake, who entered into some arrangement with John Knisell, the occupant thereof, in pursuance of which he was to enter upon tenantry to-day. But Knisell, being of a perverse disposition, flew from his contract, and, when Cake came up, with his family and goods, this morning, refused to

46. Richard M. Johnson (1781–1850) of Kentucky had been Van Buren's vice-president. South Carolina Senator Calhoun (1782–1850) had served in several high government posts since 1817 and had been vice-president from 1825 to 1832. His break with Jackson and his strong states' rights views made him an unlikely presidential candidate for 1844.

47. The *Spirit of the Times* was an influential Democratic journal published at Third and Chestnut Streets in Philadelphia.

evacuate; and, standing in a menacing position in the door, forbade the new-comer to enter the premises. Mr. Cake has moved clear from Cape May; and will be obliged to board at some of the taverns until Knisell's lease expires, and the Company can use compulsion to rid their property of its malicious incumbent. . . .

28 March, Sunday.

I arose earlier than common this morning, and called upon my friend Sam, by appointment, to accompany him to the annual examination of the Sunday School pupils attached to the Jewish Synagogue in Cherry Street, Philadelphia.[48] We crossed the river with the belles of Camden, the Cooper Street Constellation; and saw, on board the boat an amusing scene between a drunken sailor, and a dandy Frenchman. They had quite a flurry, arising in the sailor's striking the favorite dog of the Gaul; but the matter was ended without any broken bones to either side. A Frenchman and his dog are, seemingly, parts of the same being; you cannot strike one of them without the other's avenging the blow.

Being come to the Synagogue, we entered, and found three or four hundred people, with their hats on, and talking, and laughing and skylarking, just as much as Christians would, at an ordinary meeting, on Saturday. I was reminded of a theatre's pit just before the curtain has risen—for it was all bustle, and nodding of heads, and roaring with laughter, and winking at the females, and moving about, as one is accustomed to see at the play-house. Presently a little hand-bell was jingled; when we all sat down, but did not remove our hats. A prayer was then read in broad English by a German in a civil dress, and with his hat cocked on the side of his head with an air of nonchalance that surprised me. A Christian I am sure would uncover himself to pray on the Jew's Sabbath, as well as on any other day. After the prayer, about two hundred little children chanted in Hebrew, and then were examined by their teachers on the history of the Old Testament. Before this was over, we became tired, and departed; but all the responses that we heard from the little followers of Abraham, Isaac and Jacob, were delivered promptly, distinctly and correctly.

I have often noticed the extreme ugliness of Jewish men, but never till to-day had a chance of observing the great beauty of Jewish women. Their faces, for the most part, are no more than agreeable; but they have forms which will give one a better idea of an angel, than all Milton's poetry or Angelo's painting. I sat, to day, close to one of the teachers, a girl about sixteen or seventeen years of age; and after examining her with a critical eye—and alas! a critical heart,

---

48. Temple Mikveh Israel stood near Third and Cherry Streets.

too!—for an hour and a half, I came to the conclusion that her form has no superior on this side of heaven. Her dress—being low in the neck—revealed her round, snowy breast, and dimpled and voluptuous shoulders, far enough down to captivate the heart of a Stoic, but not far enough to wound the delicacy of the most fastidious saint. Her complexion, pure as the whitest snow, was contrasted with ringlets of the most jetty blackness. Piety beamed from her blue eyes, while mirth and mischief reigned about her ruby lips. Her whole contour had the symmetry of an angel, and her movements an angel's ease. Her hand was more perfect, if possible, than even her form; soft, small, white and flexible, ungarnished with trinkets, and by warts unsoiled; and her foot was the quintessence of grace and elegance. In short, she was the Statue of a Phidias[49] inspired with life—the dream of a Byron invested with reality. Equal to what celestials can be, she surpassed everything that mortals can imagine.

Edward Cole called upon me this afternoon; and I gave him a lesson—in playing chess! He learned the moves like an apt scholar, as he, and all other young men, are, when any thing unprofitable is to be acquired. Who cannot learn the game of cards in half the time required to commit the ten commandments to memory? A moralist, in answering this question, might make a very handsome sermon.

I went to Baptist Meeting this evening, but I looked in vain for the match of my pretty Jewess. I saw those whom, this morning, I would have called elegant. To night, their beauty is insipid, not to say actually disgusting.

29 March, Monday.

I have been at work at "Scrapio" to-day, pretty industriously; but notwithstanding my mind was engaged on that nonsensical thing, I have scarcely ever felt more wretched and melancholy. I have read that Cowper wrote his *Johnny Gilpin* in one of his desponding fits; and have heard it argued that a person must have the "blues," in order to compose any thing laughable. If there be any truth in that, "The Adventures of Scrapio" will produce the effect upon the countenances of my hearers, that I desire—for, really I am most prodigiously down in the mouth to day.

There was a full attendance at the meeting of the Institute to-night. The following question was discussed with very great animation: Can treason to one's country be justifiable, under any circumstances? . . .

While the coxcomb Clement was speaking in reply to me, I observed an expression in the face of the wiseacre who presided, that I could

49. Phidias or Pheidias (*c.* 500–*c.* 432 B.C.), an Athenian sculptor, was noted for the perfection of his creations.

not resist. I burst out in a laugh. Hereupon Clement, thinking I was making game of him, said something that I was in no humour to pass by. I rose and spoke as follows:

Mr. Chairman: The gen—I mean, the **member**, has taken to himself an honour from me, which **I would never have thought** of bestowing on him. **What!** laugh at **such a thing** as that to which you listened but a moment ago? **Laugh** at him? I would as soon laugh at the **wind.** He is a thing too contemptible to meet or merit a laugh from me. **For ten thousand just like him** I would not move a muscle of my countenance. **Were I to spit up on him accidentally, I should never feel clear of degradation,** UNTIL I HAD WASHED MY MOUTH WITH SOAP AND LYE! . . .

30 March, Tuesday.

. . . Cowperthwaite spent the evening with me. We played a game or two at chess, and then amused ourselves by the following experiment: He, with two castles and two bishops attempted to beat me, with one knight. After he had tried a long time, to no purpose, we swapped sides, and at length I succeeded in penning his horse-head up. One knight is about worth the four peices I have mentioned.

31 March, Wednesday.

A Doctor Patterson[50] from Philadelphia lectured this evening, on the "Age of Chivalry." He opened with Burke's celebrated sentence, "The age of chivalry is gone!" and exclaimed "would to god, its effects had gone too!" We have been accustomed, said he, to regard only the bright side of the picture. We dwell with delight over the exploits of Amadis de Gaul and others of the knightly order, during the age of chivalry. The prowess of imaginary heroes meets our admiration; but the groans of nine-tenths of Europe for long, long ages; the real groans, and sighs and sweat and tears of millions of vassals, at whose expense the lords maintained their splendor, have had no troubadour to commemorate, and now have but few hearts to sympathize with them. He painted the classes of the middle ages, forcibly and faithfully. He then spoke of the remains of chivalry among us: duello, and the empty titles which yet disgrace this republic. He traced the downfall of feudalism to Christianity; and concluded with a long digression upon the state of the working classes at this day in England. "If" said he "something be not soon done in relation to them, something will do itself in a way no one will like."

50. Dr. Henry S. Patterson (1815–54) had recently completed his medical education at the University of Pennsylvania and was currently a resident physician at the Philadelphia almshouse.

The lecture abounded in anecdotes and rich historical allusions, and gave complete satisfaction. The Doctor's hair and eyes are red; his voice, strong, his manner tame. I procured an introduction, and think he is a very clever fellow. After the lecture I called at a Billiard Room, and staid a few minutes to please a friend.

1 April, Thursday.
As Pythagoras exclaimed, when he first discovered that the square of the hypotheneuse of a right-angled triangle is equal to the square of the two other sides; or as Archimedes cried when he ascertained the true value of the crown, so I now exclaim, so I now cry—"I have found it! I have found it!" But great as my joy is at the discovery I have made, I will not let it transport me so much as to sacrifice a hecatomb to the gods, or run through the streets in my shirt-tail, as the worthies I have just mentioned are said to have done.

If the reader wishes to test my theory by an experiment, let him obey the following instructions. My discovery is, **that one may see with both his eyes shut**; and the matter can easily be proved in this manner:

Go into a dark room and close the door after you; then wash your eyes in a decoction of *morus-multicaulis* leaves and Bateman's Drops; and closing them up, lay a finger on each, to prevent the possibility of any delusion. Remain with your eyes thus shut, for two or three minutes; then incline your head forward and downward, until your face is level with your knees. Now separate your legs as far apart as possible, and at this interesting crisis of the experiment, you will see (if, indeed, you have not seen before)—**That you have been made a fool of!**

After working awhile in the garden this morning, I went to Philadelphia, and took a long walk. I fixed my eye upon the attorney's office of James Page, late Post-master of Philadelphia, and thought to myself—"pleasantly located, ahem!" It is in Walnut Street, above Third. Colonel Page is a tolerable lawyer, an excellent politician, an entire gentleman; and just such a man as I would like to read black-letter under. I did not go in, to-day, for fear I should be reminded, in a way by no means agreeable, that it was **All-Fool's-Day**.

2 April, Friday.
The doings of this day are so important that they deserve to be classified, as follows:

I. I crossed the river, this morning, to do myself what the business of my uncle and guardian will not afford him time to undertake. For a year back it has been fixed that I should read law; for a year back my guardian has delayed to see to procuring me a place; and for a year back, in consequence, I have led a life, of uncertainty and unpleasantness. To-day I resolved to end my perplexity; and so called upon Colonel Page, introduced myself, and asked him if he was willing to receive a student at law. He raised his eyes from his book, viewed me from top to toe, and replied "I have not much occasion just now for a young man," and then commenced turning over his leaves again. My dress, I am convinced, had some part in prompting this equivocal reply; I had neglected my toilette most unpardonably; I had on my oldest pantaloons, a vest frayed with hard service, and a shirt by no means the cleanest that ever was. From my dress he argued poverty, from my poverty, a brainless head—a mode of argument which in some cases traps us into great errors. Nothing daunted, I asked him if any of his professional friends were desirous of receiving a student. He showed me an advertisement in the *Ledger* for a young man who "had a liberal education, could produce good recommendations, and write a legible hand," as a student in the office of Mr. Jack.[51] "Such," said the advertiser, in conclusion, "would be received without any compensation," and these terms Mr. Page thought (I have no doubt) would exactly suit my circumstances. Having read the advertisement, said I, "I presume, sir, I could produce recommendations satisfactory to Mr. Jack, or any one else." He looked at me earnestly, again, and then replied, "I have two students about to be admitted to practice, and my office will then be vacant; but much depends upon the terms." "I trust" I said, in a firm tone, "we will not find any difficulty as to them. However my guardian—" "Who is that?" he here interrupted. I had not whispered my name before, nor my uncle's, although I knew him and Page to have been, for a long time, political and personal friends. When I mentioned "Captain Mickle, John W. Mickle of Camden," the negotiation received a new face. "O yes," said he, "I know him, know him well—very well! Call again, and bring him with you. O, Mickle, eh? Well!" I promised to wait on him again in a few days, then thanked him, and with divers bows on both sides I took my leave.

I have entered into the details of this interview, because it may prove to be a very important chapter in the book of my life. I assumed throughout it an assurance altogether foreign to my nature; but I am convinced that bashfulness and the law do not belong together, and I hope the former will go out as the latter comes in.

II. On my return from Philadelphia, I heard that Will Jeffers had arrived in Camden, and so started off to hunt him up. Meanwhile he too was hunting for me. We met after a while, and adjourned, with a hearty shake of the hand, to my sanctum. There he explained the

51. Attorney Charles James Jack had offices on North Seventh Street.

cause of his not having answered my letter of the 26th of December. He had been at sea, on relief service, and got his fingers so frosted he could not hold a pen. This was perfectly satisfactory. We then talked an hour or so upon old times, and parted, *a revoir*. With his midshipman's undress, he cuts a noble figure. His morals, however, have not been greatly improved by his uniform.

III. There was a violent hurricane this evening from the west, accompanied by thunder, lightning and rain. Trees were bent nearly to the ground, and the steamboats on the river were for a time unmanagable. I have heard as yet of no great damage.

IV. I went by invitation, to see the collection of plants owned by Richard Fetters, Esq. He has two houses full of the most beautiful flowers, and the rarest spices; but as I have an invite to go again, which I shall not fail to do, I will put off till after then, some remarks which I have to make.

3 April, Saturday.

My friend, Will, and I, have been together for the greater part of this day. He went this afternoon to see the Cooper Street Constellation; and there is much cause for me to dread the effects of his gallant uniform upon the mind of Miss Josephine. Gold lace and eagled buttons cannot be met by any arguments. They are like whig logic; they reach the heart by way of the eyes; and the heart once reached, the head is completely turned. . . .

President Harrison has been dangerously ill for some days past. Yesterday it was said in Philadelphia that he was better, but many predict with obstinate confidence that he will die.

4 April, Sunday.

I went to church in Race Street with my aunt Eliza,[52] this morning, and heard a missionary sermon. Mr. Berg made an eloquent prayer "for the head of this nation, who now labours under a severe attack of disease"—he might have said, "who now lies upon that cooling board, where sooner or later, Presidents and people all must lie"—for while he prayed, the object of that prayer, who but a short month ago, was called to rule over the destinies of this great nation, was indeed stiff in death!

Many were the sad faces in the peaceful streets of Philadelphia to-day! From the north came the tidings of threatened war—from the south the dismaying news of the death of the chief of the people. The steamer *British Queen* had just arrived at New York, bringing intelli-

---

52. Eliza Hogeland, Mickle's maternal aunt, lived at 31 Cherry Street in Philadelphia. Her daughters, Adelia (Delia) and Mary, are mentioned later in the diary.

gence that ten ships of the line had been ordered to cruize off our coast "until the demands of the English Minister, Mr. Fox, for the liberation of McLeod,[53] had been complied with," and that Victoria's government had also ordered several additional regiments to Canada, to be prepared for any emergency. The British lion couches for another spring, and shall not the American eagle plume her wing, as in days of yore, and bear to the clouds the starry banner of the free—triumphant, and yet more radiant from the taunts cast upon it? I trust to God, she may!

General Harrison died this morning, between twelve and one o'clock; of a combination of diseases brought on by a sudden change of diet, from that of a log cabin to that of the White house: by being worried out with the applications of beggarly office-seekers; and by old age. The news of his death reached Philadelphia in the afternoon, nearly simultaneously with the intelligence of the war movement in England. The last was communicated to about five hundred persons in the Exchange; and when they heard the distant grumbling of the twice repulsed war-dog, "to arms" seemed to burn in every eye, and quiver on every tongue. Then the brief but eloquent bulletin of Webster, announcing that **Harrison was no more**, that he died with prayers for the happiness of his country and the sanctity of the Constitution—then, I say, this was read, and grief took the place of defiance on the countenances of the astonished auditory. The news flew far and wide, and soon the sadness pervaded the whole city. Here and there, at every corner, in the market places, every where, might be seen groups standing together, discussing the national calamity; for such I consider it, and such must every one consider it, though he opposed the election of the deceased hero never so violently.

In speaking of men's characters while living, we are allowed to tell a little more than the truth; in speaking of them when dead, a little less than the truth is expected. When **William Henry Harrison** was a candidate for the office which, by the unfair means resorted to by his friends, he obtained by a tremendous majority, I opposed, with all my little influence, an event which I really believed would be for my country's harm. On the pages of this book, carried away by party heat, I may have said some things which were better unsaid; but I am not aware of having said anything in relation to the now illustrious dead, which in the least transcends the bounds of truth. Harrison is now no more! His fame is now his country's, and his country is bound to vindi-

53. Alexander McLeod, a Canadian citizen, was arrested and jailed in New York State in November 1840, as one of the participants in the Canadian raid on the steamboat *Caroline* (see entry of 11 March 1841). He was acquitted at his trial in October 1841.

cate it. An American myself, everything American to me is dear; and I feel a just pride, to-day, in owning for my countryman a man like him whom, to-day, a nation deplores. His faults (if any he had) be buried with him; his virtues (and them we know him to have possessed) live on the annals of his country forever!

The Whig party in Philadelphia are in great trouble. They fear Tyler, who is now President, will not follow the path which Harrison was elected to pursue. In fact "the great Whig party" will now crumble to peices. General Harrison was the only man, perhaps, in their whole ranks, in support of whom Abolitionists and Anti-Abolitionists, Tariffites and anti-Tariffites, Bank men and anti-Bank men could rally. The heterogeneous mass under Tyler, whose feelings are all Southern, will soon dissolve—and the sooner it does, the better for the country!

The Democratic party, so far as I have seen, maintain a decorous show of grief, at the death of the head of the other party. They however, bewail **the President**—the Whigs bewail **the man**.

Will Jeffers spent the afternoon with me, in playing chess, telling yarns and so forth. I learned from him that Paulding, the late Secretary of the Navy was very unpopular with both men and officers, from one end to the other of "our right arm of defence." Harrison's appointment of Badger,[54] he says gives better satisfaction. Will starts for Bridgeton to-morrow morning.

5 April, Monday.

The bells in Philadelphia have been pealing muffled chimes to-day in honour of the late President. The flags on all the vessels are at half-mast, and all the newspapers are in mourning. The *Spirit of the Times*, a daily democratic paper, recommends a meeting to be called, to show a proper respect to the memory of the departed, and that every republican wear crape on the left arm for thirty days. With this suggestion I presume many will comply. . . .

I mentioned, last Friday, that there was a violent hurricane on the afternoon of that day; but I did not know till this morning that it was the cause of my losing an acquaintance, and schoolmate. John Hinchman . . . and two other young gentlemen were pleasuring in a wherry on the Delaware, near Gloucester Point, when the storm burst. None of them knowing how to manage a boat, they did not furl up the sail at the approaching gust; when it first broke upon them, the mast was snapped off, and they were left to drift about the river at the mercy of the wind and tides. The wind blew so hard and the lightning

54. Harrison's choice for secretary of the navy was George E. Badger (1795–1866) of North Carolina.

flashed so vividly and incessantly until late in the night, that those on the shore were afraid to attempt to assist them. Nothing was known of them until the next morning, when the wherry was found on the shore, near the Point, with the bodies of two of the company in her, killed with light'ning. The hat of Hinchman was also taken up on the surface of the water, telling too plainly the fate he had met. May he rest in peace! . . .

6 April, Tuesday.

Nothing is talked of but the death of the President, and nothing is seen but bears an impress of the sorrow which such an unexpected event is calculated to cause. Even those who but lately predicted and prayed for the decease of the hero of Tippecanoe (for some such there were) now partake of the strange feeling which they experience who were his warmest friends. The faces of some exhibit a confused expression of grief and joy, as if they had at once lost their best friend and worst enemy. The mail from Washington this afternoon brings the announcement that the funeral will take place to-morrow at noon. The Councils in Philadelphia have recommended all places of business be closed, on that day, from ten in the morning till two in the afternoon.

Samuel Cowperthwaite spent the evening with me, and we played a game or two of chess. He learns rapidly.

7 April, Wednesday.

General Harrison was buried to-day at twelve o'clock, according to the announcement made by Webster, and the other members of the Cabinet. Wherever the news of his death has reached, unfeigned grief prevails. In Philadelphia the stores were shut up, (though business was not altogether suspended) from ten till two o'clock. At twelve, the hour at which the illustrious ashes were committed to the earth, a salute of twenty-six guns was fired from the Navy Yard. Similar tokens of respect were also heard from some of the small towns down the river. Now that the last duty of a nation towards the dead are over, their eyes will be fixed upon the living. John Tyler, of Virginia, and Samuel L. Southard of New Jersey, the President and Vice President of this Country,[55] by accident, will, for some time, be the most unjustly praised, and most unmeritedly abused, men between the lakes and the gulf. . . .

A low fellow was committed by Esquire Gray this evening on suspicion of murdering his brother and burning his house and body to

---

55. Senator Southard of New Jersey was not actually vice-president, of course, but, as president *pro tempore* of the United States Senate, would succeed to the presidency in the event of Tyler's death.

escape detection last night. The supposed crime occurred on the Burlington road, three miles from Camden.

8 April, Thursday.

Although I did not get to sleep till three o'clock this morning, yet I arose an hour sooner than common, to wit at seven, to see my friend Will off to New York. He had leave of absence for a week, and was obliged to return to-day. When it came to starting, his face was long, and his lip quivered, as if he was not a little reluctant to bid his friends "good bye," perhaps forever. May God protect his body in war, and his morals in peace. . . .

I went this evening to Cowperthwaits', to hear some music. Sam plays the flute very well, and he engages a ferryman named Bishop[56] to come to his residence occasionally with his violin. Besides those two performers, Stivers to-night sung base, while I listened. The last named gentleman informs me that Miss Mary Turner has read my Oration for the Twenty Second, and that she entertains of it a very favourable opinion. Miss Mary's approbation is worth having. She is a sensible woman—very.

9 April, Friday.

There is a great excitement in Philadelphia about the report of the committee of stock-holders of the United States Bank, which was published in yesterday's papers.[57] This rotten institution has now received its last stab, and with falling Caesar it might exclaim at the report of its friends, "*Et tu, Brute?*" with much reason. In the apt quotation of the *Chronicle* newspaper, "Good night to Marmion!"[58] But the people have been cheated, oppressed and tantalized by the banks so long, that they have no tears to shed for the monster that is gone. They who but a year or two ago lauded Nicholas Biddle to the skies, as the greatest financier of his age, now damn him as a knave with all heartiness;[59] and the former enemies of the illustrious Jackson now admit his sagacity in all the stands he took against the Bank of the United States. His predictions have been proven true, and his apprehensions not without cause.

In this connection, to show the ruin to individuals which is wrought

56. Mickle apparently refers to a man named Bishop Ivins whom he sometimes calls by his first name and sometimes by his last; see entries of 14 August 1841, 4 May 1842, and 24 September 1842.

57. Angry stockholders, dismayed at the bank's reckless policies and declining financial position, eventually sued Nicholas Biddle and accused him and other former bank officers of criminal conspiracy.

58. The newspaper apparently meant to print "Mammon."

59. Biddle (1786–1844), though he had quit the presidency of the bank in 1839, had remained active in bank affairs and was partly responsible for its demise.

by the means of Banks, I will mention the case of a Colonel Dobbins, who now lives in Camden; or rather stays, for the Bank's have scarcely left him the wherewithal to live. He is a gentleman of a good education and respectable family; an Englishman by birth, a soldier by profession. He was at the Battle of Waterloo under Wellington, and won, on that immortal field, the laurels that are due to the brave. He was promoted to a Colonelship, and in that capacity served long and honorably in the wars of his country. Having amassed a fortune of ninety thousand dollars, and finding age approaching, he resigned his commission in the army, and emigrated to America. With six or seven loving and lovely children, the still beautiful wife of his youth, and a fortune, sufficient to gratify their wants and his; inhaling the free air of a republic, and conscious of an unsullied fame; what could have added to his happiness? Alas, though sometimes the world can bestow nothing, yet it always has the power to take a something away! Mr. Dobbins was anxious to invest his money with safety, and was referred to Biddle, then the President of the United States Bank. By him he was advised to buy stock in the Vicksburg bank, in Mississippi, and reposing on the high financial reputation of his counsellor, he did so. In a few short months the Bank exploded—his scrip for ninety thousand, was not worth a dollar—and he was plunged from the height of affluence to the depth of a hopeless beggary. My uncle, Doctor Mulford, now attends his broken-hearted wife; his "lovely children" go dirty and ragged; and he who could face French bayonets undauntedly at Waterloo, now seeks in vain an escape from the despair of poverty. And he, too, is but one of thousands! . . .

10 April, Saturday.

To use a homely, but a very expressive word, I have loafed this day away completely. I went to market in the morning, after returning whence, I read a little in Lamartine's *Travels.* Then I went to a carpenter-shop, and conversed an hour with the knights of the plane, *de rebus variis*; and after that returned home.

There was a considerable fall of snow, this afternoon, and ice is forming now (twelve o'clock, midnight) pretty fast.

I attended a meeting of the citizens of Camden this evening, at the City Hall, called by the Mayor, to give an expression of the public grief at the death of Harrison. Owing to the snow storm there were not many present. Doctor Mulford made some appropriate remarks, and proper resolutions were adopted.

11 April, Sunday. Easter.

Verily, verily I am improving! I have been to church three several times this blessed day! In the morning I went to Saint Augustine's in Fourth Street, in Philadelphia, and heard a most eloquent sermon preached by Doctor Moriarty. . . . Although I got to the Cathedral a half an hour before the time, I could get no seat outside of the orchestra; but I was invited to sit among the singers, and accepted the polite offer. I think there were two thousand pious Catholics in attendance. The house was perfectly crammed. The priest drew a comparison between the Catholics, and "the heretics," and made it out to the satisfaction of the former that the latter are a sorry set of devils enough. The Catholics, said he, worship now just as they did in the beginning; their ceremonies and implements are the same as those which the fathers attest to have been in use among the primitive members of the Only and Holy Apostolic Catholic Church. Heretics, despising the examples of the Saints, have modelled outward religion to suit their own convenience. They study a short time at some ordinary college, come out, and set themselves up as heads of the people; claiming the right of altering or abolishing things holy, as they please; instituting new sects; and forming new divisions; and leading weak mortals astray, even unto their damnation. "We, of the Apostolic Church" said the enthusiastic priest, whirling his little cap high above his fine head, "We worship God according to the practice and precepts of the Evangelists, while others follow their own whims, or obey the commands of a tyrannical, a monstrous, Henry VIII. We love God and exalt him, because he is, in himself, lovely; others aim at Heaven because they fear Hell." When he spoke of the ancient power and splendor of the church of Rome, his eloquence almost drew plaudits from his serious audience, *ut ante scenam*; and when he foretold the rising of another glorious day upon her annals, it was with the greatest difficulty that some of the faithful restrained themselves. It is one of the most objectionable features in Catholicism, I think, that while the priests are dangerously talented and learned, the laity are equally dangerously besotted in ignorance and bigotry. Such a firebrand as Moriarty among such combustibles as the Catholics to whom he preaches, might do a vast deal of mischief. I really believe that one word from his mouth to day would have set a thousand armed men upon any "heretical" church in Philadelphia.

In the afternoon I attended Saint Paul's, in Camden. Mr. Burroughs[60] held forth from Joshua's "as for me and my house, we will serve the Lord." In the evening I went to Baptist Meeting, and was invited into the choir. Two or three of the goodly singers were fast asleep, as not

60. Henry Burroughs was rector of St. Paul's from 1838 to 1843.

unfrequently occurs under the drowsy sermons of Mr. Tyndall, and some of his narcotic brethren. One of the latter was the orator to-night. For a dull preacher there is no excuse.

12 April, Monday.

. . . I read Tyler's Inaugural last night. It has the merit of brevity, at least. It leaves the Whig party in as much doubt as ever. He says nothing against a second Presidential term, nor the exercise of the Veto; which leads some to suppose that he will not carry out the avowed principles of his lamented predecessor. Upon the Bank question he does not commit himself; and as to the Tariff he maintains a silence which leaves the friends of that measure here at the north, but little to hope. He has studied to escape committing himself on many of the engrossing topics of the day. In short his address is void of subject, and weak in style.

13 April, Tuesday.

There was to have been a grand Funeral Procession in Philadelphia to-day in honour of General Harrison; but owing to the deep snow which fell yesterday, it is adjourned for a week. I doubt much the propriety of the intended parade; for it seems to me that respect to the dead can be better shown by other means than those which tend to make the people a tumultuous, noisy, frolicksome and ungovernable mob. The banners and ribbons would be well enough, if they were not attended with rum and rows. The mock solemnities of the day might do, were they not sure to be followed by a night of inconsistent and disgraceful debauchery. Men who devote the daylight to national grief, balance the account, in most cases, by giving the night-time to individual jollification. . . .

14 April, Wednesday.

About three inches more of snow fell this morning; but it began to melt fast at ten o clock. The wind blew fresh from the west this afternoon, and it is now (ten, at night) quite cool. . . .

I spoke to one of the Constellation, and got an introduction to another sweet little girl. I am certainly enlarging my female acquaintance, and am determined to try whether the company of the angelic fair will have the desired effect of relieving me from the blue-devils, under which I have suffered for some time past; and moreover (to use another I) I am resolved to read Chesterfield's *Principles of Politeness* forthwith, to the end that I may make my entree into society with becoming flourishes. The first bow that the reader's humble servant ever undertook to perform before ladies—was his last! He caught his feet in the carpet, and fell sprawling upon the floor; and since then, at introductions, recognitions, and salutations, he has never ventured beyond an inclination of the head, or a formal touch of his chapeau. But inasmuch as this stiffness brings great scandal upon him, from the other sex, in general, and the polite part of that sex, in particular, he is resolved to begin de novo, as aforesaid, to wit, by reading Chesterfield.

15 April, Thursday.

My mother being gone to Philadelphia this afternoon, I was left to keep the house, in which irksome duty I was fortunately assisted by the timely visit of my friend Sam. We played three or four games of chess, and, at last he nearly succeeded in making it a drawn match. He is an enthusiast in the noble science, and progresses in it with wonderful rapidity, by the aid of *Chess Made Easy*, a valuable little work by Walker.

In the evening I took a stroll over the town, dropped in at Delacour's Drug Store,[61] and then returned to my sanctum, and began a series of "Secular Sermons on Several Subjects" with which, perhaps I may edify the world in general, but the readers of the *West Jersey Democrat* in particular, during the coming summer....

16 April, Friday.

I took a long walk in company with Sam this afternoon, through Fetterville, and down to Kaighn's Point, and from there up the river-road, **to the place of beginning.** Sixty houses are engaged to be built in Fetterville this summer, as I was told to-day by Mr. Fetters himself.

I spent this evening in company with Mr. Gray, the editor of the *Mail* newspaper. He has a pretty daughter, with whom to-night I renewed a dilapidated acquaintance. In coming away—would the reader have thought it?—I really executed a bow—yes, an actual bow! This speaks well for my improvement in the fine arts....

17 April, Saturday.

In pursuance of my resolution of Wednesday last, I have read closely and attentively, Chesterfield's celebrated *Principles of Politeness....*

In many things, Chesterfield speaks like a man of sense; but, upon the whole I think his little book is calculated to do more mischief than good. I am sure the majority of mankind are prone enough to be formal apes, and scraping, smiling coxcombs of fashion, without his eloquence to set them forward.

---

61. Joseph C. Delacour (1813–91) operated a drugstore at Third and Plum Streets in Camden.

18 April, Sunday.

I went this morning to Doctor Ide's[62] church in Second Street, Philadelphia, at the solicitation of my friend Sam. By some mysterious coincidence, the Constellation from Camden were there too, and by another strange accident I happened to procure a seat within the influence of Phoebe's dangerous eyes! The house was dressed in mourning, and I observed before the pulpit a basin in which they immerse their candidates for membership. This is called The First Baptist Church of Philadelphia, and for beautiful girls, it is the first.

This afternoon I heard Mr. McCalla[63] deliver what he called an Eulogy of General Harrison, at the Baptist Church in Camden. This man is a Presbyterian clergyman, of great learning, and, I guess, with not a little of intolerance. His address was replete with invective against the Church of Rome, lugged in for what purpose, on such an occasion, I cannot see; and his text was that one in Isaiah which, as the newspapers say, struck Harrison's attention very forcibly, a few days before his death: "The burden of Dumah. He calleth to me out of Seir, Watchman, what of the night? watchman, what of the night?" Chapter XXI, verse 11. David Paul Brown, the vainest and the most eloquent of all the inhabitants of the city of brotherly love, honored us with his presence. He is of opinion, perhaps, that they on the other side of the river have looked at his gold snuff-box and ruby-finger-rings enough, and is willing consequently to astonish our humble eyes.

In the evening I went again to Baptist meeting, and heard a sermon about Education by a Doctor Samis. It looked very like an advertisement to those who know he is going to open a school, to-morrow in the Academy.[64]

19 April, Monday.

My skiff, which has been painted and fixed up in style, was launched this morning; and in the afternoon I sailed down to the fishery, got a shad, and came back, and actually put it in a tub of water, to clean it, before it was done floundering. I had two men in the boat, and started at slack-tide; there being a fresh breeze from the west. We went in twenty seven minutes, and returned against the ebb, in twenty three. The distance is about three miles. I have been boating pretty

62. George Ide (1804–72) was pastor of Philadelphia's First Baptist Church.
63. William L. McCalla (1788–1859), a highly controversial Presbyterian clergyman, had served as minister at various churches in the Philadelphia area since 1823.
64. Dr. O. K. Sammis apparently did not start his school in Camden. He was active in the town in late 1841 and early 1842, however, with his course of lectures on phrenology.

industriously all day, in order to restore the roses to my cheek, which studying Virgil the past winter has nearly wiped out. . . .

20 April, Tuesday.

To those who believe in the mediation of Providence in human affairs, proofs enough have been given, I think, to convince them that the people of this country, in electing Harrison to the Presidency, committed an error at which the very heavens are displeased. For my part I believe most sincerely in the existence of an all-wise God; I believe that in his hands the destinies of nations are placed; and I believe that from his hands this country has been punished, for its wild enthusiasm in elevating, by appeals to the basest passions, a man into official power and station, from which a better was removed.

Pending the election, misfortune began to lower upon the fireside at North Bend; for a son of General Harrison died suddenly in the vigour of manhood, and the prime of his career. While tears yet dimmed their eyes at the loss of one of their beloved members, acclamations from Maine to Missouri hailed the bereft father the Chief of the People. But the joy attendant upon the attainment of the pinnacle of their ambition was short. Ere the particulars of his inauguration had reached the extremities of the country, the news of his death was on wing; ere the shouts that hailed him President had died away, the lamentations for his death began to rise. The illustrious man had scarcely been consigned to the tomb, when his family's residence at North Bend was burnt to ashes: thus realizing the saying that "misfortunes never come single!"

Since Harrison's death, there have been processions in most of the large cities in honour of his memory; and it is remarkable that the days appointed for those ceremonies have invariably been untoward. At the parade in New York (on last Saturday two weeks) there was a violent rain. A severe snow-storm caused the honours intended to be shown in Philadelphia on last Tuesday to be postponed until to-day; and to-day, although the morning was bright and promising, yet it began to rain as the procession was about to move, and continued raining until to-night. . . . If all this be hap, chance, I must own, is most wonderful—if all this be hap, let us hear no more of providential interference in human affairs.

I repaired to the city pretty early this morning, and walked about it until noon, when hearing the sound of the approaching drums, I drew up upon the curb-stone, and saw the procession continue to pass for an hour. This was not one quarter of it; but I got tired of standing in the rain, and came home. The military was splendid, but

many particulars of the parade were excessively ludicrous, especially
the clergymen in full robes, as, trudging along through the mud, they
held umbrellas in one hand, while with the other they held up their
gowns, and looked most irresistably rueful. Artillery was discharged
all the time in Washington Square; muffled bells sent forth their dole-
ful sounds and many of the fronts of houses were hung with heavy
festoons of black crape. It was, altogether, an imposing sight, and but
for the rain, the pageant would have passed off very well. Philadelphia,
I guess, was never so populous as to-day. People flocked into the city
from all parts of the country, by hundreds; and hundreds left it with
the conviction that something was wrong in the election of Harrison....

21 April, Wednesday.

Joseph R. Chandler, Esquire,[65] lectured this evening before a full
audience upon "Parental duties." His address was written in pure
English, and in some parts was read with much eloquence. He has a
comical way of shrugging up his shoulders and blinking his keen eye,
which would forbid any one from ever forgetting him....

22 April, Thursday.

My uncle promised me this morning that he would see Colonel Page
about my reading law with him. He said he would go over perhaps
to-day, at all events before long....

24 April, Saturday.

... In the evening Master Sam paid me a visit; in gratitude wherefor
I beat him in a rub at chess. Notwithstanding his scientific openings
and tricks, I checked him in nine moves. The best way of beginning,
as I have found in all my experience, is to advance the king's pawn
one square and then to play the queen and the released bishop. I
have often won a game with these two pieces without even a pawn's
being captured on either side.

By the newspapers to day, I see that "on motion of James Page,
esquire, William D. Kelly has been admitted to practice in the Common Pleas and Quarter Sessions of Philadelphia." Now is my chance! I
must read law with Page!

25 April, Sunday.

Three times at church again to-day! In the morning I went to Doctor
G. Ide's, in Lagrange place, near Second and Market Streets, Phila-
delphia, where the same coincidence occurred that I mentioned last
Sunday. There is not a Jordan artificial before the pulpit, however, as
I thought I saw on my first visit. I had been told that there was one,
and found but little trouble in translating the sacrament-table into it;

65. Joseph R. Chandler (1792–1880) was editor of the *Gazette of the United
States,* 1822–47.

"For what a man's resolv'd to spy
He can detect with half an eye."

In the afternoon I went to Harry VIII's church[66] and heard a learned extemporaneous sermon from some stranger. This was in Camden. The pretty little girl to whom I was introduced last Wednesday week sat just before me. She has not the most beautiful hand in the world—and that's enough.

At night I heard Mr. Tyndall attempt an Eulogy on Harrison.

26 April, Monday.

I received a letter from Samuel Foster this morning. . . . This young man, when I got acquainted with him, was an apprentice harness-maker, and very fond of books. His master lived next door to us, in Garrett's row, here in Camden; and he used to walk along the rain-spout, at the eaves of the building, after they supposed he had gone to bed, and thump at the window of my study, which was in the attic story. Often have I let him in, and, sat up till the night was far advanced, instructing him in the little that I knew, and listening to the good stories which he used to tell so well. . . .

My guardian made arrangements to-day for me to read law with Page. I calculate on commencing on this day week.

27 April, Tuesday.

. . . I sailed down to the fishery this afternoon, with Gideon V. Stivers Jr. and a little negro wharf-rat that I picked up for ballast. The wind was north-west, the tide slack—the sea high—the negro scared—the voyage fine—the weather ditto. Coming back we were obliged to reef, notwithstanding which, the spray wet us to the skin.

28 April, Wednesday.

. . . To-night Doctor Isaac S. Mulford delivered the nineteenth and last lecture of the present course before the Washington Library, upon "the influence of the mental upon the bodily powers." The audience was larger than at any former lecture, and showed by their close attention how much they were gratified. For my part I derived more instruction from it than from any other one we have had; and were it not that I intend to borrow and copy it entire, I would here make an abstract from it, for future reference. . . .

The Camden *Mail* of this morning contains a flaming compliment to the Library Company, for procuring the past course of lectures. Gray, the Editor, says that we, the sons, have undertaken what the

66. Mickle refers to St. Paul's Episcopal Church in Camden.

fathers neglected—that we have made another place of Camden, and a great deal of the same kind of stuff.

29 April, Thursday.

I have kept close to the house this rainy day, busied in reading Gillie and in finishing the first book of "the Scrapiad." By the by I had an offer a short time ago for the copy-right of my Hudibrastic—and that too from no less a personage than the Town clerk of this right goodly city of Camden![67] Ever since I read the adventures of my ragged hero to him, he has never seen me without having something to say about the man or the man's wife or the man's and wife's mare. With the members of the Institute some of Scrapio's smart sayings are bandied about like household words. I'm on my road to fame, eh reader?

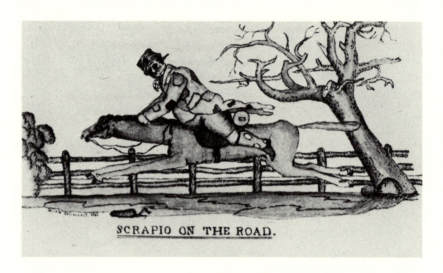

SCRAPIO ON THE ROAD.

30 April, Friday.

. . . Doctor Mulford lectured this evening before The Howard Beneficial Society, to a larger audience than could have been expected, when the proverbial meanness of our Camden people in matters of benevolence was remembered. His address is to be published, and it well deserves it. I joined the Association; which makes the fourth society of which I have the honour to be a member. The other three are: The Washington Library, The Henry Institute, and The Camden Literary Association.[68] By paying four dollars a year to the last of

67. Mickle's friend, Josiah R. Atkinson, Jr. (1811–81), son of a Camden justice of the peace, had been elected town clerk on 8 March 1841.

68. The Camden Literary Association had been founded sometime since 1838 and, apparently, did not last much beyond 1841.

these I have access to about twenty five of the best periodicals of this country and England. The newspapers which are taken by our family of three, are *The Saturday Courier* and *Pennsylvanian,* of Philadelphia; The Trenton *Emporium*; and the *Mail* and *Democrat,* of Camden: weekly; Kendall's *Expositor,* Washington; irregularly; and *The Spirit of the Times* Philadelphia; daily. In addition to these I receive every few days from some old schoolmate papers from all parts of the country. What with the above and my own library, I have sufficient means of enjoyment; and between these and the reading of law, and the business of love, and the exercise of benevolence, in which I have commenced to-night, I have plenty of work in prospect.

The lecture mentioned above was delivered in the Methodist Church—Richard Fetters, Esquire, presiding. A collection was taken up, and twenty seven new members were added to their list.

A deficiency has been discovered in the Camden Bank, which to day makes a good deal of talk. J.W. Peterson, a clerk employed by that institution in an office in Church Alley, Philadelphia; a worthless, dissipated fellow, has robbed it, as they say, of thirteen thousand dollars. This is an underestimate, I dare believe. But whether the default be much or little, it tends to prove the dogma of the demo-cratic party, that there is something in the very atmosphere of a Bank that is detrimental to honesty. "There's something rotten in" the whole "Denmark" of banking, and nothing, I fear, but a great popular com-motion can purge it away. This, were it to happen to-morrow would cause, in me, no wonder.

Almost a month has now passed since, by the death of General Harrison, John Tyler was called to fill the Presidential chair of this country. It was hoped that the professions made in his inaugural address would have been carried out in practice; but four weeks have shown those hopes to be idle, and doomed to disappointment. Tyler has abused his accidental power more than his enemies feared, and more than his friends can excuse. Notwithstanding a direct and solemn protestation to the contrary, he has carried on a continual proscription of honest and able officers, from alpha to omega; filling their places too, with men in many cases far inferior. Thus Colonel Page was removed from the Philadelphia Post-Office, and John C. Montgomery[69] appointed in his lieu, although his honesty is so doubt-ful that he could hardly procure the necessary sureties even among his warmest friends. This particular proscription, made by Harrison, is far surpassed by many others made by his bastard successor. Not only the highest must "pack up and begone," but the lowest are not lowly

69. Montgomery, a railroad executive, served as Philadelphia's postmaster from 1841 to 1844.

enough to escape the besom of removal. From Secretary to bottle-washer, all in the public service are now or soon will be Federalists.

To the principle of this thing I would not object. The laws of justice and gratitude require the President to prefer a friend to an enemy, when both are equally capable of doing their appointed duty. But when a party that has always professed to consider every removal by the opposition a grievous proscription, comes into power, and in the teeth of all consistency rewards its favourites without any regard to capacity or honesty, then indeed I cannot suppress the exclamation, o Hypocricy, thou art detestable!

The past month has been excessively rainy, and the river has been continually swelled in consequence thereof. Fears are entertained for the crops by many farmers. But the measure of our country's misery is full; there is no room for famine.

1 May, Saturday.

The forepart of this merry day of the olden time was cloudy and unpromising—many an intended excursion I ween, was marred, and many a bright young eye suffused in tears of disappointment. This holy day is of very ancient origin, and of a very natural one too; for nothing can be more natural than to feel joyful at a period when the flowers of the field and the trees of the forest awake out of the torpor of winter, and put on their brightest garbs; when the birds begin to sing, and the air to be redolent with balmy incense. This is the time of Nature's festivity; and in the day thereof shall man also not be joyful? Let the curious search among their musty tomes, and, as Burns says, "Mickle Greek and Latin mangle," to ascertain the origin of this merry anniversary: its history is found in the human heart, which in every age and clime spontaneously rejoices at the return of spring after the hardships of winter.

I went a-Maying this morning with Master Frank Ogden, a good-for-nothing, good-natured, gallows-doomed, clever scamp: to wit, around by Cooper's Creek, and "the Woodlands." At the latter place we played a game or two of ten-pins, at which the rascal beat me. I had my revenge however, for as he stooped down to take better aim than common, he tore his trowsers most extensively in a place where a rent is most provokingly perspicuous.

This afternoon I called again upon Colonel Page, and fixed it that I am to commence the *lucubrationes viginti annorum* on next Monday or Tuesday. I had a good deal of conversation with him, and think he is a very gentleman. . . .

2 May, Sunday.

In company with Master Sam Cowperthwait I went to old Christ

Church this morning, and heard a good sermon. At evening I attended Baptist meeting on my own side of the river, where a discourse was preached from Luke XIV, 18. . . .

It is very cold, for the season, this evening. Farenheit indicates thirty-two degrees. It will freeze before morning.

3 May, Monday.

To-day I commence a new life—the study of the law! To-day the die is cast upon which depends my future success or ruin, honour or disgrace, happiness or misery; and to-day therefore let me throw off my idleness and resolve to do my best! If I triumph, well; if I fail, let me fail with stout resistance!

The particulars of this day will serve for those of days succeeding; to wit—at nine o'clock I begin to read; at twelve I come home to dine; at half past two I return to my study; between five and six, I come home for the night. In the morning I intend to cross the river at the Public Ferry, by which my walk is only about three squares; at night, for more exercise, I will cross at English's ferry.

The office is pleasantly situated in Walnut near Third Street, opposite to the old Almshouse of the Friends. Colonel Page, being an active politician, has an army of friends, some of whom are stopping for him at every minute. To day, I think, there were fifty of these visiters at the office—all genteel men, and warm politicians, and good democrats at that. Notwithstanding their intrusions however I read fifty pages of Blackstone whom I like, so far, exceedingly. Mr. Page put me under the charge of Mr. Kelly a young practitioner who occupies a part of the office. Thus far things work bravely! The first day is a promising one!

At noon I walked with Gideon V. Stivers, Junior. down to the Navy Yard to see the steamer *Mississippi*[70] which is to be launched next Wednesday. She is a noble vessel, and noble deeds may she perform in her country's behalf! Her pumps (o the shame!) are of English manufacture, and bear the crown and lions over the patentee's name. Are there no Yankee pumps, I wonder, for Yankee ships? If not, some Connecticut blacksmith should set his wits to work forthwith. . . .

Towards evening I visited the Exhibition of paintings in the Artists' Fund Hall, and was much pleased.[71] There are several hundreds of fine paintings there.

70. The *Mississippi*, a side-wheel steamer, had been built under the personal supervision of Commodore Matthew C. Perry. The vessel served as Perry's flagship during his famous voyage to Japan in 1852–55 and was eventually destroyed during the Civil War.

71. The exhibition hall was built by the Artists' Fund Society, on Chestnut Street above Eleventh, in 1840.

To-night, there being a full meeting of the Henry Institute, I read the first book of the Scrapiad. The broad wit produced a great laugh, while the finer strokes were heard quietly, or not heard at all. . . .

4 May, Tuesday.

The second day of my sergeantship is over, and as yet I am well enough satisfied with the study itself, and with all the circumstances under which I study. I read about fifty pages in Blackstone to day, which is twenty five more that the number Mr. Kelly recommended. Sir William is so interesting indeed that it is a task to lay him down. . . .

5 May, Wednesday.

I remained at the office till noon to-day; at which time, *avec tout le monde*, I went to see the launch of the Steamship *Mississippi*, from the greater house at the Philadelphia Navy Yard. I got on board the *Hornet*,[72] and away we went, with flying colours and gallant music, through a floating world, and past wharves and vessels crowded with living masses, to the scene of action. There were steamboats, and sail-craft, and row-barges, ornamented with flags and crowded with people *omnis generis*, while on every one the sweet strains of music were heard, the martial drum and the mellow horn, the shrill fife and the hoarse bugle. Our boat procured a good station; and a great many of the passengers getting on that side which was next the Yard, she was so listed over that all had a clear view; the deck ascending like the seats in the pit of a theatre gave those in the rear an equal chance of seeing with those in the front. Doctor Harris[73] was not a little discomposed lest we should capsize; but this catastrophe did not happen, although the boats' lee guards were even with the water, several times.

At quarter past one a gun was fired. At precisely half past a general flourish of trumpets, and a subdued cry of "She moves! she comes!" from thousands of throats, announced that the event was at hand. Slowly, and almost imperceptibly at first, then faster and still faster, she glides—the water foams before her elegant stern, and now, like a graceful swan she rides her native element! A commotion among the thousand craft ensues, and nine thundering cheers rend the welkin, as the *Mississippi* rounds to on the failing flood. Artillery was discharged from the shore and answered from a revenue cutter lying in the stream, immediately after the launch. The densely crowded steamboats passed in turn under the new vessel's lee, and hailed her with cheers and

72. The *Hornet*, built in 1839 for the Camden and Philadelphia Steamboat Company, was a wooden paddle steamer.
73. Dr. Samuel Harris (1781–1843) had been, in 1811, the first physician to settle in Camden.

music. Our excellent band performed *The Star Spangled Banner* as we passed by, on our way home, and those on other boats played appropriate national airs as they followed, in turn. There were more people afloat to-day, I think, than when three or four years ago the famous *Pennsylvania* was launched from the same place. Some of the boats were crowded to excess; and the *Clifton*[74] steamboat was on the very point of rolling over, by reason of so many mounting upon her upper deck. For a moment or two the whole assemblage breathlessly awaited to see her upset, but after several heavy rocks she became steady again, and stood it out.

It rained a little just as the people began to disperse, but not enough to mar their enjoyment. This has been a kind of holy-day with all classes; and one class has kept it as they keep all other such days, by getting, like Tam o' Shanter, and Sonter Johnny—"glorious—O'er all the ills of life victorious."[75]

7 May, Friday.

. . . I reached the office before nine o'clock, and immediately went to work; and spent the day in reading Blackstone on the Parliament, and copying political notices for Mr. Kelley. From what I can learn a move is about to be made to throw off the state debt of Pennsylvania!

After I returned from the city this evening, I played a game or two of tenpins with Robert W. Ogden, Jr., which cost him (o the misery of dressing in eel-skins!) a rent in his coat. After supper I had a bout at chess in company with Gideon V. Stivers, the son of Gideon, and beat him. He then defied me to check his king with two bishops and one knight, which after an hour's work I did. This triumph gives me but little satisfaction, when I ask myself the question, How many pages of Gillie's *Greece* could I have learned during the hour that the game took up? . . .

8 May, Saturday.

I to-day finished Blackstone *de familia regali*; and after the experience of a week I conclude that the study of law is far less dry than it has the character of being. He who cannot admire Blackstone has no relish for pure and simple style, combined with forcible conception and profound—but I forget the world has long ago heard his merits discussed.

At Mr. Kelley's request I also read *An Address to the Democracy of Worcester, Mass. on the Fourth of July, 1841,* by the famous Brown-

74. The *Clifton,* built in 1837, was a wooden paddle-steamer, owned by the Salem and Delaware City and Philadelphia Steamboat Company.
75. In short, by getting drunk. Mickle quotes Robert Burns' *Tam o' Shanter.*

son, the leveler, the eloquent Editor of the *Boston Quarterly Review.*[76] There are many propositions in this pamphlet which will bear debating, but that it is a well-composed thing none can hesitate to admit. Brownson says it is his aim to bring all men upon a common level, and to disenthrall them from every kind and description of tyranny, whether it be to the priests, that they bow, or to the strong man, or the rich. On another occasion I wish to notice this address more largely; for the present suffice it to say that Brownson is the leader of the radical part of the democratic party, that Kelly is one of his converts, and that Mr. Page himself preserves, as yet, a silence from which I can infer nothing of the opinion which he entertains of the principals which the Review and its editor advocate. Doctor Patterson . . . is at the office every day to talk with his intimate friend Kelley; and although the lecture which he lately delivered in Camden was fraught more than any other of the course with pious reflections, yet I find he too is a Brownsonite, and can swear like a trooper! How detestable is hypocricy when we find it out!——yet how often does it escape detection, and pass for true piety! He who professes holy things in public, and despises them in private, is the most contemptible of all animals. . . .

10 May, Monday.

I read sixty pages of Blackstone *hodie,* besides copying some resolutions to be presented by Mr. Kelley at a radical meeting in front of the State House, (to consider "the iniquitous and anti-republican bill of indulgences" lately granted by the legislature of Pennsylvania to the rotten banks) this evening, at eight o'clock.[77] Kelley and his radical Brownsonite companions wish to throw off the enormous debt of their commonweal, and to let its creditors whistle for their due; but Mr. Page, Congressman Brown and others of the milder democrats, oppose, as well they may, this shameful measure. The Colonel took a stand in the middle of the office this afternoon, and made a long and truly able speech in oppugnation to the wild schemes of Kelley, Patterson and their clique, "who," said he, "by persevering in their determination of becoming notorious even at the expense of the public honour and the commonwealth's honesty, will work the defeat of the whole democratic party in the state election for governor at the coming fall; and "the Keystone" once federalized, the whole country will be thrown into the hands of the federalists for twenty five or maybe

76. Orestes Brownson (1803–76), a prominent reformer and writer from Boston, had written and delivered *An Oration Before the Democracy of Worcester* on 4 July 1840.

77. The so-called "Relief Bill" suspended state penalties against defaulting banks. Whig legislators passed it over Governor Porter's veto.

thirty years." Kelley could not answer by argument, and dared not by sarcasm, his usual and effective weapon; and so the conversation was changed. There are, I find, two distinct divisions in the democratic party; Brownson, armed with brand and sythe, heads one, clamorous for equality between all men in all things, and disseminating doctrines subversive of all order; while the wiser and more honest portion altogether repudiate his theory, and remonstrate with his followers in a tone addressed indeed as to friends, but as to friends who to-morrow may become their enemies. The *Pennsylvania* is the organ of the Moderates, in Philadelphia, and the *Spirit of the Times* of the Radicals. Colonel Page has a great respect for the talents of Kelley, and it pains him that he should have adopted such fantastic notions. Mr. Martin,[78] who was admitted on the same day with Kelley keeps up a neutrality, and so, as yet, have I. When the matter shall have been discussed more completely I will decide the question of, "Moderate or Radical?" For the present I have only to pity the pecuniary pother and perplexing politics of poor Pennsylvania! The gallant ship upon a lee shore—the noble charger rushing headlong to a fatal precipice.

At the Institute to-night the question was discussed, Should the Bible be used as a class-book in common schools? A pious church member presided, notwithstanding which we of the negative carried off the palm of victory. For my part, I argued against my convictions; but not the less strenuously for that.

11 May, Tuesday.

. . . I took a walk out to the Woodlands this afternoon; then came back to Heyl's Garden and rolled a game or two of tenpins for exercise. In the course of my peregrination I saw about fifty men moving the large Coach-shop of the exploded firm of Scull and brothers.[79] It is to be converted into a town-school house. Prosper the cause of public education! for in that is the hope of our republic.

Doctor Dyott, who made such a noise in Philadelphia about two years ago, was yesterday released from prison, *jubente Gubernatore.*[80] His time was half endured out, but the Governor was of opinion that he was too big a knave to receive the honour of being kept in the

78. James K. Martin, who had just passed his bar examination a month earlier, was another lawyer in Page's firm. Mickle describes him in detail in the entry of 15 May 1841.

79. Samuel Scull had founded the first of several coach factories in Camden in 1800 and, by the 1820s, had a large factory on Arch Street, between Front and Second. The company apparently folded, like so many others around the United States, in the severe financial difficulties following the Panic of 1837.

80. Thomas Dyott had been found guilty of fraudulent insolvency after his glassworks failed in 1836 and was sentenced to prison in 1837.

penitentiary, and so reprieved him from the civil death thereof. The times are such, and rogues and murderers are so thick now, out side of the prison walls, that honest men will be obliged to shut themselves up in limbo to keep their characters from being suspected. Even to-day, to wear a broadcloth coat and afford a coach and two subjects one to the imputation of being a bank-man—alias a thief. . . .

12 May, Wednesday.

. . . The weather for a month back has been almost continually cloudy and rainy. The crops, say the farmers, will, in consequence, be much retarded, if, indeed, some of them are not entirely ruined. William Bates,[81] the most experienced agriculturist in the vicinity of Camden, told me a few days ago that the seeds in the ground are all rotting, while the long rains prevent the planting of later produce, and the preparation of the soil for truck. Peas have been in market of former years, by this time; but now the vines have scarcely begun to blossom. The cost of all this will have to be defrayed by the consumers in the cities, the poor portion of whom are now, by the cursed operations of Bank speculations, reduced almost to starvation.

This is the first evening I have spent at home for the past six weeks, with no company with me. And the merit of this self-denial belongs rather to the untoward weather than to any will of mine.

13 May, Thursday.

With the same horse and wagon used by Sam and myself on our Haddonfield jaunt, I took my respected mother and her sister Eliza to see the Huggs. We arrived at their farm, which is near Moorestown, about ten o' the clock, this morning, and found them all well. Little Joe is brimfull of mischief, and Mary is as lively as ever. We returned before dark, having ridden nine miles in an hour and a half, notwithstanding the roads were in some places very bad. A shower of rain fell as we were coming home.

Joseph Hugg, my aunt Hannah's father-in-law, is an old man to whose conversation I could listen day in and day out, so full is he of well remembered tales of the olden time. He lived on Timber Creek, in this county, in his boyhood, and was in the fort at Red Bank on the day after the overthrow of the Hessians under Donop. He says that not one third of the men under the command of Greene on that glorious day, were white. The majority of them were Indians, with some negroes and mulattos. When Donop marched down from Camden, (where he quartered in the house now occupied by Joseph W.

81. City directories list William Bate simply as a farmer, residing on Fifth Street below Market.

Cooper, at Cooper's Point) he ordered all the bridges over Newton and over Timber Creeks to be demolished after him. He had a peice or two of artillery, also, which increased his hope of bringing to a stop the Yankees about, as he thought, to run away. Sure of success the three thousand hirelings marched against the little band of Freedom's soldiers: being arrived at the fort, a demand was made for a surrender of the same to "George the Third, King of Great Britain, Ireland, and these Colonies, of the faith the defender," and so forth, to which Green deputized one of his officers to say that "George the Third might be damned first"—in which reply was more perhaps of sincerity than politeness. The fortification had been intended for a garrison of fifteen hundred men, but had been reduced to the convenience of five hundred, whereby a large portion of the embankment was thrown out and left unguarded. Through the gate of this undefended outwork the Hessians rushed without order, though with a loud shout for what they thought a bloodless victory. When the enclosure was nearly filled, and Greene could distinctly see the whites of the enemies' eyes, the word was given, and a crossfire from the hitherto masked battery of the fort mowed down the foes of Freedom in scores and hundreds. The victorious shout soon changed to the wail of defeat. Death rode on every volley. Donop fell, at the head of his miserable countrymen. The survivors hastened back to Philadelphia, by way of Chew's Landing, where some farmer's boys resisted them a while, and induced them by their resistance, it is supposed, to throw their artillery into the Creek; certain it is they were never taken over it, nor have they to this day been found. Mr. Hugg saw the Americans, the next day, burying the slain, some of whose bodies were perforated with the wads, or literally blown to peices with the shot—so near were they to the fatal muzzles. He confirms also the anecdote of Miles Sage . . . and of the Spartan Mistress Whitall . . . as I have narrated them.[82]

Between "uncle Josey" and the delightful children I had a very pleasing visit, and was sorry when it was at an end. Talking of ends, by the by, Mr. Hugg predicts that the Union will come thereto before seven years. Why he, an inveterate federalist, should think so in these times of federal ascendency, I cannot see.

Mr. Chapman[83] (*eruditissimus homo*) invited me into his library,

82. Mickle's account of the Battle of Red Bank comports with modern versions in most particulars, but Donop was not quartered in Cooper's house and recent studies suggest that there were more white troops at the fort than Hugg remembered. For the story of Mistress Whitall, see the entry of 17 July 1840; for that of Miles Sage, see 7 March 1841.

83. Thomas Chapman (d. 1845), a native of Salem County, was a prominent Camden lawyer and a collector of fine books.

this morning. He is an antiquarian in the way of books, and his house is full of old, curious, new, common, good, bad, big, little, and other, tomes, from the garrett to the cellar. He is the most complete book-worm I ever knew—but a very clever, good-natured man, notwithstanding. I am to show him my copy of Livy some time soon, and to buy a copy of Malte Brun[84] of him, for six dollars.

14 May, Friday.

Agreeably to the recommendation of President Tyler, this day has been observed throughout the country "with fasting and prayer" upon the account of the decease of General Harrison. In Philadelphia the stores were closed, and all the churches open. The streets bore the appearance of a Sunday—but few people stirring there-in, and those few looking unusually sad. But notwithstanding all this outward hypocrisy, many transacted business in their shops by the light of the back windows; and some, I guess, attended church with no certain object, or more for the purpose of thanksgiving than prayer, or most of all to see and to be seen. The appointing of this day of dissembled grief is one of a series of steps by which the "powers that be" are attempting to do penance for the iniquitous means by which they succeeded. Montgomery, the whig postmaster in Philadelphia, or as the *Spirit of the Times* calls him, "saint John" lately discharged a letter-carrier because he subscribed to a liberal periodical; and Mayor Swift,[85] a notorious gambler, has used his influence to stop omnibuses from running on Sunday—not even he blushing to aid in carrying on the scheme of hypocrisy.

It rained, of course, during the ceremonies at the churches. Through-out the whole day black clouds have been hurrying to and fro across the skies, now and then weeping tears, as it were, for man's burlesque on grief. For my reason for saying it rained of course, see [*entry of 20 April 1841*]. . . .

15 May, Saturday.

I carried my old Livy around to Mr. Chapman's to-day at noon, and remained some time his fine library. He thinks that my relique is what I bought it as being, the copy owned by Melancthon, and says it is worth twenty dollars. Some allowance must be made however for his enthusiasm. . . .

It is worthy of note that the sturgeons in the Delaware began to leap on yesterday. How they do this, philosophers are at a loss to determine. Some suppose they sink to the bottom of the river and then

84. Conrad Malte-Brun (1775–1826), a Danish geographer, was author of an encyclopedic geography of the world.

85. John Swift was mayor of Philadelphia, 1832–38, 1839–41, and 1845–49.

swim obliquely up with great swiftness; but were this so they could not leap in shoal water, which I know they can. Four or five years ago my uncle had some of these fish in a fish-pond on his place, which was only six feet deep; but notwithstanding this, they used to leap twelve feet out of the water, which is as high as they ever jump in the deepest rivers.

Having now been reading law two weeks, I have become well enough acquainted with my office-mates to know their respective characters, and understand their particular eccentricities. But since the reader of this may not have had the same chance of knowing them, he will be obliged to me for the following sketch:

I. James Page, Esquire, Ex-Post Master of Philadelphia, Colonel in the volunteer corps of State Fencibles, Attorney-at-law, and professional politician; is a fine looking bachelor, aged I should suppose about forty five years. He has a martial gait and carriage, dresses well but not fashionably, is a very happy speaker in the comic way, and by no means a common one in serious argument. He is a democrat to the spine, and in speaking of the nomination of Commodore Stewart the other day he said he had rather a civilian should be taken up than him; but if he, nay if the devil himself, were taken up, and were a good democrat, he would go for him to the death. Mr. Page is very popular with his party, and is respected by his opponents as a clever and an honourable man. He has a fund of original wit, from which he is ever willing to draw for the amusement of a public meeting or a private circle. At the former, his is always the first name that is clamoured after the organization, and he no sooner rises to speak than his audience begin to shrug with satisfaction at the drollery they anticipate. As a lawyer his character is fair; he attends punctually to the business with which his clients entrust him, and if he ever fails of success it is not through a want of industry. He is in moderate circumstances, neither rich nor poor; but his practice is extensive, and might be profitable, were it not that many of his political friends consult him on legal questions, and forget the fees. On an average fifty persons a day call to see him, and the confusion attendant upon their coming and going impedes, not a little, my progress in Blackstone.

II. George Washington Page, like his brother, a bachelor, sits in the office opposite the door, leaned back against the wall, with some miscellaneous volume in his hand, which ever and anon he drops upon his knees, while he edifies some new comer as to the politics of the state in general, and the Bank question in particular. He is rich, and has retired from business; and his time is devoted to reading, thinking and talking about the knotty politics of his native state. His first question to every acquaintance is "what about the banks to-day?" or

"Well, what are the whigs about?" He has a noble forehead, and is, by nature, a superior man; but his parts have never been improved by a good education. He is, however, well-informed, full of sound advice, (which he deals out generously to me) and an exemplar of moral rectitude. Less liberal than his brother, he is in consequence, more opulent.

III. William D. Kelly, (of whom I have often spoken before) was apprenticed to a jeweller, at which trade he worked in New England until he was past twenty one. He posesses quite as much talent, I guess, as integrity. He is too open to flattery, and too fond of display-ing his powers. His forehead is low, and his physiognomy rather disagreeable. In religion and politics he is too wild, radical, and theo-retical; in his converse pointed and satirical; but a very clever fellow withal. He read law two years, and passed his examination with flying colours. If he do not get too deeply into politics and theology, he may make an eminent lawyer; for his voice is deep, full, and powerful, his apprehension quick, his gestures appropriate. Of him and O. A. Brownson's principles I have more to say at another time.

IV. James K. Martin, a stout, sallow, aquiline-visaged young man, has his table, along with George Washington Page, Kelly and myself, in the front office, which connects by folding doors with the Colonel's sanctum in the rear. He has been reading law four years, and is no lawyer yet; although, after a frying examination of two hours, he was admitted to practice by the merciful Court. Kelly passed the same day, but with far greater ease. He was only examined fifteen minutes. Jim is not so brilliant as Kelly—but he is better-principled. He rejects Brownson's notions of things altogether; is moderate in politics, in religion somewhat pious. He has read Blackstone through five times, but, (as Washington Page says) not having reflected on what he read, he knows but little about it. He talks but little, but is pretty good-natured. He sleeps but little, but is surpassingly lazy when awake. In short he promises but little as yet, but may, by dint of perseverance rise to mediocrity, or, maybe, above it.

This is a brief, but I think a faithful sketch, of the four persons with whom, six days, full, out of the week, I spend five or six hours a day. I am perfectly satisfied with them as companions, and will endeavour to give them cause to say the same of me.

16 May, Sunday.
My sweet young cousin, Adelia Hogeland, spent the present, or rather the just past, day, with us. I remained at home to entertain her; and here endeth the record, which is the first part—and now for some reflections, which are the second:

It is a fact evident to myself, and of course more so to others, that for some time back, I have fallen in *malos socios, mala loca, malesque habitus,* or at least upon such as will not bear a close examination. The cause of this is plain. Confined by my studies all day, I have right and a reason to devote my evenings to recreation. For this purpose I start out from home after supper, and for want of agreeable acquaintances upon whom to call, for want of friends my own age, I fetch up in public places, where looking on may lead me, as it has led others, to participating in. From this, defend me, gods! from this, my own principles of right defend me!

This danger would be removed by an extension of my female acquaintance—by changing the billiard-room, for the drawing room; and this change I will make. I had a long walk and a corresponding talk with Lemuel H. Davis this evening, which confirms my resolution to seek the society of the ladies more than I hitherto have. Lem was born, I believe, on the same day with myself, his parents having married on the same day with mine. He went into a book-store and I into a lawyer's office simultaneously. We are just equal in stature and in bashfulness; and the morals of both of us are running to ruin . . . for lack of having the company of divine women to preserve them. To-night we resolved unanimously to begin instanter, and henceforth to become beaus wherever there is a belle; to be ladies' men, with right gallant earnestness; in short, to fall in love to keep out of worse mischief. Prosper the wise resolve! . . .

17 May, Monday.
I reached the end of Blackstone's first book to-day, and underwent a short examination by Mr. Martin upon its contents; of which, as yet, I have but a very crude knowledge. Repeated readings and reflection are required to form an acquaintance of the right sort with Sir William.

At the Institute this evening the following question was debated until near eleven o'clock: Which has the more benefitted the world, Washington or Franklin? For the former Clement, Stivers, Hazard; for the latter, Davis, Fortiner, and myself. An intelligent and unprejudiced council decided in our favour, which I consider a triumph to be boasted of. To obtain a decision from American judges, unfavourable to Washington, is a thing of rare occurrence.

I have heard it suggested within a day or two back, that the ungenial weather of this spring is owing to five maculae on the surface of the sun, which impede his life-giving rays, and make the success of some of the crops a matter of much doubt and solicitude. In 1817, they say, there were two spots on Sol's disk during the spring and summer; and in that year there was but one month in which there was no frost. This thing is worthy of some attention; for such a cold and rainy season never before, in the recollection of the oldest men, stunted the flowers, and repressed the fruits. The trees are as yet almost destitute of leaves, and the face of nature has the appearance of March more than May.

The *West Jersey Democrat* not having come, as it was wont, last Saturday, I called, this afternoon, at the office to learn the *cur* and *quare* of its non-appearance. I found Irwin most miserably dejected.[86] His paper is to issue to-morrow, for the last time! Shame it is, that the only democratic paper in West Jersey should be allowed to die for want of support! but so it is. Democracy, just now, is in bad odour—papers, principles, and all!

Irwin came out last week in favour of the movement of Philadelphia to nominate Stewart for the presidency. His paper's dying wish was for "Old Ironsides."

19 May, Wednesday.

. . . This evening one of the new sect of Mormons,[87] (who have been persecuted into much consideration)—called Newton, had a meeting at the City-Hall. He talked nonsense for an hour and a half to about an hundred people. He is an illiterate fellow, and by reason of a natural impediment in his speech it was most laborious for me to listen to him. The Mormons he says believe the Old and New Testaments with the completest belief, and from them he would bring texts to show that the Book of the Mormon (which was exhumed in the western part of New York state in 1830, and translated by Joe Smith) is authentic. They hold that this continent was inhabited by a branch of God's people at a very remote day, the record of whose doings while here, kept by the scribe Mormon, constitutes their third testament. The meeting was broken up in a blackguard manner by Tyndall and some of his Baptist laughers-down. After showing themselves to be as great fools as the Mormon himself by arguing, or rather attempting to argue, against his ridiculous absurdity, they proved themselves more void of decency by dissolving the assembly in a manner altogether unworthy of the dignity and kindness which we are accustomed to attribute to the character of a minister of the gospel, and professors in the religion of Jesus Christ.

As one of the humbugs of the day, Mormonism deserves some notice

---

86. Samuel Irwin had edited the *West Jersey Democrat* since late 1840.

87. Mormonism had begun only a decade before with Joseph Smith's (1805–44) testimony about a divine revelation and the founding of the church in Fayette, New York.

in this, my diary, of these, my times. This shall be given when I have more of history and knowledge upon the subject than I now have. For the present I shall say but little, and that as follows:

It is no matter how preposterous any new creed may be that is started; in this country, it is not to be crushed by persecution. Religious liberty is guaranteed by the Constitution; and they who think different from the churches now existing, only use the same privileges which those very churches used when they were instituted. If dissention from the popular and established opinions was justifiable formerly, it is as much so now.

Secondly. If we know a new creed to be wrong and injurious to man, we can prove it to be so; if we cannot prove it, we do not know it. But now, if we can expose the danger of a new doctrine by argument, there is no cause for persecution; if we cannot so expose it, we have no right to persecute, for it may be true. So that in both, and in all, cases, persecution is incapable of defence, as certainly as it is incapable of producing the desired effects.

Thirdly, If any man really believes what he preaches, his sincerity sho'd command our respect, however much his doctrines excite our contempt or our disgust. The parson of no church would tell his flock that what he was about to preach exceeded belief, and then look for their respectful attention to his discourse: And as a hypocrite preaching truths deserves not the civility of attention . . . a sincere man even though preaching the most evident absurdities, does deserve it.

For these reasons (and many more that I might give) the very reverend Mr. Tyndall behaved wrongfully at the meeting this evening. And for his exceedingly mean conduct I despise him far more than the fanatical fool for whom he condescended to throw off the dignity of a man, and the humility of a holy man. At the close of the Mormon's bungling speech, after a good deal of confusion by the Baptists and Methodists, the parson of the former arose and said something to this effect: All those who have heard enough about Mormonism to-night and who want to hear no more such nonsense, will please to manifest it by going out of the house. Thereupon a dozen jackasses set up a great braying, and by their noise broke the meeting up in tumult and noise. . . .

21 May, Friday.

The races over the Camden Course closed to-day; they have had elegant, delightful weather for their celebration from the first to the last of the four days, which they have never had before. Our town was lively enough with gamblers, jockies and other knaves, from nine o'clock this morning till night. Pity it is that the efforts of Doctor

Mulford, Mr. Gray and others, for the abolition of this nuisance of horse-racing were not successful.[88]

I engaged a violin to-day at Osbourne's Music Store.[89] It may serve, when I shall have learned to scrape a tune or two on it, to amuse my evenings and keep me out of other company. The sound of the fiddle is the most admirable that can enchain the ears of man; and the name of the instrument itself, when called a viol, is liable to no objection, although I own that when denominated bluntly a fiddle, it conjures up associations of Bedford Street. . . .[90]

22 May, Saturday.

. . . I brought home my violin this afternoon, and borrowed a *Preceptor* from my friend Sam, who by the by, is also commencing the science. When I went for this book I stumbled into the parlour with some outlandish speech or other, without knowing that Miss Eastlack and another young lady were sitting in the corner. When I perceived them I made all haste to speak and bow, and edify them as to the state of the weather! This evening I have been scraping a discord of horrible sounds, doubtless much to the discomfiture of dame Scull, whose young ones have slept hitherto, but will hereafter only try to sleep, in a room adjoining my study.

I took a short sail after my return from the office this evening.

24 May, Monday.

I closed Blackstone at four o'clock this pleasant afternoon, and wended my way to Independence Square, where a Sunday School Celebration took place, as was advertised. Twenty five thousand children of all ages joined in the exercises and listened to an Address by the reverend Mr. Chambers,[91] which was an excellent thing, with the exception of an eulogy which he introduced upon Mayor Swift, for reviving and enforcing an ordinance against using carriages on the Sabbath. The mayor is a notorious gambler and drunkard; and this hypocritical affectation of respect for God's day merits rather the censure than the praise of a clergyman. After the celebration I returned across the river with Misses Clement and Hugg, and had some conversation with them.[92] I also saw Miss Josephine in the square—but

88. Reformers did help close the race track in 1845.

89. J. G. Osbourne's "music saloon" was located at 27 South Fourth Street.

90. Bedford Street was a lower class neighborhood where, presumably, beggars and "loafers" might be heard playing the violin.

91. Rev. John Chambers was pastor of the Independent Church on Broad Street below Chestnut.

92. Probably Miriam Clement, whom Mickle mentions later in the diary, and Anna Hugg, daughter of William Hugg of Fifth and Cooper Streets.

did not speak to her. My acquaintance with this lovely girl has by some mishap, so far decayed, that we pass as if we had forgotten the happy days of other years, without appearing to recognize each other at all, and without seeming to wish a revival of a friendship in which, I think I can say, we both once found pleasure without alloy.

Master Sam gave me my first lesson on the violin this afternoon and assured me I made some progress; which fact however was by no means very evident to myself. According to Shakspeare's rule I am "fit for treasons, strategems and spoils" for I fear I have "not music in my soul." But nothing is to be despaired of: I may become a fiddler yet! . . .

26 May, Wednesday.

. . . There was another Mormon meeting to-night at the Court House; and by reason of the row which Tyndall the Baptist raised on the other occasion, the house was jammed full. Had it not been for the intolerance manifested towards these fanatics I, (and, I dare say, many others) would not have attended this second time; for though as fools their doctrines deserve our contempt, yet as men their rights are entitled to protection.

A much more witting speaker addressed this meeting than Mr. Newton who spoke at the other, and the audience listened and departed decently and quietly. There was not one word said to-night about The Book of Mormon, but the preacher confined himself to the two principal ordinances in which his society believes—baptism by immersion, and laying-on of hands. In the obeying of the former of these, he taught us, is the pardon of sins and the guarantee of reaching heaven; while repentance, if necessary at all, is only a secondary point, and is as well after as before the ceremony of baptism. The virtue of the thing, he contended, lays in its being a fulfilling of a divine command; and were we ordered "to run three times around a tree, and be saved" it would be the same. With such cobwebs as these, and by keeping dark as to the famous Book of Mormon, in which Newton so stupidly professed his belief, he got along without any interruption other than the snores of a goodly number whom his metaphysics had put into a most irreverent nap.

This sect of fanatics, under the leadership of one Joe Smith, are said to be making many converts, not in this country only, but also in England. . . .

29 May, Saturday.

. . . I . . . took up Caesar's *Commentaries* awhile this evening and read his remarks on the Britons. His description of their mode of fight *armatis essedis*, with armed chariots, is perfectly Caesarean. No man ever lived who could both fight and describe a battle so well as the immortal Julius. . . .

30 May, Sunday.

This morning, at the request of Mr. Kelley, I went over the river to "Clarkson Hall," to hear a Transcendental sermon; but when I got there I found an advertisement on the door, stating that there would be "no service here to-day, owing to Mr. Channing's visit to Philadelphia."[93] William Channing is a celebrated Unitarian preacher from the eastern states, and as he preached this morning at one of the Churches, the Clarksonians had all gone to hear him.

Being thus disappointed, I went next to Doctor Ide's sanctuary where some one preached from "I come not to call the righteous, but sinners, to repentance." I have forgotten the place; but the reader, being of course a good biblical scholar, can easily turn to it.

In the afternoon, I heard Mr. Burroughs in Camden speak from "Commune with your own hearts;" and

At evening I listened to a discourse by Tyndall the Baptist, from "the harvest is the end of the world." This may be found, if the minister informed us right or I have not forgotten, in Matthew XIII, 39.

31 May, Monday.

To-day I finished reading Blackstone's Second Book of the *Jura Rerum*; and Mr. Martin tells me that this is the dryest part of our author's work. If this be so, if I have nothing more tedious to read than the Second book aforesaid I shall be agreeably disappointed in the study I have chosen.

I crossed the river this afternoon with Miss Phoebe, and—would the reader believe it?—did not take the pains to walk across the boat to hear her divine voice. We merely spoke, and went each our way. But *quaere*, why is it that I feel so much interest in this lovely family? This must have a cause, and that cause I must find out. "Commune with your own hearts," as the minister showed yesterday, is a good lesson; and especially so when we suspect that love lies thereabouts.

There was no quorum at the Institute to-night wherefore Sam and I adjourned to his parlour and exercised a little in music. He performs on the flute very well; and I too can scrape *Yankee Doodle* on the violin right bravely!

1 June, Tuesday.

When, on the fourth day of last July, I began to keep a record of my daily actions and observations, I had no anticipation of making

93. Clarkson Hall was located at 103 Cherry Street. William Ellery Channing (1780–1842) of Boston was a founder and leader of Unitarianism.

more than a brief note of what I might do and see; but the task growing by degrees more pleasant as I continued, and I suffering my love
for scribbling to carry me away—lo! here I am beginning a third volume in less than eleven months. Compactly, too, are the former
volumes written; insomuch that, if printed, they would make a folio
of respectable size.

I have become so accustomed to retire into my library at the close
of every day, to record in what manner I have spent the hours; and
have contracted such a fondness for the exercise, and for the books
themselves, that I could not discontinue the one nor lose the other,
without feeling deprived of a part of my life, or a part of its enjoyment. For certainly there are few things in which I take a greater
pleasure than in reading in my diary what I have written therein in
the past; and but few things now come more natural than for me to
write in it that, the reading of which may afford me amusement or
instruction, and the same perhaps to others, in the future.

Of the utility of keeping a journal I spoke at large in the *Ad
Lectorem* of the first volume; and I have only now to add that the
experience of nearly a year confirms me in the belief that it is an
occupation in a better than which no one can pass his odd moments
and his scraps of days. It combines amusement with instruction, and
against these there is no disadvantage to be off-set. A diary, to its
writer and to all others, now and through all time, is a lively monitor,
a joking sage, to which the wise can listen and learn, the gay hearken
and laugh, all attend and be interested.

I arose so late this morning that I deemed it useless to go over to
my studies before dinner; an omission for which the lenient reader,
(especially if that reader be Isaac Mickle) will excuse me when I
inform him that I did not fall asleep until near two o'clock this morning aforesaid. I however made amends to Blackstone, this afternoon
for having spent two of his hours in playing upon my violin this—but
it were tautological to say—morning again.

The Message of the President by accident, communicated to the
extraordinary Congress which met yesterday, reached Philadelphia at
about half past five o'clock this afternoon.[94] I heard it read by Joseph
R. Chandler, at the Exchange, as soon as it could be got out of the
mail-bags. There were not more than an hundred people present at
the reading; and so dubious is the import of it in relation to many of
the great questions in which the country is interested, that neither
Whigs nor Democrats ventured to applaud it. I begin to suspect, with

94. The Twenty-seventh Congress held a special session to consider the Whig
program for revenue and finance.

Doctor Mulford, that Tyler is a kind of trimmer. He wants to carry water on both shoulders; but between two chairs he will most likely come to the ground. In point of composition it does—not excel the state papers of the elder Adams. . . .

2 June, Wednesday.
. . . There was another Mormon meeting to-night at the Court House. Gideon V. Stivers and I walked up to hear the fanatic. . . .

3 June, Thursday.
I had a long discussion to-day with Mr. Martin whether the law of libel in Pennsylvania is a good one or not. He said Yes; I contended No, and Washington Page, Messers. Kelley and Patterson agreed with me. I will some of these times report the grounds and the arguments at length.

I spent this evening at Sam's domicile, playing on the fiddle and on the chess-board. He can beat me on the former, and I him on the latter.

4 June, Friday.
Masters Charles West and Henry Edwards,[95] two of my school-mates at Burlington, called upon me at the office this afternoon, and staid a short time, talking over our ancient pranks. Edwards invited me to accompany him to his home in Chester on next Saturday se'en-night, and I promised so to do. He is a good-natured, clever fellow—just one of those who make good citizens in any country.

There was a discussion last evening at the Court-House between a Mormon and a Mr. Rhees,[96] wherein it is said the latter was entirely discomfited and put to rout; although he was backed by a posse of Baptists and other anti-Mormons, who of course applauded all he said, and hissed whatever his opponent advanced. This is the course which the followers of Joe Smith like; for they know well enough that persecution and opposition always help the passive, to the injury of the active, party.

Our churches are too fond of bickering. Church members are too eager for conflicts. When they have no infidels nor heretics to quarrel with, they turn one upon another; for quarrelling with somebody or something must be done. Of this I saw an extraordinary proof, about two years ago, here in Camden. There was a Methodist minister named

95. West's identity is unknown. Edwards, from Chester, Pennsylvania, cur-rently attended school in Philadelphia.
96. John Rhees was a Camden school official in 1842 and became a Camden city councilman in 1844.

Joseph Ashbrook,[97] and a Baptist named Napoleon Bonaparte Tyndall, both holding "protracted meetings" at their respective churches at once. It became a matter of rivalry between them, who could make the greater number of converts; and from this they began to make faint allusions to each other from their pulpits. At this point the women of both congregations took the thing up, and circulated divers scandalous tales about each other's parson—the Methodists of Tyndall, and the Baptists of Ashbrook; whereby both of these worthies were made exceeding wroth against one another. . . .

5 June, Saturday.

. . . I saw one of my old sweethearts—Miss Caroline Cole—to day.[98] She has just returned from boarding-school in Pennsylvania, improved bodily and mentally. . . .

6 June, Sunday.

I walked out this morning to see the venerable John Ward, with his grandson William Ward.[99] We dined there, and remained until about three o'clock, enjoying the substantial conversation of the good old octogenerian; who really seems to belong to another, and less degenerate, world. He has frequently sent word to me by his grandson, that he wished me to come and see him; and it appeared to-day that his reason for wanting to see me is this: He had heard that I was going to begin the study of law, and he had a desire to inform me that lawyers were great knaves, and were very apt to turn out dissolute men. All this I had some suspicion of before; but he told me too that our country wanted more tillers of the soil, and that I owned "a good peice of ground, and enough for any man." Upon this he left me to put my own construction, which I did as follows: "Go to hoeing corn and digging potatoes, Isaac and let the law alone." He told me too the anecdote of my ancestors, the Woods, who settled Woodbury in this county. It is as I am about to write:

About one hundred years ago the Woods and Wilkinses sailed up Woodbury-Creek (as it is now called) and located at Woodbury.[100] The little colony soon after became short of provisions, and none being to be had nearer than Burlington, the male colonists started off in canoes to that place to obtain some; leaving, most ungallantly, their

97. Ashbrook served at the Third Street Methodist Episcopal Church in 1830 and again in 1838–39.

98. Caroline Cole (nicknamed Caddy or Cad) was the sister of Mickle's friend Edward and daughter of wealthy coachmaker Isaac Cole.

99. John Ward (d. 1842) was an octogenarian farmer with lands in Newton Township.

100. Woodbury was founded by the Wood and Wilkens families in the 1680s.

wives and children behind to await their return on the third day. A violent storm prevented the canoes from coming back as soon as it was expected they would; the provisions left for the women were exhausted and the poor creatures, overwhelmed with grief, looked for nothing but strvation in a strange land, with none of their kindred near to soothe their dying moments. Thus they were grouped together at the bend of the creek where now the graveyard is watching with tearful eyes the flowing tide, and listening in vain for the sound of the returning paddles, when an Indian woman appeared on the opposite shore. She saw they were in trouble and stopped. They made her understand by signs what they wanted—and she disappeared again in the shade of the forest. In an hour or two (for she had travelled several miles) she came back loaded with venison and cornbread. These she placed on a long piece of bark, and walking a good way to tideward set it afloat and gave it a push across. It came to where the White women were, and its contents saved their lives; for their husbands came not back, till such length of time that, but for them, their starvation would have been certain. From these circumstances, the Wards, Woods, Wilkinses and Mickles have always treated the red-man, whether young or old, drunk or sober, as a friend, and the benefactor of their ancestors.[101]

I heard Mr. Tyndall preach a sermon to-night at the Baptist Church. After service Mr. Stivers introduced me to some, not very pretty, ladies.

My cousin Emma is recovering. Yesterday she was extremely ill.

7 June, Monday.

Mr. Martin came over the river with me this afternoon and spent an hour or so in my sanctum. I read Scrapio's Adventures, Book I, to him, and he seemed to understand its drift pretty well.

SCRAPIO, CONVERSING WITH THE LITTLE PEDLER.

It was carried at the Institute this evening that we should celebrate the approaching fourth of July in an appropriate manner. I was placed on a Committee to procure an Orator, and that orator shall be William

101. All four families had intermarried since the event Mickle describes.

D. Kelley. The question up to-night for debate was, "In which sex is the passion of jealousy the more predominating?" Our side, for the male, won the decision.

8 June, Tuesday.
The thermometer stood to-day, at 3 o'clock at 98 degrees; notwithstanding which I read my usual portion of Blackstone and a little over. I find the book on Private Wrongs less tedious than I expected.

There was another Mormon meeting to-night in the Court House, but not more than thirty persons attended. There were several ladies on the stairs and outside, who thus gratified both their curiosities and their ministers; the former urging them to go, the latter commanding them to stay away from the heretic gathering. . . .

9 June, Wednesday.
I crossed the river this morning with the eccentric John Landis,[102] of the city of brotherly love. He had been over to Jersey to peddle some of his own books, but had not, (I suspect from his long face) met with much success. He is a middle-sized, swarthy fellow, with long hair and beard (whence his nick-name of the "goat,") and wears an old frock-coat reaching nearly to his feet and a pair of trousers which would be a prize to a tallow-chandler. He has two or three times been arrested for insulting women in the streets, and that notwithstanding his great air of piety; and on the whole I should take him to be far more a rogue than a fool.

This evening I spent with Sam, practising on the violin.

10 June, Thursday.
. . . I met George Harvey evening and walked with him up to the Woodlands, where we played a game of tenpins, and took a swing. He had a rowdy friend with him, to whom he introduced me; but it is more than probable I shall not recollect him when next we encounter each other.

There is a Benton Meeting to be held in Philadelphia to-night in opposition to the Stewart movement. "Of two evils chose the lesser." I prefer Old Ironsides to Tom Benton, because, (if for no other reason) he is a common fellow enough, whom the country only know by a nickname. The Missourian, albeit his nomen ends in "o-n" will never, I guess be President of this country.

11 June, Friday.
Although I did not get to sleep last night until—to use a bull—one

102. Philadelphia city directories list Landis as a "stove finisher" on Germantown Road above Franklin Street.

o'clock this morning, yet I arose a little after four, and took a long sail before breakfast. How much better it would be to do this daily than to lie abed till breakfast-time, as I most generally do!

I finished the third volume of Blackstone to-day; and in the evening went to a singing meeting at the Baptist Church.

12 June, Saturday.

My friend Harry Edwards called upon me at the office this afternoon at three o'clock and I started with him off to Chester, as per promise. His accomplished young sister and Mrs. Matlack[103] accompanied us down in the cars, and we arrived at our place of destination after a pleasant ride of an hour and a quarter. A grand introductorial ceremony being gone through with, Harry and I took a sail upon Chester creek, while the ladies honoured us with their presence on the bank. After tea (which was most splendidly served) Miss Edwards played some tunes on the piano in a most enchanting manner; and then we ended the day by promenading to town with our fair friends, and in making divers calls; in all which I was most highly delighted, and verily most greatly edified—for the conversation of Miss Edwards, whom I escorted, is no less intelligent than her face is handsome. Our walk being over, we had more music, ice-cream and lemonade, and bidding *Bon soir* to the ladies I went to bed.

13 June, Sunday.

The style in which my entertainers live is almost princely, and Miss Edwards is really a princess. Chester has always been famous for pretty girls, as my dear mother, who was at school in Wilmington with Mrs. Edwards, then Miss Engle, informs me; and its reputation therefor is not likely to be diminished. Miss Thurlow, a sun-burnt, black-eyed, laughing girl of sixteen, the daughter of a rich farmer in the neighborhood, came into Chester this morning to see her friend Mary, and with those two lively companions I passed the day most agreeably. Mrs. Matlack too was all vivacity; and notwithstanding the feud between the family of her late husband and ours, we became quite intimate. I find the Edwardses, to be very amiable and hospitable. The father is quiet, but affable; the mother gay and noisy; the son will make a good citizen; the daughter a splendid wife.

Our party were walking along the creek this forenoon, when Harry slipped into the soft mud bordering upon it, to the infinite amusement of Misses Thurlow and Edwards, and the more infinite annoyance of

103. Mrs. James Matlack was the wife of the former congressman, now deceased, with whom the Mickle family had disputed the will of Dr. Andrew F. E. Mickle. See the first entry in the diary.

said Harry himself, whose white trousers were completely spoiled. We looked at the ancient house in which William Penn lived, and at whatsoever else the town contains worth looking at.[104] After many calls and much feasting we went to Episcopal church and heard a pretty good sermon, during which Master Harry set himself about tickling his pretty sister's ears with a straw, with laudable perseverence and most exemplary industry. And after church we made more calls, took more walks, and had more treats, till bed time. So ends the second day.

14 June, Monday.

I left Chester this morning very reluctantly. Harry, his sister, and Mrs. R. Matlack returned to Philadelphia with me. The enchanting Mary rode all the way directly facing me; and who knows what might have been the consequence if I had forgotten Miss Thurlow's pearly teeth and rosy cheeks? But, more of this anon.

Harry accompanied me over the river, and spent a short time in my studio. He did not go to school, nor I to the office, to-day; for which dereliction the Chester ladies must stand responsible. My friend is to return my visit on next Saturday and Sunday week.

I went to Woodbury this afternoon on business. This evening the abolition question was discussed at the Institute; Samuels and Stivers, pro, Cowperthwait and myself, con. Our side came off victorious.

15 June, Tuesday.

I began the fourth volume of Blackstone to-day and read fifty pages, notwithstanding—I left Chester yesterday! My lucky escape from any discomposing result to my visit may be accounted for in this way: I cannot tell whether to fall in love with Miss Edwards or Miss Thurlow—they are in *equilibrio* for loveliness—both alike loveable; but as I cannot love both at once, and cannot (as aforesaid) prefer either one to the other, therefore of needs I must love neither one at all.

My acquaintance with the Edwardses may now be considered as fairly established. Harry, who goes to school in Philadelphia, and boards at Mrs. Simmons'[105] in Second Street, called upon me at the office this afternoon, and promised to stop in as often as he can. We took a walk through the unfashionable part of the city together, and went up the steeple of the State House. He improves upon a more thorough intimacy, and is (I begin to suspect) *haudquaquam stultus.* . . .

104. Mickle refers to the Caleb Pusey house, of 1683, in Upland, just outside of Chester. Penn frequented the house, but never lived there.
105. Mrs. R. R. Simmons' boarding house was at 144 South Second Street.

16 June, Wednesday.

This evening first I took a walk with Frank Ogden, then called for a moment upon some ladies, and then went to Master Sam's, where I heard some good music. Baxter performed on the bass viol, Bishop Ivins on the little viol, and Sam himself on the flute. My love for sweet sounds is increasing to a degree of which I never dreampt when I got a fiddle for myself, to counteract a slight touch of the blue devils brought on by the decease of poor Hinchman. The remedy is likely to remove the disease.

Gray's paper of to-day contains a very flattering notice of the lecture delivered by "the good Doctor," my uncle, which we have had printed.

A letter is published in the *Pennsylvanian* of this morning from Colonel Benton, in which that gentleman declines a nomination to the Presidency. It is thought that the Benton men will now go in favour of Buchanan, in preference to Stewart.[106]

18 June, Friday.

I did not go over to the office this morning, having arisen so late that the trouble of such going would not have been repaid. But in the afternoon I did go, and found the town full of foreign news. Canton has been captured by the British, and a great slaughter made among the inhabitants of the Celestial Empire, by way of forcing them to eat British opium, that British pockets may be filled. The war now waging against China by England is one of the most unexampled injustice. Ambition and avarice are at its bottom; cruelty and coward-ice in its execution; and I hope to God the downfall of the proud oppressor may result from it. When I remember the burning of *la Pucelle*,[107] the execution of Mary Stewart, the exile of Napoleon, and this present hellish war upon an unoffending people—all British acts and applauded by the British nation; when I remember these things, I say, I burn with the thought that in my veins there courses a drop of British blood.

The *Times* of this morning proposes Colonel Page as the Democratic candidate for Mayor of Philadelphia. It says he would be to the present incumbent, Hyperion to a Satyr; but has some doubt whether his heart is not too humane, and his face too good-humoured for the awful seat of justice.

I practised a good deal to-day on my violin, and this afternoon, at

106. Thomas Hart Benton (1782–1858) was a United States senator from 1821 to 1851 and a figure frequently mentioned as presidential material. In Benton's absence from this race, James Buchanan (1791–1868), a United States senator from Pennsylvania since 1835, seemed to be in a better position than Commodore Charles Stewart to run for the presidency.

107. *La Pucelle* was Joan of Arc, the Maid of Orleans.

my uncle's suggestion, stipulated with Osbourne in Fourth Street for a quarter's tuition therein. I am to commence next Monday to go twice a week and pay fifteen dollars a-quarter.

19 June, Saturday.

Not having much to write down to this day's account, I will go back and record some few trifles that I omitted to mention on last Monday. And first of all, why did I go to Woodbury on that afternoon? On business. With whom? My Aunt Haines. About what? The sale of the late Benjamin Mickle's share of the Mickle fishery. This was advertised to be sold by John Kaighn, administrator to said decedent's estate, "by virtue of a writ of the Orphan's Court," on last Wednesday. My uncle was willing to give $800 dollars therefor, which is in truth quite its value, considering it is but a sixth part of the whole, and that fisheries are fast depreciating, in consequence of the imperfect execution of the laws against gillers;[108] and he sent me down to my aunts to request her not to bid any higher than said sum, unless she had some very good reason. She told me she had no wish nor intention to buy it at any rate, since it was a very unsafe investment; and with this answer I returned home. But the next day John Kaighn called upon her, and induced her, I suppose, to offer a thousand dollars; for on Wednesday it was struck off to her name at that price.

And secondly, what did I hear on that occasion worth remembering? James Sloan—Esquire James, forsooth!—happened to be there at the same time, and he and my aunt were speaking of an incident of which I had never before heard, although it seems to be pretty notorious throughout all the ramifications of our family; to wit:

My grandmother on my father's side, Sara Wilkins Mickle, had a brother William Wood Wilkins, whose superior talents and early death I will take occasion to speak of at another time. He studied law with one Todd,[109] and contracted an intimate acquaintance with his family, whereby he was enabled to do one of them a good turn, as I am about to describe. Todd dying left a young, beautiful and accomplished widow, qualified to do dreadful slaughter among the hearts of men. She could sing like a siren, converse with the most fascinating ease and elegance, and spin withal, unlike our more modern belles; and none of these accomplishments were impaired by the year of grief for her lost partner; she arose, like the phoenix from the ashes, more than ever beautiful and perfect, from her deepness of sorrow. In Philadelphia, when that city was the capital of our country, she one evening met a member of Congress, in company. The legislator at first ad-

108. By "gillers," Mickle means fishermen using gill nets.
109. Philadelphia attorney John Todd, Jr. had died in 1793.

mired her beauty; then engaged her in conversation; and from that fell headlong in love with the splendid widow. But he was a prudent man, albeit he was a bachelor, and he resolved not to commit himself too hastily in so grave a matter as matrimony. He told some of his friends that if Mrs. Todd was really the woman she seemed to be, he would have no hesitation in wedding her instanter; but to satisfy himself that the powers displayed in her conversation were not merely superficial, aped from the high circles in which she moved, he intended to address her a letter requesting an answer. The widow got wind of this; and sure enough, soon after, the letter came. But although she could compose as readily as she could talk, yet this was an occasion on which her usual confidence forsook her. She had no objection to marrying the Congressman, but did object to telling him so; and the letter must be more than commonly excellent, for it was to be read by more than a common man. Under these circumstances she requested my grand uncle to frame her answer, and he did so to the best of his ability. The widow copied it, the congressman received, read and was satisfied with it; and (to cut the story short) in a little time afterwards, Mrs. Todd became MRS. JAMES MADISON. . . .[110]

There is no new news in Philadelphia; but a general indignation is manifested by the citizens against the British for their outrage upon the Chinese.

21 June, Monday.

. . . I did not begin to take lessons on the violin as I expected to, to-day, owing to a mistake of my tutor in appointing the time.

At the Institute to-night the question was discussed, "whether a lawyer is justifiable in pleading upon what he knows to be the wrong side." I was on the affirmative and succeeded in convincing the President that such pleading is perfectly excusable and proper. I have happened to be on the victorious side of every debate for ten or twelve nights back.

24 June, Thursday.

I finished Blackstone's excellent *Commentaries* to-day—having been almost eight weeks in reading them. As yet I have but a faint perception of the general outlines of the law, which the study of three years will, I hope, fill up; so as to make a complete map upon any city or mountains of which I may be able, from thorough knowledge, to put my finger. . . .

This evening I carried my violin to Sam's—entering by the back

110. There is no documentary confirmation of Mickle's story, but Wilkins was Dolly Todd's lawyer and close friend and may have helped her in the way indicated.

way—and played some duetts with him. I am making some progress in the ancient and highly respectable science of drawing a horse's tail over the entrails of a cat.

Bob Matlack has advertised the property in Newton, obtained by a fraud of his father's from our family, for sale at public vendue, in the Woodbury *Constitution*. Of this business I have much to say at another time.

25 June, Friday.

I did not go to the city this forenoon, and I might as well not have gone at all to-day; for I did nothing in the two hours that I staid at the office this afternoon but laugh at the drollery of the famous Murdoch,[111] a player, whom the rain forced into our sanctum and detained until after I came away. He gave some pretty strong hints at three o'clock, when he found the Pages were about going up to dine, that he lived away down in South Street, and had not had his grub, nor e'en had an umbrella under which he might go after it; but it would'nt do. This popular son of Momus is a remarkably fine looking young fellow.

Kelley gave me a letter to read which he received to-day from Edgar A. Poe, the poet and scholar.[112] It was concerning Brownson's *Review*, and I find from its contents that Mr. Poe is a transcendentalist of the most ultra stamp. He uses the phrases "the inspired man, Christ," and "the incomprehensible doctrine of original sin and the Salvation of man by the Redeemer," in such a way that there can be no doubt of his religous opinions. I am inclined to think that there is a band of infidels in this country more numerous and dangerous than is generally supposed. There are, I know, many talented men professing outwardly the Christian religion whose hearts are poisoned with new fangled theories of the rights of man, and French notions of the nature of God. There are thousands now who, with a proper leader, would throw off their hypocricy to morrow, and vote, like the revolutionists in France, that Reason should henceforth be their deity, and none other. A leaven is at work in every section of our country fomenting a batch of radicalism in religion and government which will equal, if not surpass those of the days of Robespierre and Voltaire. The witch of Anarchy and the warlock of Atheism, together with sundry miscellaneous devils, are already walking round and round the hellish cauldron, throwing in the horrid ingredients, and repeating their dreadful incan-

111. James Edward Murdoch (1811–93) was a Philadelphia native famed for both comic and tragic portrayals.

112. Poe was currently living in Philadelphia where he was literary editor of *Graham's Lady's and Gentleman's Magazine*. Many of his best short stories were in print, but they had produced little acclaim and virtually no income.

tations to "black spirits and white, blue spirits and gray." When this pot boils over, wo to them that are in the way of the hot ashes!

Sam brought his violin around to my room to-night, and we performed a few pieces together. I can now play several tunes so correctly that my dear mother can tell me what they are, although she has not heard some of them for a quarter of a century before. And I can name an air first and play it afterwards, unlike uncle Job Wilkins who used to christen his tunes after having performed them, to avoid any mistake that might otherwise occur.

26 June, Saturday.

I read some little in the *Spirit of Laws* this forenoon at the office. In the afternoon I went on an excursion to Gray's ferry,[113] by the Steamboat *Ohio*. She started from Dock Street wharf at half past four o'clock, with about three hundred people aboard; among whom were Doctor Harris, my uncle, and the famous Frank Johnson and his band.[114] Frank and I got pretty well acquainted and I found him to be very intelligent for a negro. He loves to talk about flats and sharps and naturals, and to tell of his visit to Europe, his reception in Paris, and his interview with queen Victoria. This musical genius has lately applied for the third time, I believe, for the benefit of the insolvent laws: from which it appears that however fast he may make money, he lives it away faster. There were nine other Ethiopians with him to-day, whose music delighted the party in general and the ladies in particular, not less than the rich ice-creams furnished by Mrs. Wood, the wife of the filiacide.[115]

On our way home we landed at Fort Mifflin and took a promenade; then re-embarked and had a fine, cool, run up to Philadelphia, which we reached just after the Camden boats had stopped plying. After running up and down the stream, once or twice to serenade the city we went ashore. I crossed in a wherry, and got home about nine o'clock; glad that I had begun and by no means sorry that I had ended the trip. Never having been up the Schuylkill before, I enjoyed the romantic scenery on its banks with all the zest that novelty lends.

113. Gray's Public Garden, on the west bank of the Schuylkill River where Gray's Ferry had once docked, was a popular spot for picnics, concerts, and other outings.

114. Frank Johnson (1792–1844), a leading popular musician of his day, conducted his band frequently in and around his native Philadelphia and also won admirers in other states and in England. Johnson was an accomplished composer and arranger as well as master of several instruments.

115. James Wood, who operated a confectionery on Philadelphia's Chestnut Street, killed his daughter in September 1839 because he disapproved of her marrying Edward Peak. Wood was tried and acquitted. See entry of 17 March 1843.

Captain Davis at first refused my ticket money, but I forced him to take it—not liking sponging in any way. My jaunt (refreshments and all) cost me a dollar.

28 June, Monday.

. . . A splendid silver urn was presented to Colonel Page to-day by the clerks and carriers late of the Post-office under his management. It is beautifully chased, with a view of the Exchange and an appropriate inscription, upon it. The Colonel wrote a handsome reply, which he gave me to read and—ahem!—to correct; remarking that young folks often made very excellent suggestions in such things. Of course I found no room for improvement. . . .

The steam ferry boat *Delaware* sunk at English's wharf last night. This same boat's boiler exploded two or three years ago, killing the engineer and another man. Lem Davis . . . was on board of her at the occurence of the accident, and was shot twenty feet into the air. He landed—or rather, he watered—in the river, and came pretty near fetching up in the other world. Being destined perhaps to stretch hemp without foothold, he proved steam-and-water-proof.

29 June, Tuesday.

I read pretty industriously this morning, notwithstanding *tout le monde* were dropping in at the office to see the Colonel's urn.

This evening I and Sam—No!—Sam, Mr. Thompson, my uncle, and I, went on an excursion in the Steamboat *Burlington* to the old city of the same name. . . . We started from Arch Street at eight o'clock, reached Burlington a little after nine, and the company separated then to promenade. Sam and I, having got some ice-cream at Mitchell's went with the band down Green Bank, to serenade the young ladies' Boarding School.[116] After an hour or so spent very agreeably on shore we reembarked, and got under weigh for home, amid deafening cheers from the town-people assembled on the wharves, and the noble air of *Hail Columbia*, happy land, pealing from twenty instruments. Coming down, a cotillion or two were danced on the promenade deck, and we had abundance of music and other refreshments—not omitting the serene moonlight, without which the whole affair would have been intolerable. We arrived at Philadelphia before one in the morning, and a little after two I was asleep at my home in Camden. These excursions are becoming very fashionable, and the people who go on them are generally of the better sort.

116. George P. Mitchell's "Ice Cream and Refreshment House," a few doors from the steamboat landing, was a popular spot among visitors to Burlington. The highly respected St. Mary's Hall had opened, under the auspices of the Protestant Episcopal Church, in 1837.

The present trip cost me about fifty cents.

30 June, Wednesday.

I arose about nine o'clock this morning, and went to Market. Not feeling in a reading humour, I concluded not to go to the office until afternoon, and so spent my time, after my return from market until dinner, in fiddling—or rather in playing the violin. By the bye, I went to Osborne's again yesterday, with the intention of beginning to take lessons of him on the instrument just named, but as usual, "he was really engaged just at that hour—but if I would come next week"— and so forth. I told him in very polite language to go to the devil, while I would look up some other fiddling-master.

There was a salute fired from the Navy Yard at noon to day, in honour of General McComb, who died on the 25th of the present month. . . .[117]

It is the province of a diary to note as well the mere whims as the reasonable actions of men; for the former are often no less valuable as monitions than the latter as examples. A history of the whims of our race, in general, and of its whims in regard to dress, in particular, from Adam's fig-leaf down to the French blouse, would be a book of vast interest. It would convince us, I think, that in proportion as men advance in civilization, they retrograde in their habiliments. First we should see the fig-leaf changed for the skins of wild beasts, those for garments of divers kinds, flowing freely about the person, those for habits of a more confining and less graceful cast, and those again for the imprisonment of tight coats and small trousers. But at all these improvements for the worse we would cease to wonder, when we came to look at the French Blouse, which has come in fashion in Philadelphia during the past month. This is a thing intended for summer wear by gentlemen, although as yet I have seen no gentleman, not indeed any man of any kind, have one on, although the dandies are wonderfully taken with it. It is made of calico, in the shape of a fish-woman's petticoat, and reaches nearly or quite to the knees. There is a belt set in at the waist, above which it is gathered before and behind, and these gathers, inflating with the wind, swell out till the fop who is inside has the contour of a Falstaff. In short they are lacking of any recommendation but cheapness, being worse than nothing for comfort, and for looks as ugly as the devil.

The brains of civilized nations are always engaged in an upward direction, exploring the skies, and studying the stars; hence it is, no

117. Alexander Macomb (1782–1841) had been an important figure in the War of 1812 and was commanding general of the United States Army from 1828 until his death.

common sense is ever applied by them to the clothing of their feet, which, indeed, have good cause to regret the moment they first trod enlightened soil. The hottentot can luxuriate in nature's stockings and reason's shoes; but we, more civilized and consequently more cruel to ourselves than even the Chinese, who thwart nature by degrees, and as though they thwarted her not—we, I say, obeying fashion's call, jamb our big feet into little shoes of one shape to-day and of another to-morrow, until the pangs of our corns make our very lives to be burthensome. These and a thousand similar miseries attend civilization. Tight shoes and corns; tight hats, and headaches; tight vests, and consumption; French blouses, and empty pates and purses—the catalogue is endless! . . .

The disposition to nominate Stewart for the Presidency is evidently increasing. All the disappointed office-hunters are leaving the Whig ranks and declaring for him. Songs have already begun to be written, into which "Old Hick'ry of the sea" is woven in a manner that will convince the mass much sooner than any argument.

It is thought Scott will be the Federal candidate.[118] Some papers indeed in the interior of Pennsylvania have actually nominated him, so far as their influence extends. The Keystone state is the maker of Presidents, as old Warwick was the maker of kings.[119] She moves first and fights harder on both sides than any of her sisters.

1 July, Thursday.

I finished DeLolme's *Constitution of England* this forenoon, and came to the following opinion about it: an Englishman can not read it too often, an American cannot read it too cautiously. His arguments in favour of monarchy, as restrained in England, are ingenious and well-framed; and if we acknowledge his premise, that there needs must be orders or degrees in every state, we cannot help agreeing with him in his conclusion, that those orders are better distinguished in England than any where else. But we republicans deny that some are born to govern, and some to be governed; further than superior virtue or abilities distinguish men, we admit of no distinction, and these, we hold, will be sufficiently appreciated without a constitution of government especially adapted to display them. . . .

This afternoon I began Kent's *Commentaries*, and after reading twenty-five pages therein, went with Kelley up to Alderman Bians', where said Kelly had a suit against Moyamensing Bank of some importance. It was postponed. . . .

118. Winfield Scott (1786–1866), now commanding general of the army, would be the Whig candidate, but not until 1852.
119. Richard Neville, Earl of Warwick (1428–71), was known as "the King-maker" during the War of the Roses.

2 July, Friday.

The remains of Colonel Haslett who was killed at Princeton,[120] and buried in Philadelphia, were removed to-day to Dover, in Delaware. The military paraded—the flags floated at half-mast, guns were fired in Washington Square, and the bell of freedom in the State House added its muffled sounds to the other tributes of respect to the fallen brave. Colonel Page's Company of Fencibles[121] paraded among the rest, and looked very soldierly. After looking at the display at the foot of Arch Street, whence the corpse started in the *Kent* Steamboat, I read a good deal in the *Commentaries on American Law*.

I called at Edwards's boarding-house this afternoon. . . . He has gone to Chester to spend the Fourth. I came over home soon after . . . and encountered two of the Misses of the Constellation. We had quite a familiar talk, and the one with whom my acquaintance is owing to a mistake I made . . . was particularly lively. They are all virtuous, intelligent, beautiful, and lovely girls. I am resolved to ken more about them. They would not, I imagine, repel my advances to their friendship.

Cowperthwait and I wrote and posted some Notices of Kelley's Oration to-night. I fear we are not going to have a very full house.

My uncle went to Salem by invitation of Jacob Ridgway the millionaire to-day in the new steam-boat *New Jersey*, owned by said Jacob. This is the first time she has ever run. She was commenced for an opposition line to the Company in which my uncle is an officer. "We know not what a day may bring forth!"

Mrs. Finch was at our house to-night. She told me she had heard I often called upon Mrs. Budd, and that she began to feel jealous at my not calling upon her, the said Mrs. Finch, too. She is a lively woman—very. . . .

3 July, Saturday.

I waited upon Mr. Kelley this afternoon at four o'clock at his residence in Southwark.[122] He took me through his garden and showed me a splendid collection of flowers which he takes great pleasure in cultivating. I was obliged to admire, of course; but preserve me from having to talk another half hour upon a subject of which I am entirely ignorant!

About five o'clock, we crossed the river, and (after I had introduced

120. Col. John Haslett was commanding the Delaware regiment at the time of his death, in 1777.

121. Formed during the War of 1812, the Pennsylvania State Fencibles was a Philadelphia militia unit, often used during ceremonial occasions.

122. Southwark was a small urbanized district on the Delaware River, just south of Philadelphia in 1841. It became part of the city in 1854.

him to my mother) took a walk around to Delacour's and up to the Woodlands, at the former of which places we encountered Clement and several of his friends, and all drank some mineral water together. Kelley was all the time in very good spirits, but I felt not a little uneasy, knowing as I did, that nothing like a full advertisement of our Oration had been made. Clement, so far from being apprehensive of a thin attendance, expressed his fears that the house would be uncomfortably jammed, and some of the members even proposed procuring the up-stairs room which has galleries that hold two or three hundred people. Whether we had "ample space and verge enough" below stairs, will be presently told.

My uncle being gone to Bordentown, there were only three of us— Mr. Kelley, my mother, and myself—at tea. From some expressions dropped by the orator at the table, I found that he calculated on making a decided hit. He refrained from eating heartily, in order to have a free respiration, and after tea went into my library to put a finishing polish on one or two paragraphs of his oration. At eight o'clock we went to the church, and looking in at the door, found six or seven persons only collected. Kelley's countenance fell below zero, and my anger rose to the boiling point. We took counsel of some of the members who were standing on the pavement in front of the house, and resolved to begin in a half an hour. We then walked leisurely out Cooper Street and returned by way of Plum at twenty minutes of nine. Forty persons had gathered by this time, but in so large a room they could hardly be seen. I was mortified almost to death at so complete a failure, and Kelly himself, altho' he affected to laugh at it as a joke, was, I know, infinitely chagrined. I proposed to put off the thing until a complete publication could be made; but to this he objected; several of the members too thought it best "to go ahead now"—so in we marched, and escorting the orator to the desk, took our seats.

In a few minutes our Cicero arose. His eye glanced with almost a devil's gleam over the house. The blood mounted for a half a second to his cheek, then vanished, and again for a half a second he was more than usually pale. Collecting himself with a philosopher's readiness, he unfolded his manuscript, and commenced in a voice by no means proportioned to his feeble audience. It was strong and deep, like the mutter of distant thunder, or soft and melodious as the murmur of a cascade as it gently descends a channel edged with flowers and paved with musical pebbles. For more than an hour he held his audience entranced by the originality, the pathos, the variety of his eloquence. His positions were entirely new, his arguments in support of them completely satisfactory. He considered the struggle of '76 as a war of

Revolution, that of '12 as a war of independence; and he convinced all who heard him, I think, that this is a correct view of the subject. If I can borrow the Oration I will make a brief of it, and so at present forbear any further remarks upon it. . . .

The orator and two or three of the members came down to our house, and remained smoking cigars and telling anecdotes, until the mail-line came in from New York, at eleven o'clock.[123] He then went over the river, damning Jersey and Jerseymen, I dare say, and I went to bed soon after, half inclined to say amen! to his supposed maledictions.

4 July, Sunday.   Columbia's Sixty-fifth Birth day.

. . . A year is to-day completed since I began this diary, or, as I say in my laboured preface to the first volume, since I declared independence of Prince Ennui, and resolved never to give myself reason to say, *Diem perdidi*, again. The reader will have observed that, so far, I have not lost a day. For twelve months back I have every evening made a note of what I have done, seen, heard or thought of in the hours preceeding. Sometimes, (as will be evident from reading the two first volumes) I have sat down to my task fatigued and wearied; sometimes sick or sleepy, sometimes angry or disgusted; but I can safely say I never took up my pen to set it to this journal in any other disposition than not to relinquish my undertaking. In some places my style may be more than commonly weak, in others extraordinarily diffuse, and in others again severe and crabbed beyond my general tenor; but these discrepancies, as the thermometer (if I may so speak) of my feelings, are invaluable, since from them I know that at one time I was tired, at another, good-humored, and at a third out of temper. Even from the penmanship of the different entries I can form an idea, or recall the memory, of my feelings at the times they were made. My gammas have a more gracefully turned or more spitefully twisted tail, I fancy, in proportion as I was in or out of humour when I made it, and so of the rest of the alphabet. . . .

This memorable day has been cool and pleasant, but notwithstanding this, none of the frolicking and noise with which its return is usually welcomed, has been seen or heard. A salute was fired from the Philadelphia Navy Yard between midnight and four o'clock this morning; but for which one would have supposed that the city in which, sixty five years ago, the great declaration of Independence was made, had forgotten the existence of such a declaration—so superior is religion over the feeling of patriotism! There were but few people

123. The mail-line was the train which carried mail.

over from the city opposite to day, and they who were over behaved very well.

Sam and I walked up to the Tamany Fish House this afternoon. It is on Pea Shore,[124] about four miles from Camden.

5 July, Monday.

As an Irishman would say, the Fourth of July this year came on the Fifth. All the ceremonies and festivities which belonged to yesterday, took place to-day, and as Thomas Hague . . .[125] predicted, the weather was unusually pleasant and favourable for the manifestation of a nation's gratitude.

In the morning, Sam, Lem Davis and I went to a church in Tenth St. Philadelphia, to hear Doctor Patterson[126] deliver an Oration. His house was about as full in proportion as Kelley's was on Saturday night, but the address was vastly superior in point of elegance, to any thing Kelley can produce. It savoured however pretty strongly of Brownsonism, and therefore, deserves condemnation. I am sick to death of such wild notions of man's equality. It is absurd to contend that such a state can be realized while human nature is as it is; and he who thus contends is either a fool or a knave. My radical friends will fall under the latter epithet.

There were some of the most magnificent tunes played upon the organ at the above church, that I ever listened to.

In the afternoon the New Jersey Cincinnati Society had an Oration delivered before them in the Baptist Church, by Colonel Scott.[127] The room was even more empty than when Kelley spoke in it, and I do not regret that it was so. I will inform that gentleman of this fact to-morrow, for, since as the proverb says, "misery loves company," such information will be a balm to his wounded pride.

Thousands upon thousands of Philadelphians came over to Camden today, but behaved themselves very well. The notion, so prevalent a few years ago among the denizens of the city of brotherly love, that Jersey has no laws, is exploded. Some of them however had to experience the contrary before they showed their belief of it by their conduct.

124. The Pea Shore was a popular bathing and fishing area on the east bank of the Delaware, north of Camden, in present-day Pennsauken.

125. Philadelphia city directories list Hague as a "planet reader" of South Thirteenth Street.

126. Patterson was probably speaking in the First Unitarian Church, at Tenth and Locust Streets.

127. Joseph Warren Scott (1778–1871), a New Brunswick lawyer, was vice-president of the New Jersey Society of the Cincinnati, 1840–44. The Society of the Cincinnati was a fraternal, patriotic organization founded in 1783.

At eight o'clock this evening the most violent thunder-gust I ever saw passed over our neighborhood. The lightning was terrific. It lasted, with a high wind from the north west, until ten o'clock, at which time a large fire was seen in the west, and another in the north, which I suppose were ignited *"fulmine Iovis,"* that phenomenon which no philosopher can explain nor entirely keep from fearing. In consequence of the heavy rain, we had no meeting at the Institute room.

7 July, Wednesday.

This morning I took a fresh start in my legal studies, which have been broken in upon by the fourth of July and its attending festivities. I read to-day an hundred pages of Kent's *Commentaries*, in which learned work I find a defence of the dubious right of searching neutral vessels by a belligerent, that is sufficiently ingenious, but to me by no means satisfactory. . . .

The *Mail* for this week has not yet appeared. Since Gray's appointment to the Collectorship he has become negligent of his paper. Some of his irons, I'm afraid, will burn. . . . Gray got his appointment about a week ago. Croxall is still alive, but is not expected to continue so from day to day. Gray is a strong friend of mine, or I would say something hard of his inconsistency.

8 July, Thursday.

. . . I referred to the Directory this morning for the address of Frank Johnson, the famous black musician, and having ascertained it to be in South Eleventh Street, I sallied forth from the office with the intent of proceeding thereto forthwith, to engage him to give me lessons on the violin; but opposite to Independence Area I met Frank himself walking down street with an air of great consequence and self-sufficiently. I accosted him, opened my business, and fixed it that I am to commence my pupilage on next Monday, for eighteen dollars a quarter—one third in advance. When I came home and told my uncle what I had been doing, I found that he did not altogether like the thought of my learning even to fiddle of a "damned Negro," as he very emphatically terms every individual of the unhappy race of Ham. He did not object to my whim, however, very seriously; indeed, that is what he never does.

9 July, Friday.

The town is rife with a romantic incident that occurred on Wednesday night and appeared in print this morning. On the evening mentioned a young woman of about nineteen, of very good looks, and a man aged about twenty six, having tied themselves together with a handkerchief by the arms, jumped off the Arch Street wharf into the

Schuylkill and were drowned. Yesterday morning a gentleman fishing at the place caught his hook in the lady's dress, and the bodies, thus discovered, were taken out of the water, and carried to the Dead House. A loaded pistol was found upon each of their persons, but nothing by which they could be recognized. They were both well dressed, and a man who came immediately from the scene of the inquest to the office, yesterday afternoon, told me that the lady was really beautiful. Ten thousand rumours are afloat concerning the cause of this melancholy act, but nothing can be ascertained about it. The general impression is that love and crime are at its bottom. How incomprehensible is the human heart, to quail before the trifling greivances of this life, and brave the terrors of the unknown grave, infinite punishment, and unrespited misery through eternity. . . .

11 July, Sunday.

. . . Not being very well to-day I did'nt intend going to church; but hearing that a reformed tippler was to preach in the woods, between the circular and the oval rail-roads, I hobbled up there, and got disappointed. The man did not come. My cousins the Hogelands, were over in the afternoon, and borrowed some books. By the by my bookshelves begin to look bald in a good many places. Mrs. Budd and Mrs. Fisler, and Mrs. Finch all have more or less of my dear tomes.[128] The first and the last of the Mistresses just named visited me again on last Friday, and borrowed several of my novels. . . .

12 July, Monday.

I read a hundred pages of Kent's *Commentaries* to-day—finishing about four o'clock. Then piling my books up upon my table, and bidding the Colonel "*au revoir*," I sallied forth in quest of Frank Johnson's domicile, as per agreement on last Thursday made and ratified between said Frank of the one part, and myself of the other. After a long walk down to Eleventh and Lombard Streets I found the residence of the sooty Apollo—a fine three-story house, with "Francis Johnson" in capital letters on a stylish door-plate, and other appendages from which no one could possibly infer that its owner was just taking the benefit, as is the case.

Having found the *locus in quo*, as I have intimated, of the scientific African, I rang the bell, and a young darkee about thirteen years old appeared.

"Is Mr. Johnson in?" I inquired.

"No sah!"

"Are you right sure?"

128. Mrs. Fisler was the wife of Dr. Lorenzo F. Fisler (1797–1871).

"Yes sah."

"When will he be in?" continued I.

"About five o'clock, sah!"

The young ape looked at me above half a minute with much earnestness, as if to see if I were on a dunning errand; than

"Is you de gem'man what's goin' to take lessons on de violin?" asked he.

"Yes."

"O well den, I guess he is in—I'll see—walk up stairs sah."

I was now introduced in to Frank's sanctum, a pleasant room on the second floor filled with articles of his profession. Immediately opposite to the door, and suspended in a gorgeous frame, was my visitee's portrait, representing him in his uniform, with a bugle in his hand. Over the mantel was another likeness of Boyer, the President of Hayti, in whom all negroes so much glory. The wall was covered with pictures and instruments of all kinds, and one side of the room was fixed with shelves whereon were thousands of musical compositions, constituting a valuable library. Bass drums, bass viols, bugles and trombones lay in admirable confusion on the floor; and in one corner was an armed composing chair, with pen and inkhorn ready, and some gallopades and waltzes half finished.

After I had taken a good look at all around me, Frank came in, yawning most gracefully after his afternoon nap, and dressed in fashionable dishabille in which he sported with as much ease as ever beau Brummel himself could have done. Bowing very politely, he sank, rather than sat, into a chair; and our business began. I told him I was going to Bethlehem next Monday, and that I had concluded not to begin to take lessons until after my return. He said he would leave it altogether to me; so I fixed next Monday week as our starting time. After talking a while on matters and things, he played me some airs on a violin; and then I bade him good day. He told me it would do no harm to thrum away at my fiddle before commencing to take lessons, and he promised to make me master of the instrument in three months, if I have any taste for music. He has about a dozen young men receiving instruction from him, and he says it is hardly respectable now to say you cannot perform on the divine violin. The students he has are of the most decent families in the city, and the fashion of fiddling is soon to be one of the most universal of all fashions in the higher circles. So, at least, he assures me.

I got some advertisements of Kelley's lecture printed this afternoon, and began to put them up, but was obliged to stop by the toothache, that "hell of 'a' diseases," as Bobby Burns calls it.

13 July, Tuesday.

Not having been able (for the tooth-ache) to sleep much last night, I arose too late to go to the office this forenoon. I went however earlier than usual in the afternoon and finished the first volume of Kent's *Commentaries*. Perhaps I ought respectfully to submit to the authority of the learned work put into my hands by those older than myself; but I cannot agree with Mr. Kent in his defence of the consti-tutionality of a Bank of the United States, nor his vindication of the right of search by a belligerent over a neutral vessel. As to the first, he is guilty of a *petitio principii,* in taking for granted that a bank is necessary for the proper operations of government; and for the last, he says when we come to be a great maritime nation we will enter-tain more favourable opinions of the right of search than we do now when it is our interest to preserve an unmolested neutrality in all the naval wars that agitate the world. And how absurd does it not seem, to apologise for a present wrong, because, in the future, it may be our policy to acquiesce in it? If an act be unjust to day it will be unjust to-morrow; the line between right and wrong is unvarying, immutable, eternal.

Harry Edwards called at the office this afternoon, with his burnt hand. We agreed upon next Saturday for his visit.

Lem Davis and myself distributed the notices of Kelley's lecture to-night around the city.

14 July, Wednesday.

The evening of this day is past, and as Webster said on some occa-sion, now I can breathe "freer and deeper." Since the third of July I have looked forward to this, the period of the re-delivery of Kelley's address, with an apprehension of meeting with a disappointment as great if not greater than before; and this notwithstanding the pains and expense bestowed by the society in general, but myself in particu-lar, to ensure a full house. My fears were greatly increased by the threatening of a storm just before sunset. Thunders were heard and lightning seen in almost every quarter of the compass, and the whole sky seemed to prognosticate an unfavourable evening. After a slight fall of rain however, which served to cool the atmosphere, it cleared away, and with the appearance of a storm vanished my anticipation of empty benches. At eight o'clock we proceeded to the church and found it already well filled with beauty and respectability, and before the orator commenced speaking our audience was larger than any one could have expected. He re-delivered his admirable address with more than usual brilliancy, and the congregation dispersed in good humour with all around—which is saying all that is necessary to constitute a compliment.

Messrs. Clement and Dudley[129] accompanied Kelley down to our house, where we—that is they—took a glass of wine, and remained until the mail-boat started for Philadelphia at eleven o'clock. . . .

I availed myself of my privilege as "a member of the Philadelphia bar" this morning, and went into the sanctum of the Court of General Sessions, where none but the counsel, witnesses, judges, jurors and parties are admitted. The case that was before the Court will be a novel one in the Reports, where it will be found, I suppose, under the head of "*Burr* versus *Baggans*, on indictment for larceny." The circumstances are as follows:

Baggans is a minister of the gospel, and Burr and his family attended his Church, situated in Kensington.[130] The friendly connection which ought to subsist in general between a pastor and his flock was carried to a greater length between Mr. Baggans and Mrs. Burr, than the plaintiff in this suit, as a man of honour, could endure. His nuptial bed had been defiled—to submit to which was beyond the power of even the phlegmatic Mr. Burr, (who is, by the by, a little Dutchman, with a comical blinking pair of eyes, but a face otherwise very philosophical.) But what was he to do? Expose the adultery of his wife? That would have been to dishonour himself. Prosecute the reverend sinner for a criminal connection? That would have been to do the same. Apply for a divorce? With all her faults he loved her too well for that. Yet something must be done. He and his lawyer having satisfied themselves that Mr. Baggans had received a sum of money from the frail creature as a kind of deodand, laid their heads together and procured the clergyman to be indicted for larceny; for by the law, though a woman cannot be guilty of stealing her husband's property (man and wife being by a legal fiction, one)—yet if she gives it to another, without her husband's knowledge, it is felony in the receiver. I left the lawyers arguing the case, with by no means the talent for which the bar of Philadelphia is so famous. Hubbell was for the Commonwealth, Hannah for the defendant.

15 July, Thursday.
Kelley's Oration is spoken of by the whole town as a splendid affair.

129. Thomas H. Dudley (1819–93), a native of Burlington County, had recently arrived in Camden to study law with William N. Jeffers. Later he would become active in Whig and Republican politics and would play a major role in the nomination of Abraham Lincoln in 1860. During the Civil War, he gained fame as the Union's highly effective consul in Liverpool.
130. Newspapers identify the two men as Frederick Baggans or Bargans and Nicholas Burr.

The reverend clergy praise it as loudly as any body, not having perceptions acute enough to see the strain of radicalism which pervaded it throughout. A certain Yankee schoolmaster declares that he has often heard Webster, but never heard from him any thing to equal the address he listened to last night! The ladies, too, are in ecstacies with it—or maybe with the deliverer of it. By the by, I am told by Stivers that the audience sat still last evening several minutes after Kelley had stopped, to see if I was not going to make some remarks. I observed them to be very backward in breaking up, but I did not know the reason of their being so. A lady told me to-night that she halted for that express purpose! I met Gray in Chesnut Street this morning, and he requested me to give him a notice of my friend's address for his paper, which I promised to do. . . .

There was a display of fireworks with music, rum, and so forth, at the Camden Garden this evening. A good many were over from Philadelphia, and I saw most of our Camden people there. I had a talk with some young ladies, and with Mistresses Budd and Finch. . . .

16 July, Friday.

I borrowed a copy of my friend's Oration to-day, in order to comply with Mr. Gray's request, that I would write a notice of it for his paper. This evening I sat down to my task, and tried over and over again to get through the first paragraph, but without succeeding. I find it difficult so to split matters between my respect for Kelley and my suspicion of his principles, as to satisfy myself. If I laud his radicalisms my conscience will wriggle about as though it had a thorn in its side, and if I do not laud them, he will think I had done better not to have touched the thing at all. Which of the two ought I the sooner offend? The answer is plain.

My face has been swollen up with the toothache for two or three days past.

17 July, Saturday.

My friend Harry Edwards came upon his long-promised visit today at two o'clock. Having partaken of as good a dinner as ever he sat down to at home, we sallied out, and spent the afternoon in wading through the sand to call upon my acquaintances. The evening was passed pretty exclusively in the same manner too. This exercise being new to him, a Pennsylvanian, it tired him very much, and he went to bed early.

Mrs. Shepherd was at my aunt's this afternoon, and after mentioning that I passed an evening at her house lately, she remarked that she had been led to believe that I was an infidel, but that she was glad to find from the soundness of the principles which I avowed, that she had received a wrong impression! Ahem! ha! ha! ! This is just what I suspected. . . . The only avowal of principles which I remember to have made on that occasion, was, to call the Mormons miserable fanatics, and the Transcendentalists dangerous incendiaries. I defended then, and always will, all the ladies in the town to the contrary notwithstanding, the civil rights of the Mormons to entertain their own opinions and hold their meetings without disturbance. And if I were required either to give up my dogma that "we should not believe what we cannot understand," or to give up all my female acquaintances and my right arm in the bargain, I think I would relinquish the latter unhesitatingly. I had rather be a bachelor for life than a bigot for a single second; and if this be infidelity, I am an infidel, and am proud of the name, but if the doubtful word has any other signification, I do not own it as belonging to me. The assassinating miscreant who has worked the minds of the amiable Shepherds up to believing the black libel which my visit on Tuesday se'ennight happily removed, is Clement. For this I will settle with him anon. If I encounter him again at the Parsonage, the insidious puppy shall be placed in no enviable light. For the present—a truce to love and theology! The less that is done in the one and said in the other, the better. . . .

18 July, Sunday.

My guest, and Sam Cowperthwait and myself went to Woodbury this forenoon. I wanted to see Aunt Mary about starting to Bethlehem, on Tuesday. We arrived at Woodbury about ten, and as the cars did not come back until two—leaving us in the dead-and-alive town four hours—we resolved to walk up as far as Timber Creek. We left my aunt's between twelve and one, declining to stay to dinner, since my mother would be expecting us home to dine; and coming through Howell's woods we stopped and got our fill of huckleberries and blackberries.[131] We reached Westville a little tired, and pretty soon the cars came along and we jumped into them, and got to Camden at half past two. . . .

William Ward gave me an introduction to my cousin John Champion this afternoon at the Woodlands.[132] I have not seen him before for several years. That Ward, by the by, is a very clever fellow, but a most perservering bore!

19 July, Monday.　Philadelphia.

Here I am, at the White Swan Hotel in Race Street, ready to start

131. The Howell family lands extended south from Timber Creek along the Delaware.

132. Ward was probably the grandson of John Ward of Newton Township (see entry of 6 June 1841). Mickle's maternal grandmother had been the former Mary Champion.

to-morrow morning for Bethlehem. Our party consists of eight, to wit: My aunt Mary Haines and my two cousins—Mr. and Mrs. Paul of Woodbury—Mrs. Ladd and her son of the same place—and myself.[133] I was introduced to the four latter this evening at the Ridgway House,[134] and like them very well. Master Ladd, is, however, richer in money than brains if first impressions be to be depended on. Mr. Paul is a good old-fashioned young quaker, who leaves his wife to do most of the chattering; and Mrs. Ladd is a very clever woman. Of myself and relations my opinions would be worth nothing if written down.

I am pretty tired with running about to see to the baggage and engage our seats, so I will haste to enjoy the maximum of all luxuries— a tavern bed with plenty of bugs. But let me first examine my purse: Here are twenty-three dollars in bills which my uncle gave me, and two dollars in silver handed to me by my kind mother just as I was starting from home, and a few Prussian thalers which I had before. This I guess will carry me through. Reader, good night! Do you wish me a pleasant trip.

20 July, Tuesday.   Bethlehem.

Our party got under weigh at four o'clock this morning in a four horse stage, after a deal of fixing and bustle with the bandboxes and carpet-bags. The morning air felt a little chilly to me, being unaccustomed to rise so early, but the sun soon peeped o'er the Jersey pines, ushering in a splendid day—neither too cold nor too warm.

I saw nothing worthy of note until we had reached the northern part of Montgomery and the southern half of Buck's Counties. Here we began to observe the women engaged in field labour—making hay, gathering after reapers, driving wagons, and the like. The least as well as the biggest of the ladies seemed to be perfectly familiar and contented with the work to which the customs of the Fatherland have doomed them ever since the time of Tacitus; but we, who have different notions of things, could not so easily reconcile the anomaly of the men loafing in the shade of trees while the women were labouring in the mid-day sun, and my cousin Sarah especially felt great sympathy for the poor little [*Pennsylvania*] Dutch girls who were spreading the fragrant hay so industriously. The country grew more hilly and the roads more uneven as we advanced, and before the blue hills of Bethlehem appeared to our view, we agreed unanimously that the

133. Besides the three Haines, Mickle's traveling companions probably were Mary Ann Paul (1792–1863), George M. Paul (d. 1858), Ann Ladd (d. 1857), and Samuel Hamilton Ladd (1826–66), all of Woodbury.

134. Mickle refers to the ferry house, formerly owned by Jacob Ridgway, at the foot of Market Street, Philadelphia.

sand of Jersey even is preferable to the stones of her wealthy sister. About three o'clock we crossed the Lehigh by a scow (the bridge having been carried away by the freshet in last January) and entered the town of our destination. It has a very pleasant location among wood-clad hills, and "its inhabitants," says the *Gazetteer of Pennsylvania,* "are remarkable for their love of music and their cleanliness."[135] We were too tired after riding fifty miles to walk about the place much this afternoon, but I inquired concerning it of the landlord at dinner, and learned that all the people, except one or two families, are Moravians in their religion, and that most of them are whigs in their politics. The history of the settlement of Bethlehem is curious; it may be found in the book spoken of above.

Mr. Paul wrote a letter from the company to Woodbury this evening, informing the good people there of our safe arrival, and of a wonderful increase in all our appetites. The party are very lively and merry, and we promise ourselves a happy time. . . .

21 July, Wednesday. Bethlehem.

I strolled away from my companions this morning and spent an hour or two on the romantic banks of the Lehigh, and on its eddying bosom. I borrowed a skiff that lay among the ruins of the bridge, and rowed across to a pleasant retreat on the southern shore, which owes its beauty jointly to nature and art. It is a semicircular recess in the mountain, a few feet above the level of the river, along the margin of which the graceful willow droops its long branches, now dipping in the babbling stream, and now wafted aloft by the wanton zephyr. The rocks rise abruptly in the background a hundred or more feet upward, and from every chink the monarch of the forest rears his hardy trunk, and covers with his grateful shade the fairy spot which I am describing. In the middle of the area is a spring of cool water, reached by a half a dozen steps downwards, and provided with goblets for the accommodation of visitors; and alongside of this stands a permanent table for sumptuary purposes, while benches fixed from tree to tree invite the lover of the picturesque to a leisurely view of as fine a landscape as mortal eye need look at. Above, the Lehigh comes tumbling over a reef of rocks, roaring and dashing like something frantic, and shaping a little oak-covered island which it meets, as though it would speedily wear it away; but opposite the romantic little niche in the mountain with which I am so in love, it flows again placidly and slowly, and so clear is its tide that the rocks at the bottom are very distinctly seen. Below, are the ruins of the bridge, beyond

135. Mickle quotes Thomas F. Gordon's *A Gazetteer of the State of Pennsylvania* (Philadelphia, 1832).

which are other rapids over which the water again leaps and foams in a beautiful manner. From this place, too, there is a fine sight of the town of Bethlehem, situated as it is on the rising ground on the opposite side of the river. The famous academy for young ladies,[136] and the extensive Moravian Church with its steeple of sunlit white appear to great advantage, and the pretty girls waving their handkercheifs from the windows of the one, and the old bell tolling the hour from the spire of the other are decidedly improving features in the scene, if I may so call that which is partly enjoyed by the ear.

After I returned to my party we went to the Academy, my aunt wishing to send her daughters there in the coming fall if the place and management suited her and them. We went through the washing rooms and the bed-chambers, into the studying-rooms and dining rooms, in short all over the house, which seemed to be well conducted throughout. The Inspector's lady showed us some splendid drawings made by the young girls, and also some needle-work, the merits of which I am unable to appreciate. They have a hundred and fifty scholars—but few of whom however were there, since it is now vacation—and there are fourteen pianos in the different rooms.

After dinner Master Ladd and I hired a horse and wagon and drove out to Nazareth, another Moravian town ten miles north of Bethlehem. I was under the impression that Miss Caroline Cole was at school there, and intended to call on her, but I found she was at Litiz Academy in Lancaster County.[137] We returned before tea-time—having had a pleasant ride, although I was somewhat disappointed as aforesaid in not seeing the accomplished sweetheart of my schoolboy days.

Supper being over we were shown the interior of the church. Here we saw the instruments on which the Moravians play at the funeral of their members—a philosophical custom wherein they are ahead of all other sects. Some of our party then went to the house of the Sisterhood—a kind of nunnery, into which old maids, widows, and young maids transgressing the irreparable transgression (I suppose) resort.[138] They bought a good many trifles of the devout inmates, and paid a pretty good price for them of course. Aunt Mary got a braid reticule for my dear mother—a present which God preserve her in health to receive on our return.

While the rest had gone to the nunnery I was purchasing a pair of shoes—those which I had having become expanded to a degree that

136. Mickle's "academy" was Moravian Seminary, founded in 1742, today part of Moravian Academy.

137. Linden Hall Seminary, founded in the town of Lititz in 1794, is one of the oldest girls' schools in America.

138. One of the Moravian buildings in old Bethlehem, "The Sisters' House," built in 1742, housed a celibate community of women.

was extremely libellous to my feet. The man of whom I bought them I found to be democratic to the back-bone. He was lately the Post-master of Bethlehem, and is well acquainted with Colonel Page. He says Porter will be re-elected by a handsome majority.

Having got a decent pair of shoes on my ambulatory extremes I rejoined our party, and we began to seek the grave-yard. Not knowing the way, we inquired of an old man whom we met, where it was.

"Go straight up this road" said he, "you can't miss it."

"True," remarked one of our party in a moralizing mood, "we can't miss the grave yard!"

And we did not miss it. Passing the house where the bodies are kept three days before burial, we entered a large grassy space, studded with numerable sycamores—"the house appointed for all living" in Bethlehem. The married, the unmarried, and the widowed are buried in separate rows, north and south. A square marble slab with the name (and of married women the maiden name) inscribed upon it rests even with the top of every grave. There is nothing like a tombstone erected in the whole ground.

Becoming tired at the solemnity of this scene, I rowed my cousins across to the niche in the mountain, where we staid some time. We then returned and got some ice-cream—and pretty soon went to-bed.

So far my visit has abounded in pleasure. The Kittanniny mountains alone are pearls in the eyes of a West Jerseyman.

22 July, Thursday. Mauch-Chunk.

We left Bethlehem at six o'clock this morning in a coach and two, and as our landlord assured us, with a very careful driver. The stage was so full that Sam Ladd and myself were obliged to ride outside on Jehu's box,[139] which we did not regret in the least, since the morning was very pleasant, and the country through which we were to pass delightful. We had hardly gone three miles when the linch-pin of one of the fore-wheels came out—letting the vehicle down, and throwing us out upon the ground. I fell among the horses' heels, while they were raring and flinging about, but received no injury. Putting a spike in the place of the pin, we started again, and soon reached a tavern; here our "careful driver" took a dram, and off we went again. Now taverns are very thick along the road, albeit it is in a neighborhood of sober Dutchmen, and our Jehu seemed to make it a point not to pass one of them without leaving six-pence behind him; the consequence of which was, as I soon observed, he began pretty nearly to nod off his seat, and to drive over the rough mountain roads as carelessly as

139. Jehu's box was the coachman's box. The term Jehu is taken from the Bible; 2 Kings 9:20.

though he were on the plains of Jersey. Sometimes he would curse his horses in half Dutch and half English, whip up, and run them full tilt down the steep hills; then almost asleep himself, he would let his team poke along as though they were asleep too. The road in several places laid within a few feet of precipices fifty yards deep, and here he never failed to whip his horses into a furious gallop, in order that he might be amused by the terror of the ladies.

We arrived safely at the Lehigh Water Gap about noon, but our driver was now so drunk he was hardly able to keep his seat at all. The ladies when they alighted to dine at this place observed for the first time the remissness of our "careful" conductor, and this increased their terror ten-fold. They refused to proceed any further with him, declaring they would stay at the Gap all night first; but there was another stage filled with gentlemen, bound also to Mauch Chunk, which stopped to let them dine at the same house with us, and these gentlemen gallantly offered to exchange coaches with our party, which we accepted—a little to my regret, for drunk as our driver was, he knew the road perfectly, and the excitement of the thing made a variety to me by no means disagreeable. After we had dined, the stages were both drawn up before the door, and our folks were ensconsed in their new quarters, congratulating each other on the change, when the drunken knight of the whip came and mounted our box, as if about to drive off with his old freight. The women began to scream, and unfastened the doors ready for a jump. I sprang out intending to turn the leaders around with their heads to the coach, so as to disable him from starting, and had just got to the reins when the mischievous fellow got down again with a tremendous roar at the fright which he had occasioned. Two gentleman (one of them Mr. Paul) being afraid to cross the bridge over a little stream in sight of the stopping place at the Gap, (and which is narrow and without any rails) in the stage, walked on ahead before we had done admiring the high cliffs on either side, and the river which flows slowly through the opening, as if reluctant to leave so romantic a scene. Presently however we started, the drunken coachee with three or four men in, and all of our party except Mr. Paul, in a four-horse vehicle, with a steady pilot. He, as I have said, and another, had proceeded on foot, expecting to get into the two horse coach when it came along. But the driver of said coach, out of pure deviltry, drove furiously past them, their cries to the contrary notwithstanding; and when he would get a little way in advance of them, he would stop and tell them to hurry. Just as they came alongside, off he'd go again like a locomotive, giving them all their trouble and fatigue for nothing. So he tantalized them for three miles. They then got in, and pretty soon after, another wheel came off and spilt them out. This was the last accident, though there was abundance of danger of the whole party being pitched two or three hundred feet down into the river, at almost every rod of the route.

Our stage came along slowly and safely, and reached this little village in the valley about sunset. The other coach got here a half an hour before us, and its passengers were surprised to find they had come over such a dangerous road, with such a drunken driver, in safety.

After a good supper, which was well used, we took a walk up the valley to the end of the town. The sun was still shining on the hill-tops, but down below it was so dark that we could not learn much about the appearance of the place. We could distinguish however that many of the houses were mere shantees. . . .

23 July, Friday.   Mauch-Chunk.

We arose this morning by crow of cock, and started off for Pottsville, intending to go from there home to morrow. We walked up the mountain just after sunrise, to get to the starting-place of the cars, and from the top of it we enjoyed a bird's eye view of the town in which we had slept. It is a dirty, lousy place enough when you are in it, but from the hill which overhangs it, it makes really a splendid view, surrounded as it is on three sides with woody steeps, and having the Lehigh winding to the eastward with its rapids and cascades, and its canal teaming with the busy coal-boats.

The rail-road upon which we embarked at the top of the hill was laid by a Coal Company to transport their merchandize from the mines a way back in the mountains, to the Canal-boats upon which are loaded by an expeditious and ingenious process, (called "shooting,") from the very cars into which the miners first heave the glistening treasure.[140] All of our party except Sam and myself went up the inclined plane in a regular passenger car; we followed afterwards in a wagon in which the mules that belong to the mines, after having dragged the empty cars up to the Summit, are placed to go down again, by their own gravity, after a fresh train. It is eight miles from the Summit to the shoot, and so great is the descent that the loaded coal-wagons often go the whole distance in twenty minutes. I was told the fall was near a thousand feet. The road winds around the mountain, and in some places is dangerously near abrupt precepices, to fall from which would be certain death.

We were going up this road in our homely conveyance pulled by a couple of mules, and I was enjoying a view of the valley that lay far

140. Mickle describes one of America's first railroads, the gravity road connecting the Lehigh Coal and Navigation Company mines, atop Mauch Chunk Mountain, with the same company's canal at Mauch Chunk.

below us, when Sam asked me the time of day. I proceeded to pull out my valuable gold watch, but could not find the seal; I looked into my fob, but there was no watch there! I then remembered having left it under my pillow at the tavern in Mauch Chunk.

In about three quarters of an hour we reached the "Summit Hill Hotel," and my mishap was communicated to the company. It was settled that I and Sam should go back after the watch, and join the rest at Pottsville to-morrow. Some of our friends sat down to eat breakfast at the Summit, before taking stage for a long and rough ride over the mountains, but everything was so dirty that their stomachs were emptier after than before the meal. For my part the thick, disagreeable, Irish smell of the establishment was enough for me—I did not sit down at all.

The stage for Pottsville being ready to start, Sam and I bade *Au revoir* to our companions, and off they went with a crack of the whip; and pretty soon afterwards we rode down the plain, and arrived again at Mauch Chunk. We found the watch safe, and ticking away unconscious of having lost its master, and put him to so much trouble. We spent the balance of the day in looking at the coal-shoot, and running about the mountains. In the evening I made acquaintance with a lady and her husband from Jersey City, the former of whom played my favourite, *The Swiss Boy* on the piano.[141]

I went to-bed early, and put my waistcoat under my pillow along with my watch to prevent future neglect.

24 July, Saturday. Pottsville.

We reached this enterprizing town about three o'clock this afternoon and found our friends at the Mount Carbon House, enjoying a bottle of excellent claret wine. After having ridden twelve miles over the Tuscarora rail-road,[142] the roughest one ever built, we partook of a glass of the juice with no little zest. Sweetened and diluted a little, this is a pleasant beverage, as my cousin Sally Haines can testify.

The house at which we are stopping is full of boarders from Philadelphia, and among them are six or seven young ladies from boarding-school, who, like all boarding-school misses, are pretty full of mischief. They keep up an industrious promenading in the mirador, where I cannot help seeing them. One of them got my cousin's fan this evening and used it apparently without knowing that it was not her own, until bed-time, when I was compelled to request of her the favour of returning it. . . .

141. I. Moscheles wrote the popular *Swiss Boy* in 1828.
142. Mickle refers to the railroad between the towns of Tuscarora and Pottsville in Schuylkill County. Within months the new Philadelphia and Reading Railroad would connect Pottsville to Philadelphia.

The following are the accidents which to-day brought forth: First, my pate got a hard thump in the stage, coming from the Summit to Tuscarora; second, the host at Tuscarora, where Sam and I undertook to dine, forgot to give us any thing fit to eat; third the car on the road from the place just named to Pottsville ran off the track once; fourth, it broke down twice; fifth, Mrs. Paul, one of our party at the house at which I am staying, upset a pudding into the lap of a fine lady who sat next to her at dinner, to said lady's great discomfiture; sixth, my cousin Sally got just one drop too much claret in her glass, whereby her face a few minutes had an elegant colour. This list is more lengthy than dreadful.

I am becoming tired of mountain scenery, and want to get home again.

25 July, Sunday.   Reading.

A ride of four or five hours this (Sunday) morning brought us to Reading in staunch old democratic Berks. It is so much like other country towns that it is unnecessary to describe it. We lounged the day away in the best possible manner, and a peevish, sickly old gentleman from New York contributed in no small degree to make it pass more lightly. He has a notion that our country is soon to become subject to Great Britain, and many other conceits, to listen to which was amusing—to cross which, dangerous; for sick as he was, he could have plied, and would have plied, the poker or tongs pretty actively about the ears of any one who might have ventured to chafe him.

There was a good deal of thunder and lightning this evening, but not much rain. Master Sam was in a complete fidget at hearing the artillery of heaven, as it reverberated from mountain to mountain around us. His mind is not, I take it, one of a very strong cast.

I was glad to-night to think that when I next go to bed it will be on my own sweet matrass at home, from which my affectionate mother keeps even the suspicion of bugs. Home: What charms has that word to the distant wanderer, and how much sweeter to reflect on it, when a loving mother prepares it with comforts for his return! . . .

26 July, Monday.

"Bock agen"—(as my ancestors would have said) in my little study! And I did not get there a minute before my purse required. My trip has cost me about twenty five dollars, and I do not at all regret the outlay.

We left Reading at six this morning, and reached Philadelphia at half past nine. The rail-road on which we came passes through a most lovely country, and several splendid towns and hamlets. In one place it runs under ground for a half a mile, and the tunnel was black as midnight and cool as November. My aunt was a little scared when the cars ran into this Tartarian place. But to my cousins it was fun. Our company were in good spirits to the last, with the exception of Mrs. Paul; she was a little sick this morning.

At Walnut Street Ferry we disbanded, and each went his own way. I hastened home, and found my mother well, and my cousin Emma improving. Being pretty tired I slept a good deal this afternoon.

27 July, Tuesday.

I called upon several of my friends in Camden to-day, to let them know of my safe return. They really seemed glad to see me, and hoped I had a pleasant trip. . . . [B]ut in the name of common sense what is the use of hoping so and so after the thing is all over? If I had a pleasant trip, I had it; but if I had it not, would their hoping give it to me?

A day or two are necessary for me to recruit in, after the jolting over the hills that I have had within the last week. Then I will lay hold of Kent again with a whettened appetite.

Crazy Joe Rozzell is wandering about our streets again. He is a son of the late Judge Rozzell[143] of Mount Holly, and he visits Camden about once in every year, roaming about during his stay, preaching and praying,* cursing the boys, who torment him a good deal, and playing the amiable with the women, to whom he professes to be the best friends. Sometimes, when the urchins carry their jokes too far, he gets the marshall to fasten him up in the jail, where he stays two or three days—depending upon charity for subsistence. He is a large, portly man, and enjoys excellent health, a disproof of Juvenal's dictum, "*Mens Sana, in corpore sano.*"

This fellow contends stoutly that he is not an idiot. He admits that he is a madman, but looks with contempt upon fools—a distinction that calls to mind personal allusions made by the pot against the kettle.

30 July, Friday.

. . . I took my violin around to Master Sam's this evening, at his invitation. He promised to accompany me on his, and to give me some instruction; but when I got there, he declined playing any—alleging as an excuse that his bow was too greasy. His two cousins and mother apologized for his unwillingness to comply with our contract, by saying that he has not performed on his instrument for three or four weeks. I begin to suspect that my master has taught me nearly all he knows

143. William Rossell had been judge of the District Court of the United States for New Jersey from 1826 until his death in 1840.

* Why is it that when a man's head becomes deranged, he begins preaching? I know several instances in which this is the case. [*Mickle's note.*]

himself. After going through several tunes by myself, we played a game or two of chess, and I came home, carrying my violin through the rain.

Sam's cousins, the Eastlacks, are neat, just-so girls, rather pretty looking, with good educations, but tempers like the devil. One of them plays chess tolerably well.

31 July, Saturday.

The month goes out with a rainy day, which the farmers are glad to see. There has been no shower before of any consequence since the fourth instant, and the weather has been uncommonly warm. On last Sunday the thermometer stood at from ninety four to a hundred. I was among the mountains then, and did not feel very hot, but the Philadelphians have hardly got over their toasting yet.

I learned several new tunes on my violin to-day, among which the prettiest is the *Cinderella Waltz*. Next week I will have better work than drawing horsetail over cat-guts, as a Quaker would designate the employment in which I have chiefly spent the last few days of my vacation.

My cousin Emma is recovering fast.

The politics of the country are in a great stew. The Whig dynasty have given evidences of a fall for a month or six weeks back. Clay is determined to have a National Bank, and some of the Cabinet want a "Fiscal Agent."[144] The Harrison papers are loud in their contentions as to which shall have the preference, and the Harrison men in Congress are split into two parties upon the same question. In the meantime the opposition chuckle with delight, and follow out their plans steadily and quietly. The fact is, Clay wants to ride into the Presidential chair—and a National Bank, a National ruin, or the devil himself may be the hobby, so that he gets there.

The Supreme Court of New York, Cowen presiding, remanded the unlucky McLeod back to await his trial for murder, in the first part of this month.[145] What the opinion in England is, concerning it, we have not had time to learn. "*Yankee Doodle* is the tune."

More than a hundred newspapers have come out for Commodore Stewart for the Presidency! "See, the conq'ring hero comes!"[146]

2 August, Monday.

I resumed my studies to-day and read near a hundred pages in Kent.

144. The Whigs fell upon hard times with the sudden accession of former states' rights Democrat Tyler to the presidency. Clay and his allies wanted a much stronger national bank or Fiscal Bank, as they called it, than Tyler did.

145. See entry of 4 April 1841.

146. Mickle quotes an aria from George Frederick Handel's oratorio *Judas Maccabaeus*.

My office-mates seemed glad to see me return. The courts have all adjourned until September, so we of the profession (ahem!) will have easy times for a month. I do not intend to read twice fifty pages every day—at least until Sirius withdraws his influence.

Mr. Kelley gave me a copy of his *Address to the Democrats of Philadelphia,* delivered in the State House Yard. It is I suppose a good Transcendental pamphlet. The Philadelphia *Gazette* of this afternoon, in speaking of it, sneers at the youth of the author. Mr. Hoover has forgotten perhaps that the slayer of the giant of Gath was a boy.

I showed [*an air I had composed*] to Sam this afternoon, and from his not having any thing to object to it, I infer that it is pretty near correct. It is—But I am getting to think too much about crotchets and quavers. The law! the law, this week, to make up for time lost!

3 August, Tuesday.

A great Anti-Bank meeting was held this afternoon in the State House yard. Colonel Page made a speech (says my uncle, who was present), and was, as he always is, loudly applauded. Kelley also addressed the people.

Mr. Dudley and John K. Clement spent the evening with me. Clement seems determined not to lack in attention to me, but I am getting tired of using forced civility towards **him**. I wonder if the Shepherds did not commission him to visit my library, to see if Voltaire's and Tom Paine's works were on my shelves? Ha! Ha! . . .

4 August, Wednesday.

Kent on Personal property went down like a nauseous pill to-day. I did not get through with more than forty pages, and I doubt whether I understood even them.

At the Institute meeting this evening our new draft of a Constitution was presented, partially discussed, and laid on the table. After we adjourned, Lemuel H. Davis and I had a little sky-larking, in which I fell over the stove and his guard chain was broken.

5 August, Thursday.

When Kelley got up on last Tuesday afternoon to address the meeting in the State-house yard, he had one of the loose "blouses" on. . . . Some began to hiss, and to tell him to take off that "petticoat;" but he braved the storm out, and finished in the same garb he began in. This was an unwise independence in him if it is his aim to increase his popularity among the operatives of unpolished Kensington and rude Southwark.[147] The smallest thing is often the means of destroying one's

147. Kensington was a small urbanized district on the Delaware River, north of the boundaries of Philadelphia. It became part of the city in 1854.

favour with a narrow-minded but numerous herd, to be found in every city and town, who measure a man altogether by his willingness to truckle to their own notions of even the most unimportant matters. Popularity is a bubble that the slightest breath may crack, and unpopularity is often the result of accident, or the unmerited consequence of a peculiarity in a man's person, for which dame Nature alone is responsible. Thus Gray, the editor of the *Mail,* has naturally an erect carriage and a somewhat pompous set of the head, which the rabble here in Camden take as indicating a pride which **Irishmen at least** have not any shadow of right to exhibit in this country. He is consequently so unpopular that scarcely a day passes in which he is not palpably insulted in some manner or other. It was used last Summer as an argument against the re-election of Martin Van Buren, that he actually wore straps to his pantaloons, and this logic of course assisted the log-cabin reasonings of the Whigs a good deal. A man who wears a white hat in the Northern Liberties of Philadelphia[148] is saluted at every step with cries of "Catch that horse thief!" "Look out for your pocket books!" and the like; and he needs say but one word to get himself severely beaten. To return to the point from which I started, I should not wonder if Kelley's blouse-bravery costs him a material diminution of his popularity with the hard fisted but soft-headed "democracy of Southwark.". . .

7 August, Saturday.

This afternoon Sam and I rode out to see Joseph B. Cooper. We were very cordially received by our visitee, and had a deal to do to keep from staying to tea. We spent two hours in looking at his collection of coins and medals, and then did not half examine it, to such an extent has he increased it piece by piece. We returned by way of Gloucester Point, and passed the road on which we had such a perilous ride together, with the same horse, a few months ago; but we did not get into the Newton [*Creek*] to day. . . .[149]

8 August, Sunday.

I finished *The Manual of Phrenology* to-day—a little work translated from the French, and published in this country anonymously. Of the truth of the general principles of phrenology I have long entertained a belief: as, for instance that the animal organs are situated about the occiput, the benevolent on the crown, and the intellectual at the forehead; but of the refinements of craniology . . . I have many doubts. The fact that certain convolutions of the brain are the seats of certain par-

148. The Northern Liberties was a large township along the Delaware River north of Philadelphia in 1841, but has been part of the city since 1854.
149. See entry for 7 March 1841.

ticular functions is too well established to be questioned by so poor a physiologist as myself; but I do question whether the exterior surface of the cranium is always a true index of the interior, and (admitting it to be), whether we can read that index as infallibly as Fowler and some others pretend to. Some of these days, however, I intend to submit my own bumps to a scrutiny, and after that I may venture a more decided opinion upon the correctness of the prenologists' solutions. I will also observe the pates of some of my intimate friends with some attention, and chew the cud of my observations until my mind is decided one way or the other. Whatever is worth looking at, is worth looking into. Let me also ponder the question whether the truth of Gall's[150] science can be anyotherwise established than on the ruins of the doctrine of free will.

My cousin Adelia spent the day with us, and consequently I did not go to church. In the evening I sat an hour with Charley Delacour.

9 August, Monday.

It is almost too hot for me even to record to-night that there is nothing to be recorded, except that there is a rumour in Philadelphia that President Tyler has vetoed the Bank Bill. I hope he has, but fear he has not. If the report be true, the friends of Commodore Stewart will be taken aback. They want the present administration to commit as many unpopular acts as possible, out of which they may make up an argument for the election of their old hero in '44.

10 August, Tuesday.

I took a holy-day to-day, and accompanied my mother down to Woodbury, to see my aunt Haines and my cousins. We dined with them, and in the afternoon I called upon Mrs. Paul, and spent an hour in talking over our trip to Bethlehem, and the ride with the drunken driver. Sam Ladd waited upon me after tea, and insisted on my coming down soon to spend a day with him.

We came back towards evening, in a heavy rain.

11 August, Wednesday.

Rain! rain! rain! When will it be done raining? I waded over to the office to-day, and waded through a hundred pages of Kent. Speaking of the wet weather, I am reminded that Kent is one of the dryest authors, when he has a mind to be, of all that ever handled a dry subject; I mean to say I was reminded of this to-day, as, with the commentaries laying on my knee, I reclined my head back and looked out the window at the large pattering drops, until I nearly found myself

150. Franz Joseph Gall (1758–1828), a German physician, was the creator of the pseudo-science of phrenology.

in the arms of Morpheus. The chapter, or rather the lecture "on bills of exchange," should have a place in every doctor's medicine chest. It is a perfect narcotic. . . .

12 August, Thursday.

The nation is standing on tip-toe with expectation as to the fate of the Bank bill—the "Fiscal" Bank Bill sooth, which has been in President Tyler's hands for some days, unheard of. The Whig papers are unanimous in calling upon him to sign it, and thereby "relieve the country;" the democratic papers remind him of what he said in 1819 against banks in general and an United States Bank in particular; they tell him to remember that he is a Virginian and appeal to him as such to veto the bill. The bank question, they hold, was not at issue at the last election. The triumph of Harrison has settled nothing but that hard cider is a pleasant beverage. Many voted for the "old hero" under the belief that he would do nothing but quaff his favourite mug and enjoy the log-cabin of state in *otio cum dignitate*. Had they entertained any suspicions that he or his party would fasten upon their veins another leech to suck them to poverty, their influence would have gone into the opposite scale, and Van Buren would have been re-elected. But these suspicions were removed by the avowal of the whole whig army militant that Harrison and Tyler were democrats, that one article of their creed was "down with the banks." The late President himself, during the canvass that resulted in his election, repeatedly declared his hostility to the banking system; and the same of Tyler. It remains now to be shown by the fate of Clay's bill whether the latter has been a hypocrite or a sincere man. Bennett is sure the scheme will be vetoed, and he has even made arrangements to have the veto message carried to New York by express for publication in his *Herald*.[151] Colonel Page says he thinks, since the delay of the bill in the President's hands, that it will be vetoed. Kelley is of the same mind.

I read pretty industriously to-day.

13 August, Friday.

The result of the state election in Indiana which took place lately, shows a great reäction in favour of the Stewart party—for that name has superseded "the Van Buren party." Every thing is coming right again. The whigs will now feel the effects of the wild enthusiasm which they fanned into existence by Tippecanoe ballads, upon their own heads. They promised better times—but better times do not come. They promised a reform of abuses—but the reform is not visible. The

151. James Gordon Bennett (1795–1872) was editor and founder of the New York *Herald*.

people see all this, and will know how to act. They may be deceived, but they will not remain deceived; and the whigs will soon learn that though power may be acquired by singing ballads and cutting antics, it will take something more to keep it. . . .

14 August, Saturday.
I did not go to the office to-day. For a week or more back I have been too much disposed to taking holydays. This will not do. It will never make me a lawyer—that's a clear case.

This morning I went a sailing an hour or two. In the afternoon Captain Ivins called and examined my violin, and pronounced it a good one. In the evening John Baxter dropped in and passed the same opinion.

15 August, Sunday.
The weather being a little doubtful, I remained *sub tectis* to-day, reading a M.S. journal, kept by a Jew during an overland trip from India to England. This interesting book was borrowed by my uncle the Doctor (who lent it to me) from a Jewish druggist, the polite but somewhat eccentric Mr. Cohen. . . .[152]

16 August, Monday.
I went to the office this morning with a determination to study hard during the ensuing week. Prosper the wise resolve!

In the evening I attended a little musical party at Cowperthwaits'. We had three small violins, one bass, one flute, and a bass voice. For fear of turning their harmony into a discord, I did not interfere with my incipient scrapes.

17 August, Tuesday.
An express arrived from Washington this morning, bringing President Tyler's almost despaired-of Veto.[153] It is a short document, remarkable rather for the correctness of its principles than the vigor of its composition. The Whigs have assumed very long faces and the democrats are proportionably elated. The flags at Holahan's[154] are flung to the breeze, and I suppose a meeting of the Anti-bank men will be got up to show their approbation of the independent course adopted by the President. It is said that a dissolution of the Cabinet will follow this Loco-foco act of Tyler's—a dissolution of the "great

152. Either S. M. or E. L. Cohen, whose drug store was on Federal, above Second Street, in Camden.
153. Tyler, after much hesitation, vetoed the Fiscal Bank bill as unconstitutional and inexpedient on 16 August.
154. Jacob Holahan's hotel was at 195 Chestnut Street, Philadelphia.

whig party" is sure to ensue.[155] What other effects it may have I cannot guess. Will the President and his friends coalesce with the democratic party, or take to themselves a name and set up for a competition with both Whigs and democrats? In the first case John Tyler, and in the second, Commodore Stewart, will be our next chief-magistrate; but in either case, the Clay faction, which is identified with the bank cause, is annihilated. Poor Harry of the west[156] was born to be a great man, but not a fortunate one. He seems doomed to fail in his every darling scheme.

The papers to-morrow on both sides will be rich!

The estate of my late uncle Andrew was sold this afternoon at Kaighn's Point, by Robert K. Matlack, under a will suspected to have been forged by said R. K. Matlack's father. My guardian bought it, through the agency of a friend, for six thousand eight hundred and some dollars. He expended near two thousand dollars in litigation to set aside the will, and after carrying the matter through most of the courts, abandoned the suit as hopeless. When I become more of a lawyer I will examine this case with more care than I have now time to bestow upon it. . . .

18 August, Wednesday.

Nothing is talked of or thought of in Philadelphia, but Tyler's veto. The whigs are out against their late chief with all the bitterness of friendship turned to enmity, which is the bitterest of all enmities. They call him traitor—denounce him as a Loco-Foco—accuse him of having availed himself of an accident, to thwart "the clearly expressed wishes" of those who elevated him to the second office in the nation, and wish the devil had him quite as heartily as they ever hoped for his success as a candidate. The whig papers in Philadelphia are however quietly awaiting further advice from Washington. A grand caucass of the lawmakers on both sides is to be held, (or on the part of the administration men, has been held); and after this the press will receive its cue. The New York papers, headed by Webb's *Courier and Enquirer,* are making a dead set at Tyler. Van Buren was never so hardly dealt with by his foes as this man is by his late friends. Fight on, ye ill matched allies, while we Locofocos enjoy our honest guffaw at your expense! What times are these for those who keep journals! and what a journal this for my grandchildren to read! . . .

Item. I paid Osbourne five dollars to-day, and took my first lesson on the violin. He says he is sure I will learn fast. My exercises this

155. The cabinet, with the exception of Secretary of State Daniel Webster, did resign but not for another month.
156. "Harry of the West" was one of the many nicknames of Henry Clay.

afternoon were confined to the gamut, and to learning to hold my instrument and bow.

19 August, Thursday.

It is a trite but sound remark that "Honesty's the best policy"—and a strong exemplification of the obverse of the adage may be found in the present dilemma of the whig party in this country. Knowing their principles to be such as, if openly avowed, would be hurled to the ground by the people who had so often before condemned them, a people who never knowingly err—they adopted at the last election a new mode of tactics, the ingenuity of which we cannot but admire. One of their measures being a National bank, a scheme to which the north was more favourable then the south—they took a northern man for their candidate as president, and a southerner for the vice-presidency; and to make the event more certain, they took care that the one should be an old federalist, and the other a democrat, alienated by some family jar, from his friends. These both took the stump, and harangued the people in *propria persona.* "I," said Harrison, "will not veto any law Congress may pass, altho'," he added, by way of carrying water on both shoulders "I deem a Bank of the United States unconstitutional." Here was a text from which the host of minor orators in the north could preach a sermon on either side, as it suited the feeling of their respective audiences. But the south could be satisfied with nothing short of a total abjuration of all idea of a bank. Accordingly John Tyler was commissioned to play out the cards of Democracy and anti-monopolyism in Virginia, and these were iterated and reiterated from the Potomac to the Gulf. This *ruse de guerre* succeeded beyond any one's expectation. The country went, we may say, en masse for "Tippecanoe and Tyler too." But Tippecanoe unfortunately or fortunately died before a bank bill could be prepared, and Tyler took his place. The great leech-law is passed by Congress, and the whigs shout hosannah at the prospect of better times. It is laid before the President. He reads it carefully, and replies, "No—you nominated me knowing my opinions to be unfavourable to this scheme for robbing the people. It was settled at the Harrisburg convention that I was to assure the public of my anti-bank democracy—and I did so. I told the truth then, and you ought not to ask me to belie my assertions now." So are the whigs taught the lesson that "honesty's the best policy." Knavery is its own antidote.

Our townsman pro tempore, Mr. Vandenburg, the composer of *President Tyler's Quick Step* gave a concert to-night at the city hall. It was a worse failure, as it respects the number of the audience than even Kelley's oration on the third of July; but some of the peices performed were splendid. The quick-step on the piano was warmly cheered and encored, notwithstanding the veto. Our people are not so violent in their feelings against the President as the Washingtonians— a mob of whom (says the *Ledger*) the other evening collected before his mansion, played the rogues' march, hissed a while, tore down a few palings and dispersed.

I observed the young and pretty Mistress Clark and her half-man of a husband. The former is of a lively temper, and loves to leer at the young men a little, and the latter in consequence keeps a close eye on her. At the concert this evening she was incessantly looking, from the corners of her eyes, to Master Cowperthwait who sat alongside of me, and her husband would occasionally glance that way too. Gray's family and Mrs. Budd were also present.

Two of the delegates to the Convention for the nomination of Mayor, Sheriff and so forth, of Philadelphia, were at our office to day. Something is in the wind. Perhaps I may have it to say that I read law with the Mayor (his honour) of the city of brotherly love. Who knows?

20 August, Friday.

I was busy to-day in counting money for my uncle. He is to pay for the estate of his brother on next Tuesday.

The weather was exceedingly warm this afternoon. Towards night I took a little walk about town, in the course of which I was stopped by neighbour Duer,[157] a shoemaker loco-foco methodist, who wished to have something to say about the veto. I find all the rank and file of the democracy hold pretty nearly the same opinion as to Tyler's act. Friend Duer, notwithstanding he exhorts sometimes at the methodist meeting, considers the death of Harrison as a Providential interference to relieve our country from the curse of a national bank; and in thus believing his pious wife, who was sitting in the door, likewise joined. There is a generality in this ridiculous idea, not among the vulgar classes only, but all, which would not have been unworthy of the darkest ages of bigotry and superstition.

21 August, Saturday.

Another day stolen from my studies! But I hope it has not been altogether unprofitably employed.

I arose at six o'clock this morning, and at seven started on an excursion to New York Bay, in the *New Philadelphia* from Chesnut Street wharf. Our party on the boat consisted of near two hundred ladies and gentlemen, and as the weather was fine they enjoyed the run to Bordentown very much. There were the happy man and the

157. James Duer's shop was at Second and Plum Streets.

wife, promenading the deck arm in arm, looking as blithe as on the day they became one; and per contra there were the ill-matched couples who can agree in nothing but to disagree whenever occasion offers. . . .

At Bordentown, (having breakfasted, or, more grammatically, having broken fast, on board the *New Philadelphia*) we took the cars and spun off at the rate of thirty miles an hour, to Amboy—stopping for passengers at the intermediate towns. At fourteen or fifteen miles from this place we begin to see the evidences of the ocean, where the earth has been thrown up along the rail road. The sand in spots is very fine, and of a snowy whiteness, and here and there were the remains of marine shells. I have no doubt that the greater part of Jersey was once submerged by the waves of old Atlantic. Irrefragable proofs of its having been under water at some time are found within a short distance of Camden in marl beds, and fossils of marine fish.

At Amboy we shipped on board the *Independence* and crossing Raritan bay came to the Narrows about dinner time. There was a little sea running in the bay—but not enough to give the steamboat any considerable motion. My uncle pointed out to me the lighthouse at Sandy Hook, and the highlands of Nevesink, neither of which I had ever before seen, although I have been to New York twice.

We dined as we were passing through the Narrows and in consequence I had not so good a view of the shores of the two islands as I would have liked. . . .

When we got near New Brighton the spires of New York were visible through the misty atmosphere. We kept close however to the shores of Staten Island, studded with elegant country seats and beautiful villages; the owners of the former of which are more vain than tasteful, I think, in not cultivating any trees around their fine edifices. We also passed in sight of Newark, went through Kill Van Kuhl and Staten Island Sound, and arrived again at South Amboy in the midst of a thunder gust about three o'clock. Two hours were given us for bathing, and two or three fools went into the Raritan and splashed about in the mud a few minutes to their entire satisfaction. I went down to the shore after the storm, and had a good deal of fun at a talk which some of our whigs had with a drunken oysterman. They had been quizzing him a good while, when he unsolicitedly began to "hurra for ole Tip, by God, dead or alive by Jesus Christ, dam' me," to their great annoyance. He is one of the party that has "all the decency." One of the Whigs offered him a dollar to turn Loco-foco, but he was too firm to be bribed!

At five o'clock we started for Camden, where we safely arrived 'mid vivid flashes of lightning, about half past eight o'clock. The storm was ahead of us when we left Amboy, but we overtook it before we got to Camden.

23 August, Monday.

I forgot to mention that Kelley went to Boston last Tuesday. I see in the *Times* of this morning that he has been making a speech there. "The talented and eloquent orator was enthusiastically cheered" and so forth. Mark my word—that man will be ruined by flattery.

This afternoon I took another lesson on the violin. I am unlearning the bad habits into which I fell when I was my own tutor. In the evening I carried my instrument around to Sam's, and accompanied him on the flute. I played Bruce's *Address* at first sight so well that he would not believe but that I had been practising it some time. I will turn round and impart instruction to him now, if he wants it.

24 August, Tuesday.

My uncle John to-day paid Matlack the full sum for which he bought his brother's estate on this day week. The feud between the Mickles and the Matlacks may now smoulder, but it can never die. We can forgive an injury—but we inherit it from our Scottish ancestors, never to forget one. . . .

26 August, Thursday.

I read pretty industriously to day, in that of all books the dryest, Kent's *Commentaries*. I am nearly through however.

In yesterday's entry I forgot to mention that Mr. Cooper and his son went in search of the *Alliance* and found her and brought off one of her timber heads.[158] They borrowed my boat, but I could not go. They left me a peice for a relique.

27 August, Friday.

This afternoon I took another lesson on the violin, and began to play tunes. Mr. Osbourne says he is satisfied that I will soon learn to play well, but whether this is a stereotype compliment which he pays to all of his students or not, I leave.

I spent the evening at Delacour's, where a party of men meet every night, to tell jokes and discuss questions of all kinds. In these debates I am always willing to participate, and have no choice of sides. Much is to be learned in this way, and no harm can come of it, provided that when one takes a certain side in theological discussion and worsts his antagonist, he does not let his love of victory carry him too far into the camp of old-established customs. I have lived too many years now

---

158. U.S.S. *Alliance* had been John Paul Jones' flagship for a brief period during the Revolution. It now lay wrecked on Petty's Island in the Delaware.

to take any but the popular side in such questions, and there is more-over an increasing conviction, that without religion men would be devils, which enlists me against all new-fangled schemes in behalf of the rights of man, which may be defined to be, the contrary of the rights of God. I like to see young men however view religious subjects on both sides. If they have common intelligence there is but one con-clusion at which they can arrive after a candid examination; and in this they will be the more firmly grounded in proportion to the magnitude of the doubts which they have surmounted in reaching their *terminum*. Newton and Franklin were both bold and noisy sceptics in their younger days; all minds above mediocrity reject with thorough con-tempt the believing of propositions without examination; and no mind above mediocrity, after an examination of the physical world even (much less reflection on its own mysteries) can deny the existence of a God; no mind above mediocrity can examine the precepts of the Naza-rene without believing him to have been more than merely human; and no mind above mediocrity can regard religion with any other or more devout wish, than *"Esto perpetua!"*. . .

28 August, Saturday.

This forenoon I actually read four pages in Kent, but in the after-noon I off-set my extraordinary industry by—reading none at all. The reason of my not making a greater progress was, I was busy in copying the Constitution of the Institute.

In the evening Master Sam spent an hour or so with me, and got beaten in three games of chess. He opens with the king's pawn, two squares, and I open the same piece, one; and herein lies, I think, my advantage over him. Mine is certainly the safest game.

My dear mother has been very unwell for two or three days back. She is now taking some pills, prescribed by Doctor Mulford; but still she perseveres in doing without any help. Such a mother—such a woman—never lived before!

31 August, Tuesday.

I dug pretty hard to-day in Kent, in that everlasting vein of re-mainders and executory devises, but whether I brought up any ore or not I am doubtful. How joyfully did I shut the book when half past four o'clock came, the time for my music lesson!

Osbourne has gone on a gunning party, but he left a substitute who attended to my fiddling this afternoon. As usual, the principal and deputy disagree as the *modus procedendi*; one tells me to hold my left hand in this position, and the other in that. The both conclude however that I improve somewhat.

This evening I went to see the famous Albino lady, at the Vauxhall.

She is indeed a wonderful freak of nature! In stature she is short, her arms and ankles are plump and well formed, and her skin as white as snow, except the scalp-cap, which is purple. Her eyes too are purple; they have a dim kind of look and are continually rolling about. But the most extraordinary part of this extraordinary whole, is her hair. This is long and wavy, of exceeding fineness, and perfectly white! Her features are a good deal negroish—her nose in particular; but she converses very well, and appears to be intelligent. She played at a tune or two on the accordion, and answered any questions put to her very politely. The room was full of spectators.

The month that has just passed will be forever memorable in the political history of this country, marked as it has been by the veto of the Bank-bill and the consequent breaking up of the Federal party. A new scheme is now before the Senate, which is called Sergeant's plan;[159] it differs from the vetoed bill in this, one is called a "Corporation," the other was called a Bank, but since it is as much the tendency of the one as the other to rob the people, another veto is confidently expected.

President Tyler's approach to democratic principles has caused "Ironside stock" to fall considerably. Benton in the Senate manifests a wish to see "the Virginia abstractionist" (as his late friends now call him) persevere in his good course a little way further. "The democracy" said he "will rally around you; they will support you through your four years term—and what they will do after that—I leave to be guessed."

3 September, Friday.

News reached town this afternoon that the English had ordered fifteen sail of the line to cruize off our coast to act in any crisis to which the McLeod affair may come. Some think this is an old story new vamped up, and others that it is the doing of the Whig ministry in England, (who are just going out of power), with the desire of leaving their successors all the trouble they can. We'll see.

I met Mr. Paul this afternoon at the Ferry-house at Market Street. He laughed heartily about his ride with the drunken driver. . . .

4 September, Saturday.

I have been so industrious for a week back that I thought I could afford to take this afternoon off, as workmen say. Accordingly I went down to the farms in my sail-boat, and staid there long enough to get thoroughly cool. My cousins were with me. We came back in twenty-one minutes, with tide.

159. The Sergeant plan was named for Pennsylvania Congressman John Sergeant. (1779–1852).

I met Charley Bontemps at Delacour's to-night, and invited him around to see how I came on in my fiddling. Always ready to teach, he complied willingly—and coming along he laded out instructions on bowing, very liberally; but when we got the instrument tuned up and I began to play a waltz, he looked astonished to find that his pupil could perform quite as well as the master. . . .

5 September, Sunday.

. . . Not having got to sleep till two this morning, of course I did not arise very early. The remainder of the forenoon I spent in my study.

In the afternoon I took a stroll through Moyamensing,[160] which is a proper school for those who wish to study human nature in the lowest aspect it can assume. After my walk I went to Saint Augustine's and heard Dr. Moriarty deliver a lecture on temperance. He was more than usually eloquent.

To-night I stopped at Delacours for one hour. The Club were for the most part present, and participated in the discussion of the question in ethics, whether if John robs Paul to relieve Peter from his sufferings he does a justifiable or an unjustifiable act. I suggested the decision that the motive was right, the act wrong. . . .

6 September, Monday.

This afternoon I walked down to Moyamensing prison with John Weight[161] who, being acquainted with the keeper, had no trouble in procuring our entrance. We looked at every thing about this elegant Felon's palace that presented any inducement for us to look; saw them boiling mush in a tremendous vessel that seemed like a steam boat-boiler; went into the bakery where they had just drawn a cartload of well made loaves from the oven; walked over the garden; sat a few minutes in the elegantly furnished parlour of some of the officers; and did divers other things, too unimportant to be enumerated.

The Keeper took us into the cell of Thomas Shuster, who is under sentence of death for murdering his wife.[162] The day for his execution has not yet been fixed by the governor. His age is about twenty seven, and he is a very good looking fellow. There is nothing of the murderer whatever in his appearance, but he has a way of talking that shows the utter callousness of his heart. He said to us that "he wished they would either hang him or take him out of that place—he did'nt care which."

160. Moyamensing was a large township south of Philadelphia in 1841. It became part of the city in 1854.

161. The Philadelphia County Prison at Moyamensing had opened in 1835. John Weight, an unsuccessful Camden businessman, was a friend of Mickle.

162. Shuster was never executed; presumably he received a pardon or commutation to life imprisonment.

The jailer replied in substance that he would be less bold when the time came. "Do you think I am afraid to die?" said he; "If I could only get a levy's worth of laudanum I'd be dead before night." Thus does this man, on the brink of eternity continually talk! He used to drink a good deal of rum when he was "outside," and as a proof of the strength of the dirty, degrading beastly propensity of the drunkard I will instance a remark he made in reply to the question if he had any books: "Yes they give me plenty of them, and I don't know what I should do without them, go crazy in a week I expect. I would'nt swap them for any thing, but a glass of toddy!" When he was remanded to prison after having received his sentence, he contrived to get some poison which he swallowed: but it was discovered, and the stomach-pump was put in requisition. He laughed to-day heartily at having come so near giving Jack Ketch[163] the slip, and then quoted a line from Shakspeare applicable to the occasion. There is nothing in his mein which betokens craziness. He was born a fool—and there's the end of it.

7 September, Tuesday.

I travelled so hard to-day in the road of the law that I came to within one day's journey of the end of Kent. The route becomes much more pleasant toward its termination; for notwithstanding the path is itself full of briars and stones in some places, and miry sand in others, yet the glimpse which you now and then get of surrounding fairy-land cheers you and keeps up your spirits. If legal writers had not Greece and Rome to make occasional digressions about, nobody would read their works—therefore there'd not be professional lawyers; therefore there would be no quarrels; wherefore it is that the world in general had been happier if Greece and Rome had never been heard of.

This evening Sam and I practised on the violin a little.

9 September, Thursday.

Evoe! Evoe! And I **have** finished Kent!—a consummation which I most ardently desired. Now, however, that I have bidd'en him farewell for a time, I begin to suspect that he is not so dry after all as I took him to be. . . .

10 September, Friday.

An express from Washington to New York bearing President Tyler's veto of Seargent's "Fiscal Corporation Bill," crossed the river at about one o'clock this morning.[164] This was looked for by many of the whigs.

---

163. Jack Ketch was a slang term for a hangman.
164. To the consternation of Whigs in Congress and at large, Tyler had now vetoed a mild bank bill which he had earlier commended.

Indeed since the sixteenth of last month the majority of the Pipe-layers[165] have considered Tyler a locofoco, and have laughed at the idea of his approving any "whig" measure. Since that memorable day the New York whig presses have been heaping the most bitter denunciation upon their late idol. Webb calls him "traitor," "knave" and "fool," and the others come not far behind him in abuse. The Philadelphia papers have preserved a wavering policy, sometimes praising and sometimes reprobating the course of the Chief-Magistrate—except the penny *Chronicle* which has at all times been open to receive the fumings of any bank-feed lawyer's disordered brain. The whig gazettes in the country, so far as I have seen, were pretty bold in their stand against the veto, and the same may be said of the party in general. Old Peter Bender, a rank Federalist, says he will go a hundred miles to vote against Tyler. Jesse Cole,[166] another Camden Pipelayer, says he hopes that some one will kill "the damned traitor," and every whig has a wish in this way more or less ardent. Chagrin and mortification prevail in the ranks of the administration party, while the democrats put their hands to their sides and roaring with laughter remind their adversaries that "honesty's the best policy" in politics as well as in other things.

I have not had time to read the second veto. From a hasty glance however at two or three paragraphs of it, I think it is a weak and conciliating thing—a kind of lemonade affair, with an offset of a spoonful of sugar to every drop of acid.

This morning I took Jim Ballantine and Frank Ogden up to the Kensington Glassworks[167] in my boat. We saw all their interesting operations, and returned about noon, stopping at Cooper's Point to play a game of ten-pins. In the afternoon I read fifty pages of Montesquieu's *Spirit of Laws,* and took a lesson on the violin. The evening I passed at Delacour's.

11 September, Saturday.

The name of our good town of Camden occurs in Tyler's message—quite an honour, this to my place of residence.[168] But the document in which the mention of Camden is made is not mentioned in Camden by any whig but with a sullen crabbedness which shows deep vexation and disappointment. The Philadelphia Pipelayer press pretends to be satisfied with the tone of the document, though it cannot altogether conceal the chagrin occasioned by the President's confirmed hostility

165. "Pipelayers," in nineteenth century slang, were manipulating politicians.
166. Bender was a Camden sausage-maker and Cole a coal merchant.
167. This was the huge factory of Thomas W. Dyott.
168. The president's message of 9 September 1841 contained only a passing reference to Camden.

to the darling scheme of whiggery. There are some paragraphs which seem intended as salves to the wounds of the Pipelayers; but the last one is eloquent and emphatic, with nothing of a trimming nature in it. A hundred guns were fired by the democrats in Philadelphia to-day in jubilee of the veto.

12 September, Sunday.

It is said that all of Mr. Tyler's Cabinet except Webster have resigned in consequence of the second veto. Several members of Congress passed through Philadelphia this afternoon on their way home; probably acting upon the modest insinuation contained in the late message of the President, that the extraordinary session of congress having been protracted several months already without any benefit to the country, it would be best for it to be broken up, and "not to press differences of opinion to any greater lengths at present." Many people begin to believe that we must have a war with England, and expect almost every hour to hear that Fox has demanded his passports. Matters look rather squally at Washington.

This afternoon Sam and I took a long walk in Philadelphia. In the evening I dropped in at Delacour's, where the Club were discussing the probability of a war. In that event we are all resolved to seek laurels—some on the bloody field of Mars, but the greater part—in the pine-barrens of Jersey!

13 September, Monday.

The Cabinet have sure enough resigned, and the men who have been called by the President to refill it are moderate Whigs, and like Tyler himself were Jackson men. This is, I guess, preparatory to another somersault which our lucky Chief-Magistrate intends turning. The Administration party are in a great dilemma: God and even their own men are against them.

Another democratic paper being to be started soon in Camden, I began a series of letters for it in imitation of those of Junius. This took up the forenoon. In the afternoon I took John Baxter down to Red Bank in my sail boat. We set off about half-past one, a little after high water, with a pretty good breeze from North East, and after a pleasant run of an hour, landed at the immortal spot where freemen fought and foemen bled. We staid on the battle field long enough to see the remains of the trenches and so forth, and made sail again for home. Our wind held us until we reached the upper end of League Island, where we were obliged to take to our oars. . . .

14 September, Tuesday.

The letters of resignation from some of the Cabinet appeared in this morning's papers. Crittenden's is short and decent, but Ewing's *tout au contraire*, they say who have read it.[169] The "great Whig party" is done for! Congress adjourned yesterday, being hurried I guess by the recent row between those two prime whigs Wise and Stanley.[170] Judging from present indications when the National Legislature meets at the regular session there will be three distinct parties in the politics of our country. Tyler has gone too far to keep in with his friends and not far enough to get in with his enemies. He will, therefore, if he remains *in statu quo*, be a nucleus around which the half-way goers of all parties will gather.

I forgot to record on last Sunday the important fact that my aunt told me that a lady informed her that a woman said—to wit: What a pity it is that Isaac Mickle . . . had been allowed to grow up without going to church, to contract what queer notions he pleases.

Quere—If the good people of Camden would mind their own business and let my opinions alone, how much more work would be done in a month? how many husbands would have less cause to complain of their heels and elbows being out?

This afternoon I took my seventh lesson on the violin, and my teacher called one of his friends in to witness my progress. He concluded I learned very fast—and so I might if I were to practice more.

16 September, Thursday.

I prepared a Sheriff's deed to-day for the Colonel, my first effort in conveyancing. It gave entire satisfaction.

The Trustees of the Library Company met to night and "Resolved that a Course of lectures be delivered before said Library during the ensuing winter." I was made Chairman of the Committee to procure lecturers. . . .

17 September, Friday.

Vanity is the failing of all great minds; read for instance Cicero's oration against Caecilius, or listen to what Kelley said to me this afternoon. He was alluding to his having addressed a large meeting last night at the State house, "with great applause," as the newspaper have it, when he broke forth with the following apostrophe:

"What are offices and public honours compared with the consciousness that I am in the front rank of those who are to regenerate the institutions of this commonwealth? What can be more pleasing than the reflection, that I have stamped my mind on such a Kingdom as

169. Mickle refers to Attorney General John J. Crittenden and Secretary of the Treasury Thomas Ewing.

170. Edward Stanley (1810–72) was a leading Whig congressman from North Carolina.

Pennsylvania, with her large cities and her numerous villages, and citizens second to those of no state in the Union for their intelligence. Able to say 'I have done this,' I could live in the meanest garrett contentedly!"

My friend is I think a little uneasy at the neutrality which I preserve with regard to his radicalisms. "Two or three young men" said he this afternoon with a significance of look that ought to have flattered my pride, "Two or three young men, with good educations, ought to colleague together, take broad ground in defence of the people's rights, and press on to a revolution which must come, and which will immortalize its promoters." And he then alluded to the enthusiastic cheers with which he is greeted whenever he appears in public, as a proof that the people will uphold radical doctrines. I said nothing; leaving him, I trust, under a firm conviction that I am a conservative. So it goes—the radicals consider me a conservative, the conservatives a radical; but I differ equally from them both, and say devil take the opinions of each.

All this afternoon, except when listening as aforesaid to Kelley, I was busy in copying another Deed poll. The Colonel complimented me as far as ever my modesty could endure on my skill in conveyancing. I will not repeat what he said, lest Kelley or Martin should chance to get hold of this book. This job being done and endorsed in due form of law I took my music-lesson, and came home.

In the evening Charles Bontemps waited on me in my studio with his flute. We played several tunes together. Charley has not the most correct ear in Camden by any means—nor have I either; but we got along tolerably well. . . .

18 September, Saturday.

Sam and I practised a good deal to-night. He has given up all idea of playing on the violin, preferring the flute, on which he has been learning four years. . . .

20 September, Monday.

Montesquieu's book is very interesting, but, somehoworother, I do not make very great progress in it. I only read twenty pages to-day—not worth crossing over for.

Sam was my guest an hour or so to-night, for the purpose of practising.

23 September, Thursday.

Mr. Lescure called on me at the office this morning, about his taking the conduct of a democratic paper in Camden.[171] He bought Cox's

---

171. Lescure, whose identity remains unknown, did not establish a paper in Camden.

school-house some time ago and got a promise of an underlease of a lot of the Ferry Company's ground in Federal Street, of Mr. Cake, and began to move his office upon it. But Gray, who is also a tenant of the Company, objected strongly to their allowing another paper to be started on their premises, and induced Cake to retract his promise. Hereupon Lescure sold the school house to my uncle, and left Camden in disgust. But William Devinney has moved out of one of Lanning's houses,[172] to make room for Mr. Lescure, and waited on him this morning to inform him of the fact: They came together to see me, and Lescure stayed nearly an hour. I almost persuaded him to say that he would try to get a footing among us Jerseymen again. West Jersey ought not to want one democratic organ, at least. . . .

24 September, Friday.

Charles Bontemps spent an hour in my study this evening fiddling with me. We then went up to the meeting of the Baptist Choir and staid till it was out. In coming home we stopped at Delacour's, where I got an introduction to Ned King. . . .[173] He and Charley then accompanied me home again, and staid till near eleven o'clock. A well-employed evening! King is one of the most comical genii I ever saw. He is a performer on a dozen instruments—plays sometimes on the stage—experiments a little in Chemistry—and what not? He was highly delighted with my room and its confused medley of music and mechanics, learning—and fishing rods! He fixed up my violin and bow, and played some splendid tunes. I am glad I have made his acquaintance.

25 September, Saturday.

I was at the office this morning, but not this afternoon. My reason for losing this time is twofold: Saturday afternoons, in general, are lawyer's holydays, and this afternoon, in particular, there was a parade of the orphans in Philadelphia which I wished to see. Bob Ogden and I went over to get a peep at them, but we could'nt find out in what part of the town they were. . . .

26 September, Sunday.

This afternoon I walked with Messrs. Cowperthwait, Devinney and Ward, up to Richmond, three miles above Philadelphia. We remained there an hour, and then walked back again—berating Mayor Swift for his hypocricy in enforcing the old and forgotten blue-law against

172. Samuel Lanning (1765–1842), a builder and Camden's first mayor, from 1828 to 1830, had erected a row of three-story brick homes on Federal Street below Second in 1840.

173. Edward (Ned) King was a Camden goldsmith and an accomplished musician.

running public conveyances on a Sunday, in a city. No cabs nor omnibuses could be procured.

27 September, Monday.

The Prince de Joinville, son of King Louis Philippe, passed through Camden to day on his way from New York.[174] He is nearly six feet high, dark-complected, well-mustachioed, and altogether good looking. He ought to have visited Haddonfield, where it is said his royal father played pedagogue while Napoleon's star was in its zenith.[175]

My friend Kelley has hit upon another method lately of reforming the age. He (and some of his chums) have collected scraps, from various authors, against a paper currency; these are neatly printed on papers about the size of a bank-note, which they paste firmly on the back of every "promise to pay" they get hold of. "This" said Kelly to-day as he had finished backing a bundle of notes, "This is a glorious idea—it make a missionary of every rag.". . .

28 September, Tuesday.

The Prince went past the office to-day, attended by a mob of republicans! It is better, however that we should run after a French Prince than an English one.

Lem Davis spent part of the evening in my studio. He makes some awful sounds on the flute.

Ned Drayton has arrived on his holy-day visit from school, with most luxuriant locks.

29 September, Wednesday.

I called on King to-day at his shop. His trade is gold-beating, and he promised to put me in posession of some interesting information concerning it when I call again. . . .

30 September, Thursday.

Cowperthwaite gave me a copy of a waltz which he composed, this morning. It is a pretty thing, but of course has none of those brilliant and difficult passages which we rather wonder at than admire. I will copy it in my Music book (if I get one) or (if I do not) in this. I am to compose a march in emulation of my friend's waltz; I have even got a few measures of it done. While on the subject of music I will mention that Sam aforesaid and Lem Davis spent part of the evening with me, practising therein.

174. François Ferdinand d'Orléans, Prince de Joinville (1818–1900), third son of King Louis Philippe of France, was currently touring parts of the United States. He was a French naval officer until 1848 and later fought with Union forces in the American Civil War.

175. Louis Philippe, contrary to these rumors, never resided in Haddonfield, though he may have passed through it on occasion while he lived in this country.

I read pretty industriously to-day, and copied a confidential letter, for the Colonel, from John C. Montgomery to Col. Todd,[176] which gave me an idea of the tricks of politicians, besides doing other things too tedious to mention.

The elections are now close at hand, and both parties are preparing for the struggle, but how different are their hopes and fears from what they were a year ago! Then the Whigs were all animation, the Democrats all despair; now it [*is*] all the reverse. The great mass that elected Harrison has crumbled to pieces like dried gingerbread. The late canvasses in Indiana, Illinois, Maine, Vermont and other states have shown them to be used up—those invincible champions of hard cider! Their log-cabins are upset—their gourds are completely squashed—their "latch-string" is pulled in! To account for a revolution which, a short time ago, we dared not hope for, (so soon at least,) we must suppose that there is an elasticity in the truth that no force can subdue. Appeal if you will to the weakest side of the people—exhibit, like Pisistratus, your mock wounds[177]—abandon reason and resort to noise; it all will not do. True, you may deceive for a while; for the principle of a republic, as Montesquieu saith and ably proveth, is virtue, and virtue is easily imposed upon; but our republicans are also intelligent, and their intelligence will soon undeceive them; they are also just, and when they have discovered your false lights, their justice punishes your deception with most righteous damnation.

The trial of McLeod was to have taken place on the 27th of the month just passed, but was put off. Great excitement is said to prevail along the frontier of the north, in consequence of which the President has issued a proclamation requesting all well disposed citizens to keep cool. Many continue to think that the speck of war which we now see will enlarge into a cloud, and then progress on to the storm fraught with fire—and bayonets! A high authority at Washington (says Rumour) entertains this opinion.

1 October, Friday.

To-day I waited on some gentlemen in Philadelphia to procure their consent to lecture before the Library Company this winter. I was pretty successful.

This evening James Ballantine and I called on some ladies. They were at home, and I passed the time very agreeably. Our visit was not

---

176. Charles Steward Todd (1791–1871), Kentucky lawyer, diplomat, military officer, and close supporter of William Henry Harrison, became minister to Russia in 1841.

177. The Athenian tyrant Pisistratus (*c.* 600–527 B.C.) gained power partly because he displayed wounds to the Athenians and convinced them that he required an armed bodyguard of fifty men.

at Sheppard's however. I am on a stand whether to go there again or not.

2 October, Saturday.

I did not go to the office to-day; but staid at home composing my march. It is an unscientific thing, and so I give it an unpretending name. It may be of some service as the groundwork of a better one when I get further advanced in music. . . .

The democrats of Gloucester County made their ticket to-day at Chew's Landing. It is composed of good men, and will tread close upon the heels of the opposition, if not upon their toes.

6 October, Wednesday.

I wrote a Circular to-day to Messrs Potts, Sherman and Thompson,[178] to get them to lecture before the Library this winter. The Colonel also gave me a letter of introduction to George M. Dallas, Esq. . . .[179]

7 October, Thursday.

I waited on Mr. Dallas to day with my letter. He received me very kindly—but said he had refused so many invitations to lecture that he could not comply with my request without showing great partiality. I then went to see Messrs. Sullivan and Buckley, who both consented to come.

Gideon V. Stivers spent the evening with me.

8 October, Friday.

This evening I called at Burrough's boarding-house for Masters King and Drayton. I spent some time with them; we then went together up to Shepherd's and staid till after eleven o'clock. Clement was there, and the girls were all at home. Between King's drollery and the ladies' singing, the evening passed very agreeably. Miss Mary was the only one who touched on sectarianism during our visit. She began to abuse the Catholics, and I was about to defend them, at all risks, when King made some hit and broke off our discourse. Josephine is getting as fat as an alderman—too fat for beauty. She spoke in a very feeling and sensible manner of the companies that used to meet at my aunts', in "the days when we went gypsying." She says she remembers them with pleasure. Enough, I've had enough!

10 October, Sunday.

I was busy this morning in copying music into my volume of the

178. Stacy G. Potts (1799–1865) was editor of the Trenton *Emporium* and held various state offices before his selection as justice of the New Jersey Supreme Court in 1852. James T. Sherman, a Trenton lawyer and philanthropist, was currently editor of the Trenton *Gazette*.

179. George M. Dallas (1792–1864), Philadelphia lawyer and diplomat, was a United States senator from 1831 to 1833 and vice-president of the United States from 1845 to 1849.

Muses.[180] In the afternoon Sam and I walked out Market street, crossed the Schuylkill, and went down to Gray's Ferry. We staid there a short time, then jumped into a car and rode in the same nearly to the Delaware foot of South Street. I got up to the ferry just in time to get over in the last boat. Sam remained in Philadelphia till the mail-steamer crosses, about midnight. He is sparking some little girl up Second Street.

This evening I went to Baptist Church. As I went in, Clement opened the door of the pew in which he was sitting, to receive me; but I deemed it advisable to sit somewhere else, so turned back a few steps and took a seat with Bob Ogden. Clement looked a little glum.

11 October, Monday.

. . . This afternoon I waited with Mr. Kelley upon the Rev. Mr. Eustis[181] and procured **his** consent to give us a lecture also. It is not much trouble to get spouters now-a-days.

This evening Josiah Atkinson and I were in my study playing together (on the flute and violin) when we heard a ring at the door. I descended and opened it, when in marched, to wit: Edward King, with a clarionet in a leather bag, John Baxter, with a double-base violin in green-baise ditto, Samuel S. E. Cowperthwait, with a German flute, and Robert (Doctor, I should have said) Middleton, with a small violin!

There was no alternative! At it the six of us went, and made night hideous until after ten o'clock, when to the great joy of the whole neighborhood, the mob dispersed. This is rather too much of a good thing.

12 October, Tuesday.

The election in Philadelphia is going on to-day with very little excitement. A few blackguards of both parties are driving about the streets with fife and drum and banners, but generally there is very little of such foolery. I saw a good many drunken men at the State-house this afternoon, but there was nothing like a row or fight. "Deep waters run still." How much will this orderly poll reduce the whig majority in the city to? Colonel Page says 1500. We'll see. In the county the Democrats have a majority, but are (as usual) split up so that there is no guessing the result.

On the Jersey side also there is very little stir. . . .

13 October, Wednesday.

The results of yesterday's election in Philadelphia is highly gratify-

---

180. This collection of Mickle's contributions to the arts is not extant.
181. Philadelphia city directories list Rev. F. Eustace as a "teacher" at 313 Chestnut Street.

ing to us Loco-focos. The whig majority has been reduced near 2000 since last year, it being then about three and now only one, thousand. A great change is working.

I waited on Doctor Moriarty to day, as Lecture-committeeman. He declined coming—though nothing would give him more pleasure, and so forth.

This evening I played till ten o'clock at Cowperthwaits', then went to hear the votes of Camden township counted off. The democratic majority is near a hundred and fifty. It had never before come up to a hundred. The good cause is advancing!

14 October, Thursday.

Hurra! hurra! Old Gloucester is partly revolutionized! The Democratic Councilman, sheriff, and two assemblymen are elected, the first time since the separation of the county.[182] Mr. Howell, whig, and Sam's father, Mr. Cowperthwait, a democrat, and both of Camden, are beat.[183] The returns so far are very different for the good cause than last fall's were. In Pennsylvania, Porter will be re-elected by near 15000 majority.

18 October, Monday.

To-day I am out of my 'teens! *Evoe!* Perhaps I ought to moralize some upon this occasion; and I certainly should if I did not feel so sleepy. As it is, the sermon I guess will have to be taken for granted as it was last year.

Mr. Jeffers mentioned to my uncle last night that he thought Samuel L. Southard would give us a lecture if we would ask him. Therefore I wrote him to day. . . . Being acting Vice President of the United States he will give the course some eclât if he will consent to come. . . .

20 October, Wednesday.

. . . In the evening at the Institute the following question was debated: Was the world more benefitted than hurt by the foundation of Rome? I was on the lucky side.

21 October, Thursday.

Master Will Jeffers arrived in town from New York by last night's mail [*train*]. He called on me this afternoon, and in the evening we went together up to Shepherd's, where we staid till near eleven o'clock. King came in about nine o'clock and amused the company a good deal by his representations.

182. Atlantic County had been formed from part of Gloucester County in 1837.
183. John K. Cowperthwait (1787–1873), father of Mickle's friend Sam, was a lay judge who held many political offices in Camden in the 1830s and 1840s. Richard W. Howell, a lawyer in Camden since 1827, was also a frequent office-holder. They both had just been defeated for seats in the state assembly.

22 October, Friday.

This evening Midshipman Jeffers and I called on Cowperthwate, and I of course took my fiddle. Ogden was also there with his flute. We had some good tunes and played them pretty well. By the by I ought to have recorded yesterday that Josephine Shepherd told me a long story about Cowperthwait and some lady at Ide's church. I will note it down anon. . . .

23 October, Saturday.

. . . This afternoon I went down to Woodbury to see my aunt and cousins, who are about moving off to West-Chester.[184]

Also, I spent the evening with the Wilkinses. Rufus played some tunes on the violin, *quanta arte* I do not say. The famous Mrs. Barton[185] was in the room; and of her more anon.

25 October, Monday.

I read harder than usual to day.

This evening Josiah R. Atkinson, jr. Town Clerk and so forth, paid me a visit and accompanied me with the flute through a good many pieces. I **must** hang up that fiddle—that's ♭—for a lawyer has occasion for a different kind of **notes** from what it makes. This drawing the bow will never learn me to C♯ into the abstrusities of the honorable science, and the ♮ consequence of not thus seeing will be that I will **stave** ahead in *prestissimo* style to the finale of a Solo commonly Called the "Ass's Quickstep." But to **bar** further punning of this excruciating kind, I will lay my pen back into its pigeon-hole. Such inflictions are decidedly **base**.

Item. There was a slight fall of snow, the first this season, on last Friday evening. The weather is right cool, and has been for some days. There was ice as thick as window glass this morning.

28 October, Thursday.

Will Jeffers bade me good by to-day for three years. He is ordered to go on board the *Valparaiso*,[186] to sail around the Horn. The poor fellow could hardly refrain from tears at his separation from the friends of auld lang syne. God be with him.

Josiah R. Atkinson, for the fourth time this week, spent the evening with me. We have played or played at all the tunes we know. . . .

30 October, Saturday.

I did not go to the office to day. At night I attended the Library

184. Mary Haines and her children, Mary and Emma.
185. Anna Barton was the twenty-five year old wife of United States Navy Lt. Charles C. Barton, of Woodbury.
186. The *Valparaiso*, a four hundred ton bark, had been built in 1836 for the China trade.

meeting, where we dispatched a good deal of business relating to the coming Course of Lectures. I am at present Secretary of the Library as well as of the Institute.

I got a letter from Foster this morning and one from Jos: B. Cooper to-night.

Mrs. Barton (see the entry for last Saturday) was buried to day! What a lesson!

31 October, Sunday.

To-day I was busy in copying tunes into my book of the Muses. I did not put my boots on till after supper, when I went around to Delacour's.

William R. Cooper,[187] the Councillor from this county, stays with us to-night. He is on his way to Trenton, where much intrigueing is afloat among the politicians. I will briefly state the case (for the benefit of posterity) in which things now are at the seat of government.

The democratic majority in the popular vote at the last election was between two and three thousand; but notwithstanding this, that party was only able, owing to the gerrymandering of the two or three late Whig legislatures, to obtain a tie in Council, while they are in a minority of some ten or fourteen in the lower house. But the governor being the constitutional president of Council, the Whigs tho't to have the whole game in their own hands, and on last Tuesday when the Legislature met, Pennington proceeded to take the Chair, to give a casting vote on the questions about to be agitated; not however until

187. Cooper (1793–1856), a farmer from near Bridgeport, had been elected to Congress as a Democrat in 1838 and had served one term before returning to his farm.

Mr. Cassady,[188] a democrat, had been elected Vice-President, by a compromise between the two parties. A Mr. Scott,[189] an able lawyer, was sent to Council by the Whigs of Somerset. He is by no means a friend to Pennington, who, he thinks, generaled him once out of the office of Governor, and the present opportunity of showing his spleen, was not allowed to pass unimproved. When the Governor came into the Council Chamber Scott arose and contended that such a step on the part of the executive was **unconstitutional**; indeed he went so far as to contend that William Pennington was no longer Governor—a few hours more than a year having elapsed since his appointment by the joint meeting last October. He in short declared he would vote for no motion but to adjourn, and so they did adjourn, without going to joint-ballot at all, and up to Friday afternoon Scott continued to vote with the democrats to adjourn, and on the afternoon aforesaid they adjourned over till to-morrow. In the mean time Pennington's commission has undoubtedly expired, and our state is without any Governor *de jure*, and is like to be so for the next year. My uncle was in caucass at Trenton two nights last week and I suspect helped a little in this thing. It is a saying that "Harrison has gone to heaven, Tyler to the locofocos, and the Whig party to the devil." They can now join Scott's name to Tyler's and say amen to the proverb with all truth.

Mr. Cooper is one of the People's Congressmen of '38, and the Broad Seal Man has little to expect at his hands.[190]

4 November, Thursday.

I went to an Auction room in Front Street this morning, to see some curiosities that were brought from the Indies and were about to be sold. While there I met two of the Shepherds in company with Doctor Burroughs.[191] They introduced me to Mrs. Smalley, the mother of my old schoolmate.[192] This incident of my meeting these ladies there would not have been recorded here, but for the fact that I bowed so awkwardly to Miss Phoebe that I have been out of humour with myself all day. Dang it, I was never born

188. John Cassedy (1797–?) was from newly formed Hudson County.
189. This is the same Joseph W. Scott who had spoken in Camden on 5 July 1841.
190. By "People's Congressmen" Mickle means the Democratic candidates who were temporarily denied seats in Congress by Governor Pennington's certification of their opponents' victory. The governor's certification, by affixing his great or "broad" seal, lent the name "Broad Seal War" to the episode. See entry of 8 January 1839.
191. Probably Dr. Marmaduke Burroughs, a local physician who had served as United States consul in Vera Cruz, Mexico, in the 1830s.
192. The mother of Joseph B. Smalley, a friend of Mickle at Samuel Aaron's school in Burlington.

> "To caper nimbly in a lady's chamber
> To the lascivious pleasing of a lute,"

or to do any of those little graces which Gloster laments his inability to do. . . .[193]

5 November, Friday.

I am still at work at the Colonel's Auditor's report. He says he likes my chiro-graphy very much; and will often trouble me to copy for him.

This evening I called at Shepherd's alone, and found them the same. I entered with a firm intention to atone for my clumsiness in lifting my hat yesterday morning and I hope I succeeded. I remained until ten o'clock conversing with them on various topics, from the latest matrimonial scandal up to the **highest** walks of science (to wit astronomy) with quite as much flippancy as I ever imagined myself to be posessed of. When I arose to come away, said Mrs. Shepherd, "Mr. Mickle, you must come and see us often," which invitation I ascribe altogether to my efforts to be amiable. . . .

6 November, Saturday.

I have been busy about the lectures all day, in getting advertisments, tickets and so forth. At night there was a meeting of the Library at which a good deal of business was done. Lem Davis appeared and paid his fee.

In yesterday's entry I omitted to mention my visit to David Paul Brown. I went about 3 o'clock and waited in his splendidly furnished office until four, when he came in. He is engaged to lecture for us on the 24th inst. The same evening that Mr. Elmer[194] has selected for his address. In order to make room for both I waited on Mr. Brown to get him to come on the 17th. So after the usual ceremonies had been gone through with, says I "Mr. Brown, I have waited on you to see if you would be kind enough to alter the time of your lecture to the 17th so that we can accommodate Mr. Elmer, of Bridgeton." The word "accommodate" set all his vanity in motion, and he replied "My engagements call me to New York on the 16th and there I shall remain some days. I have already accommodated Mr. Adams and I have accommodated Mr. Smith, and I will accommodate no body else. My consent to lecture before you is an act of pure kindness," and he swelled up until his chair was hardly big enough to hold him. My

---

193. Mickle quotes Richard, Duke of Gloucester's opening speech in Shakespeare's *Richard III*.

194. Lucius Quintus Cincinnatus Elmer (1793–1883) was a Bridgeton lawyer and legislator, later a Democratic congressman from 1843 to 1845, state attorney general, and justice of the state supreme court.

first impulse was to whistle "Go to the devil and shake yourself." I remembered however that I was acting for others, so I laid the fine words on until I got him in pretty good humour again. He is I think the vainest man that ever lived. . . .

7 November, Sunday.

There is not much to be said at this entry, so I shall say but little, to wit:

This morning I shaved for the first time in my life.

This evening I went to Baptist Church. . . .

8 November, Monday.

I sent each of the Sheppards to-day a ticket for our lectures enveloped in a note with this message: "Isaac Mickle's compliments to Mrs and the Misses Sheppard, begging them to accept the enclosed as a small token of his esteem for their acquaintance." This bagatelle can do no harm if it does no good.

9 November, Tuesday.

This evening I called with a friend at Hugg's where, awful to relate, my stocking-string (*vulgo* garter) came off and peeped out from between my trousers and my boot. Whether Miss Anna saw it or not I cannot say, but I took occasion while she was very busy playing the *Cachucha* to rearrange it. By the by I must cut this acquaintance as soon as I can with any grace at all. Anna is a very pretty girl, but unfortunately she is Bill Hugg's daughter.[195]

12 November, Friday.

. . . Harry Edwards called on me at the office this afternoon. He says the good folks at Chester are all very well. Senator Buchanan was also in towards evening. He is a large, grey-haired, queer looking man, and is remarkable for a very deliberate manner of speaking.

I heard some blackguards deliver temperance lectures to-night at the Meth. Church. During the performances Mr. Gray undertook to make some unruly boy behave himself, but the consequence of his philanthropic endeavour was a reglar fight whereout of the boy aforesaid came victorious. The urchin's mettle caused no little merriment.

14 November, Sunday.

I walked out to the Creek to-day, and gallanted my cousin home; which two acts would complete my entry but that Mr. Jeffers referred me to Mr. McCullock[196] of Salem as a lecturer, and that I spent the

195. William Hugg ran livery stables near English's Ferry and lived at Fifth and Cooper Streets. He was currently an officer of Camden Township.

196. Francis L. MacCulloch (1801–59), a leading lawyer in Salem, was currently a Salem County prosecutor.

evening at Delacour's in argument with Josiah R. Atkinson on things in general and marriage in particular.

By way of episode I would here state that the elections every where have resulted in a complete triumph to the Democracy. A change of more than 125,000 votes has taken place against the whigs since this fall a year ago; a pregnant proof that

> Truth hurl'd to earth will rise again;
> The immortal years of God are hers
> While error, wounded, writhes in pain
> And dies amid her worshippers.[197]

And by way of another episode or a metaëpisode, if you will, I will remark that Philadelphia has been thrown into some excitement within a week back by a conspiracy against Nathan Dunn of the Chinese Museum (just being removed to England) of a most horrible kind. One Curry, the plotter of this scheme to extort money is committed on a charge of conspiracy, at the trial of which cause I will have more to say about it.[198] The public are by no means unanimous in considering the matter as an ungrounded conspiracy.

15 November, Monday.

This evening I attended a lecture on Magnetism—no, Electricity, by Mr. Quimby,[199] at the City Hall. His experiments were all successful, though some of them were difficult. He burnt a town down by lightning and blew up a ship. "My lightning-rods" were, however, a complete bore.

17 November, Wednesday.

Our lectures began to-night, by Jack Sullivan the Boston rake. His subject was the Influence of the Plymouth Puritans upon the republic of North America, and he handled it very ably. . . . I promised Gray to write a kind of review of each of our lectures.

The house to-night was very well filled. I announced Mr. Brown as the next speaker. After the lecture dropped in at Hugg's with Ogden.

19 November, Friday.

. . . This day has generally been spent as yesterday. Evening at home!

197. A slight misquotation from William Cullen Bryant's "The Battlefield."
198. Dunn (1782–1844), who had amassed a considerable fortune in the China trade, until recently had operated his famous Chinese museum at Ninth and Sansom Streets. Lewis V. Curry had entered into a conspiracy to extort money from him.
199. Phineas P. Quimby (1802–66) was an early champion of mesmerism and the founder of mental healing in America.

21 November, Sunday.

I have been busy to-day composing a tune. . . .

This evening I went to Baptist Church and heard a miserable sermon. On my way home I also stopped to take a glance at the Methodists who are holding one of those nuisances, "protracted meetings." I could not stand the din long—and who with good ears could?

23 November, Tuesday.

I have not been at the office since last Wednesday, owing to a cold which I have in common with a great many others. It is now nearly gone. I played with Ogden some to day, both with the bow and **cue**. I also finished my march and in the evening took it around for Sam to perform on the flute, and to Miss Angeline Turner who played it with a bass on the piano. It goes much better than I expected. . . .

24 November, Wednesday.

David Paul Brown was to have lectured to-night, but disappointed. He told the committee who went after him that there had not been sufficient attention shown him! Now I have waited on him more than a half a dozen times and some of the other members nearly as often. The house was well filled. I dissolved it by a short speech in which I told them that we were very sorry to have called them out in vain, but that in future we would take care to have a substitute ready, and so forth. Mrs. Budd told me if it had not been for my making a good speech, she would have gone away angry. Ahem! I saw Miss Turner and gave her a copy of my march to receive a bass.

After the meeting broke up Cole and I went up to Sheppard's and staid an hour. The old lady and Josephine only were at home. I took a seat by the side of the latter and had a very agreeable chat, while Mrs. Sheppard and Cole were discussing the question whether baptism is a saving ordinance. Cole, being a Camelite, holds it is.[200]

28 November, Sunday.

To-day I composed a quickstep for my march, and am going to put it in Josephine's hands to receive a base. Miss Turner has my march for that purpose. This evening I went to Baptist Church.

29 November, Monday.

This morning I returned to the office, after an absence of nearly two weeks. After to-morrow I will read more industriously.

I got the following three things, *hodie*: my march from Miss Angeline—with a good bass—Kelley's consent to lecture on Wednesday in place of Maccullock—and a letter from Joseph B. Smalley.

200. Mickle means a Campbellite, that is, one of the followers of Alexander Campbell (1788–1866), a founder of the Disciples of Christ.

There was no business of importance done at the Meeting of the Institute—for Atkinson and I wanting to practise some in music, moved and carried an adjournment till next Monday night. We played until ten o'clock, and Mrs. Scull, our neighbour, not however a very good judge of harmony, says she never heard such music! So she told mother—**to-morrow** morning.

Doctor Mulford is writing a lecture on "The Settlements of the Delaware" for our course this winter, and some time ago he requested me to go to Burlington to examine the records of the Surveyor General's office there, to see what new light could be thrown on the matter. I consented, and fixed to-morrow as the day.

Much snow fell last night and this morning. The sleighing is good.

30 November, Tuesday.

At nine o'clock this morning I set off for Burlington and arrived there awhile after ten. I proceeded immediately to look up Mr. Woolman, and in a short time was in the little fire-proof building that contains the oldest records in New Jersey.[201]

Mr. Woolman Jr. showed me the "Concessions and Agreements" of the Proprietors of Jersey.[202] It is a quarto volume of parchment, and contains over a hundred pages of Articles (finely penned in Old English) relating to the government of the Province. It is signed by William Penn, Billinge and many others. The book is in a high state of preservation.

By Mr. Woolman's leave I took a load of old books and papers to Mr. Rogers'[203] tavern where there was a fire, and proceeded to examine them. . . .

I returned about two o'clock, and spent the remainder of the afternoon in fiddling, and the evening at Sheppard's. Browning[204] and his cousin and Clement were also there.

My Aunt Haines and cousins lodged with us to night on their way to Westchester. They leave to morrow. . . .

1 December, Wednesday.

My friend Kelley delivered our second lecture to-night on "the freedom of thought." He came over with me and supped *chez moi.*

201. Burr Woolman had been surveyor-general of West New Jersey since 1815. The little building was the Surveyor-General's Office.

202. Burr Woolman's son Franklin would succeed his father as surveyor-general of West New Jersey in 1844. The "Concessions and Agreements," issued by the West Jersey Proprietors in 1677, was the first constitution of New Jersey. The document remains in the possession of the West Jersey Proprietors in the Surveyor-General's Office, in Burlington, today.

203. Samuel Rogers was the proprietor of the City Hotel, at Broad and Main Streets, Burlington.

204. Browning is probably Benjamin W. Browning (1818–61), a sometime grocer, later clerk of Camden County.

The room was well filled notwithstanding the disappointment of last Wednesday evening, and the lecture was a powerful argument in favour of the radical views which its author entertains. I almost trembled when he gave utterance to some sentences, so *outrè* were they in spirit. See the notice of it among my printed scribblings, for I shall have to write one for Gray I suppose. By the by, as Mr. Kelley and I were going down to Turner's after the address, we heard Mr. Gray just behind us talking pretty loud about "revelation" "whole basis" "reign of terror" and so forth—from which we inferred that he had smelt that something was amiss. Mrs. Gray is a warm admirer of Kelley's—"he's so intellectual!" If some of our good people had comprehension enough to perceive the bearing of his mystic reasoning, they would drop him like a hot potatoe.

I took "the eloquent lecturer" to Mrs. Turner's, where there was a company of young ladies gathered to see him, and we staid there till ten o'clock listening to Angeline's fine playing and Mary's sprightly conversation. He went over in the mail-boat at eleven o'clock. . . .

3 December, Friday.

Having begun to make but one session at the office I cross the river now about three o'clock. To-day I met Miss Josephine Sheppard at the ferry and squired her over under my umbrella, as it was raining very hard. She is certainly a beautiful little girl, and an intelligent one too.

This evening I wrote a kind of a notice of Kelley's lecture. It is hard to carry water on both shoulders.

4 December, Saturday.

This evening I attended a lecture on Phrenology by one Doctor Sammis, an Homoeopathist at the Baptist Church. The style of the speaker was very poor, but his facts were enough to convince the boldest sceptic. After the talking was done a committee of three was appointed to select subjects to be examined.

First they took Doctor Marmaduke Burrough, whom Mr. Sammis had never seen. After exploring his bumps, the professor pronounced him to be inclined to scepticism in religion, to be fond of travelling and of pets, to have a good memory of the face of any country he might have passed, but a poor one for circumstances, to have great concentrativeness, and strong love of order (which might be inferred from his dress) to be fond of the ladies etc. The subject acknowledged the description to be true so far as he knew himself.

Next they took John Weight. The professor found him to be of that class that do not live long. "His benevolent organs were large; adhesiveness—the organ of friendship—in particular was very large. He cares nothing for money and will be likely to become bankrupt in business." [Here the house roared, for the subject has already broke in the China-business.] "He has a poor memory, and would forget his birth-day if he were not to write it down; he would not forget however to go to a good dinner" added Mr. Sammis, feeling behind the subject's ears. "He is a poor mimic"—a decided mistake; "a platonic lover of the ladies"—a decided hit; "has no curiosity and little ingenuity with tools;" all which is very true. I asked how it was with respect to tune—Weight being an excellent musician. The professor said that was one of those organs upon which he did not like to answer, lying as it does under the spinous process (I think he said) of the parietal bone. On the whole this examination was very satisfactory to the audience, though Mr. Weight blushed several times.

Lastly came Josiah Atkinson, who was examined by the professor blindfolded. He said he also was disposed to scepticism in religion (a truth)—but that he had a good opinion of the practical Christian virtues. He was like a monkey [laughter]—all activity; a poor arithmetician, but a good logician. Fond of the ladies, good dinners, and his own way. Liberal of his money in gratifying his own desires. Had language but not concentrativeness. On the whole had a very fair head. This examination must have convinced the most inveterate doubter that there is some truth in phrenology. Several persons invited me to take the subject's chair, but I declined.

Misses Mary and Phoebe Sheppard were present. Mary says she is a firm believer. . . .

7 December, Tuesday.

This evening I called around among my friends in general and those at the parsonage in particular. The more I see of these girls the better I like them, but to save my neck l cannot tell which I like best. They are to the rest of our Camden girls "as Hyperion to a Satyr."[205] I am, and always have been, received by them with marked politeness, and were it not for that the contemptible Clement goes there too I should feel quite honored by the acquaintance.

8 December, Wednesday.

Mr. Sheppard's lecture to night was well attended and well received. It was not delivered with much eloquence, but as a piece of composition was fine. William Ward accompanied him over, and after the lecture we all went up to the parsonage and staid there till the mail-train came in hearing. Sheppard is no relation to our beautiful girls of the same name, although he too is a native of Bridgeton in Cumberland.

I crossed the river with Ward and the lecturer, and got back at 11 o'clock.

205. Mickle quotes *Hamlet,* Act I, Scene 2.

10 December, Friday.

There is nothing much to be recorded to day, so I will note down that the President's message was delivered to the Two Houses on last Tuesday at noon; at a little after 5 o'clock the northern express crossed the Delaware and a little after eight the document was in New York. No deduction being made for detentions of any kind, the message was carried from Washington to New York in 8 hours; distance 235 miles; rate 29⅜ miles per hour.

I have not yet read the message, but I find that the "fiscal agent" which it proposes is not relished much by either party. To the whigs it is not a Bank, to the Democrats it is not a Sub-treasury.[206] It is thought that Webster assisted in the composition of this paper. Very probable.

This evening I was a Heyls.

12 December, Sunday.

Busy all day in writing. In the evening to make atonement, went to Baptist meeting, and saw the Constellation but did not gallant them home. Mr. McCalla, a Presbyterian and author of a book on Texas preached. He used to be chaplain in Jackson's army but now he is the shepherd of a little flock that meets in our City Hall. I waited on him yesterday to get his consent to lecture before our Company next Wednesday evening, and found him writing—with his old military hat on. He had a contest some years ago with Abner Kneeland, the author of the *Lectures.*[207]

13 December, Monday.

To-day I went to Burlington again for Doctor Mulford, and had another look into the archives of the Surveyor General's office. I got the plan of the town of Gloucester, and some memoranda which may assist the doctor some. . . .

I returned about three o'clock.

In the evening I took Bob Ogden to Sheppard's and introduced him. Ben Browning and Clement were there. At seven o'clock the four ladies took the arms of the four gentlemen and went to Doctor Sammis' Lecture, to which they listened about an hour, and then returned to the parsonage, where they staid in lively chat until near eleven o'clock. I have only two things more to remark: Bob looked as smirking as a fool whenever the ladies addressed him, and Mrs. Clark had her head examined.

206. The president's message outlined a plan for a "Board of Exchequer," which would establish agencies in the various states to handle public funds.

207. Abner Kneeland (1774–1844) was a radical Universalist clergyman and free-thinker, who published *A Series of Lectures on the Doctrine of Universal Benevolence* in 1818. Kneeland had engaged in a famous debate with McCalla in Philadelphia in 1824.

15 December, Wednesday.

The reverend Mr. McCalla lectured to night on "the Book of Job." It was a singular affair. He quoted largely from Scott's version of "the quasi dramatic poet," and contended that Job himself wrote his book long before the time of Moses. The house was very good.

After the lecture I paid a short visit.

16 December, Thursday.

During the past week a Court Martial has been sitting at the Philadelphia Navy Yard on the case of Captain Bolton,[208] charged with disobedience of orders. The Colonel is his Counsel, and I have been busy all day in copying his defence which is to be read on Saturday. I have finished Sixteen Sheets, and have nearly as many to do to-morrow.

This evening Atkinson and I had a concert *entre nous*.

17 December, Friday.

I was at work at Bolton's defence all day, and at noon sent a note over to our fold's saying I should not be home until the mail boat returned. About six o'clock I finished; then went to a refectory and got my supper, and went to the National theatre, where Forrest play'd Coriolanus.[209] I came out at the end of the tragedy, but did not get across the river until two o'clock.

18 December, Saturday.

I went down to the Court Martial this morning and heard the Colonel go through with a part of his defence. The Commodores were all in uniform and looked brave as they are.

This evening I took Miss Josephine to Doctor Sammis' lecture.

19 December, Sunday.

This evening I went to the Methodist church with all the town to hear one George Brown,[210] an African missionary, tell about the degraded state of the Africans. He told some very tough stories—especially one about forty negroes getting on a raft, and fifty of them drowning, and only a few escaping! He gave a long account of Blanco, the great slave-trader, and Cotera the Chief.[211]

208. William Compton Bolton, a navy captain since 1831.
209. The National Theatre was on Chestnut Street near Ninth.
210. Probably the G. S. Brown who had served as a missionary in Liberia around 1839–40 and returned to this country to speak in behalf of colonization schemes.
211. Don Pedro Blanco, one of the most active and richest slave traders, had retired to Cuba in 1840. Gotera, chief of the "Boatswains," a slave raiding army largely composed of Gola tribesmen, was killed by Liberian settler militia in March 1840.

23 December, Thursday.

This evening I spent at Heyl's, playing billiards. The worst that can be said of this game is that it is foolish, but I will drop it.

24 December, Friday.

At the office to-day as usual. In the evening I called upon some girls, and was feasted as to my ears with passable music, and as to my mouth, with excellent mince pies. Thank you—I'll come again before the batch is gone!

25 December, Saturday.

May the reader enjoy many a "happy Christmas!"

The weather to-day was fair, and favourable for the celebration of the holyday. The streets of Philadelphia presented from morning till night an array of happy faces and laughing eyes. Every body seemed pleased. *Sibi et suis*; and to forget the hard times and the "prophecied end of the world."[212] At Parkinson's[213] confectionary in Chesnut Street there was a figure made to resemble the child's mysterious chimney-friend, "Chriscringle." He was dressed in antique costume, with striped pants and stockings, and flying doublet; a tasselled cap on his head and a broad, benevolent grin on his face; his hands and pockets full of toys and candies, and he himself just reascending a chimney after having filled the stocking hung up by the faith of some young urchin, full of divers bagatelles.

This afternoon I amused myself by playing with the bow and cue, the former of which I find is the cheaper. In the evening I took Miss Mary Sheppard to hear doctor Sammis' lecture on phrenology. We were much amused.

28 December, Tuesday.

To-day for a wonder, I was at the office and read pretty hard. I am within a day's journey of the end of the first of Coke.[214] Two more tomes nearly as big yet remain!

This evening I went to Doctor Sammis' lecture on Phrenology. The house was pretty well filled and the success of the examinations which he made blindfolded was enough to convince any convincible person. . . .

212. William Miller (1781–1849), a New York farmer and preacher who founded the Second Adventist or Millerite sect, was currently teaching that the world would end in about 1843.

213. R. B. and J. W. Parkinson's store was at 180 Chesnut Street, Philadelphia.

214. Mickle is studying the commentaries of Sir Edward Coke (1552–1634) upon the writings of Sir Thomas Littleton (1407–81). He sometimes abbreviates the work "Co. Litt."

29 December, Wednesday.

I was at the office this afternoon, and finished the first volume of Co.Litt.

Lucius Q. C. Elmer Esq. lectured for us this evening on "Popular Superstitions." He spoke 1, of ghosts, 2 of witches, 3, of fortune tellers, 4, of dreams, 5 of "unlucky Friday," 6 of various other similar things. When he delivered this same lecture last winter, he told me he had a passage denouncing Animal Magnetism as a humbug; but during his visit to Philadelphia some weeks ago he attended one of Doctor Johnson's lectures, and was made a convert; he of course struck out his censure.

31 December, Friday.

The year goes out with pleasant weather. Farewell to it! I have no fault to find with it. The boys are very busy to-night firing guns to welcome the stranger.